DogTipper's
Texas with Dogs

by Paris Permenter & John Bigley

"Texas dogs will howl at the moon with joy for all the imaginative trips this book inspires in their people. Dog lovers everywhere will want to drive on down to join in the fun!" — **Tracie Hotchner**, author of *The Dog Bible: Everything Your Dog Wants You to Know*, host of DOG TALK® on NPR, and founder of the Radio Pet Lady Network

"Paris and John know th⟨…⟩ ⟨…⟩d and pets welcomed, and take ⟨…⟩ where both you AND Fido can e⟨…⟩ Lone Star State." - **Susan Sims**, ⟨…⟩ne

OPEN ROAD PUBLISHING
www.openroadguides.com
www.dogtipper.com

DogTipper's Texas with Dogs is the first in a series of state guides featuring the best dog-friendly hotels, restaurants, sights and activities in various states around the country. Check either website above for more information about forthcoming guides in our exciting new dog-travel series!

The authors have made every effort to be as accurate as possible, but neither they nor the publisher assume responsibility for the services provided by any business listed in this guide; for any errors or omissions; or any loss, damage, or disruptions in your travels for any reason.

Photo Credits: All photos by DogTipper.com except: p. 15: Hyatt Hotels; p. 27: wablair at flickr.com; p. 36: W Hotels; p. 34: Decker Creek B&B; p. 43: Canyon of the Eagles Resort; pp. 54, 102: Rusty; p. 57 austinevan at flickr.com; p. 59: Flat Creek Estate; p. 65: Foxfire Log Cabins; pp. 72, 112, 175, 184, 203, 230: PrestonSpeaks.com; pp. 83, 88: Rico, Nico, Nina; p. 87: syd_ney; p. 99: AAA Texas Small Business at flickr.com; p. 106: Hyatt Regency Lost Pines Resort and Spa; p. 108: WhisperToMe at wikipedia.com; p. 109: Stuart Seeger at wikimedia commons; p. 119: Hotel Palomar; p. 120: Arlington CVB; p. 133: anyjazz65 at wikipedia; p. 143: TxHC at wikipedia; p. 153: donnierayjones at flickr.com; p. 164: Mike Towber at flickr.com; p. 171: greg westfall at flickr.com; p. 174: euthman at flickr.com; p. 175: Avenue O B&B; p. 179: cortneymartin82 at flickr.com; p. 180: erion.shehaj at flickr.com; p. 187: B Rosen at flickr.com; p. 197: BFS Man at flickr.com; p. 198: Antanith at flickr.com; pp. 207: DB1911 at flickr.com; p. 208: Robert Hensley at flickr.com; p. 210: GalgenTX at flickr.com; p. 215: Brian Stansberry at wikipedia; p. 217: T. Fernandes; p. 219: Woody H1 at flickr.com; p. 223: Gage Hotel; p. 225: Nick Simonite; p. 230: ATravelingPug.com.

TABLE OF CONTENTS

Acknowledgements

Through the years, we've written many travel guides to our home state. However, this project ranks as the most fun thanks to the assistance of our dogs, Tiki and Irie. We love exploring dog-friendly locations with the help of our two furry researchers!

Many of those outings were inspired by trips shared by the readers of our DogTipper.com. We'd like to thank all the readers, fans, and followers of our site. Our network of devoted dog lovers makes us excited to switch on our computer every morning. Several of you contributed photos to this guide and shared both the love that you have for your dogs and the fun that you have traveling with them.

We're also immensely grateful to Open Road Guides, who brought together another book that we know will cause our hearts to skip a beat when we see it on bookstore shelves.

We'd also like to thank our partners at our Amazing Pet Expo booths throughout the state: Rachel and Brad Phelps of the online dog lifestyle magazine *PrestonSpeaks.com* and their West Highland White Terrier, Preston. This jet-setting dog attends expos across the country and helped us research many of the big city destinations, always with a happy wag. He happily posed for many of the photos at big city destinations.

In the course of researching and writing this guidebook, we've talked with more of our fellow Texans than we can possibly thank here, from hoteliers and tourism officials to shopkeepers and festival planners. Most importantly, we talked with the people who really know what makes a good dog getaway: the dog-loving residents and travelers of Texas. From our Amazing Pet Expo booth at events in Austin, Dallas, Houston, and San Antonio and at special dog events and destinations statewide, we talked with dog lovers across the state, people and their pets who were happy to share their favorite dog getaways, parks, stores, and special events.

They shared their out-of-the-way finds as well as their long-time favorites with us, guiding our explorations and for that we are grateful.

And, finally, we'd like to thank our dogs Irie and Tiki for traveling many of these miles with us and for showing us, once again, how much dogs add to our lives and our travels. If you are looking for a four-legged travel companion, we'd like to ask you to check out your local shelter or rescue. Both Tiki and Irie's first homes were with Texas animal shelters. We couldn't be happier with these companions in our travels and, most especially, in our hearts.

– Paris and John

1. Introduction

For years, **Texas** has promoted itself as the "land of contrasts." Rolling hills, rugged deserts, verdant forests, and sandy beaches are all found within its borders—and all await exploration by you and your dog. Regardless of the kind of getaway you and your four-legged travel companion are seeking, you'll find it in the Lone Star State. From sun, sand, and surf to big city fun to western adventure, destinations across Texas welcome dogs with open paws.

DogTipper's Texas with Dogs covers our suggestions for the best places in Texas to travel with your dog. Throughout the book, you'll see some of our favorites marked as "DogTipper's Choice." These are facilities that not only accept dogs but welcome them, and often include extras that recognize that your dog is an integral part of your vacation experience.

This book is not a comprehensive guide to all dog-friendly facilities in this state that spans over 268,000 square miles but, instead, a guide to help point the way for you and your dog to plan a memorable vacation. We hope that, like you, we'll be discovering more destinations in our home state to explore with our dogs. If you have updates or suggestions for the next edition of this book, please email us at: editors@dogtipper.com. And we'd love to see photos of *your* dog traveling Texas!

2. Overview

TRAVELING TEXAS WITH YOUR DOG

Texas Travel Regions

Texas is a big place; even during an extended vacation, most travelers will concentrate on just a few regions of the state. State tourism efforts designate seven Texas Travel Regions and, for this book, we're following those regions. You'll be able to use *DogTipper's Texas with Dogs* in conjunction with the free Texas Travel Guide and other state tourism materials and follow along as we take you and your dog through the seven regions: Big Bend Country, Gulf Coast, Hill Country, Panhandle Plains, Piney Woods, Prairies and Lakes, and South Texas Plains.

To order a free Texas Travel Guide and a Texas state map, visit www.traveltex.com, the official Texas tourism site. You can also download free podcast walking tours of the major cities, a fun way to tour destinations on your future dog walks.

When to Visit

Texas draws travelers year around thanks to largely temperate weather. The southern reaches of the state are home to many Winter Texans who come (with their pets) to enjoy the state's mild winter. Winter in the Panhandle can be quite different, however, with snow and ice a real possibility.

Summer can be a travel challenge with daily high temperatures averaging 90°–95° (but with days above 100° in many locations). Summer heat isn't just uncomfortable but it can be dangerous as well for both you and your dog.

October and April are prime months for a comfortable visit. March and April are also peak season for viewing wildflowers, particularly the state's famed bluebonnets. It's no surprise that many dog festivals are scheduled in spring or fall.

Safety Precautions

As in many parts of the country, the coyote population has grown

in recent years in Texas. Campers are urged to never leave a dog outside a tent at night when coyotes can attack. Daytime sightings are usually rare but, at night, coyotes will come close to look for a meal.

Texas is home to poisonous rattlesnakes, copperheads, water moccasins, and coral snakes. While these are typically shy creatures and would prefer to flee rather than bite, be wary when hiking with your dog. Don't let your dog put his nose in rocky ledges, beneath logs, or in holes on the river bank. If you or your dog are bitten, seek medical attention immediately.

And, if you're vacationing in East Texas or near the coast, please keep an eye out for alligators. Don't let your dog swim in waters where alligator signs are posted and don't walk your dog along the shoreline at dawn or dusk.

Texas is also home to some nasty crawly creatures such as scorpions, tarantulas, and fire ants. And Africanized bees—killer bees— aren't just the stuff of horror movies. They typically nest in hollow trees and have been known to attack the sources of loud noise: chainsaws, lawn mowers—and barking dogs.

Flash flooding is another problem that literally sneaks up on many travelers. The rocky conditions in the Hill Country and western portions of the state mean that rains will run off quickly and flood what minutes earlier may have been a dry creek bed. Some parks, like Pedernales Falls State Park near Austin, have sirens to warn travelers to get away from the river when a flash flood approaches but most of the time you'll be on your own to know when you and your dog need to get away from the water. Flooding kills many travelers every year as they attempt to drive across roads covered in water. "Turn around, don't drown" is the NOAA weather campaign to urge travelers not to try to drive across flooded roads.

But the two most common hazards are perhaps the least exotic: heat and mosquitoes. Mosquitoes can be the most annoying insects during warm-weather months; pack dog-safe repellent for both you and your dog and make sure your dog is current on heartworm preventative, no matter what time of the year you visit. Heartworm can be contracted in the middle of the winter in this state so you definitely need for your dog to be current on preventative before you arrive. (Similarly fleas and ticks can be a year-around issue.)

And although it's commonplace, heat remains the most deadly problem in Texas. Heat exhaustion and heat stroke are risks for both you and your dog, especially for brachycephalic (short-nosed) dogs like bulldogs and pugs that have a more difficult time panting to cool their body temperature. Cool, fresh water is important to provide your dog frequently on your outings. And don't forget that your dog is much closer to the hot pavement than you are and, unless you put protective booties on him, is always barefoot. Unless you'd feel comfortable walking on the pavement in bare feet, please keep your dog off the pavement.

NEVER leave a dog in the car in Texas. Temperatures can soar and your car can turn into an oven in the time it takes you to go in and order lunch. Many dogs die ever year in cars that their owners thought would be a comfortable place for them to wait.

Traveling Texas Highways

Wi-Fi is available at all Texas Safety Rest Areas and Travel Information Centers, found at the major highways into Texas as well as the State Capitol. When you connect at any of these locations, you'll reach the TexTreks welcome page with real-time information on road conditions, weather, special events, local chamber and convention and visitors bureau sites, and more. Visit www.textreks.com for more information. Safety Rest Areas have designated pet relief areas.

For current highway conditions across the state, visit Drive Texas, maintained by the Texas Department of Transportation, or call for 24-hour automated road condition information and, during the spring, wildflower sightings. From 8 a.m.-6 p.m., you can speak with a Texas tourism counselor for information on attractions and events statewide. *Info: (800) 452-9292; www.drivetexas.org.*

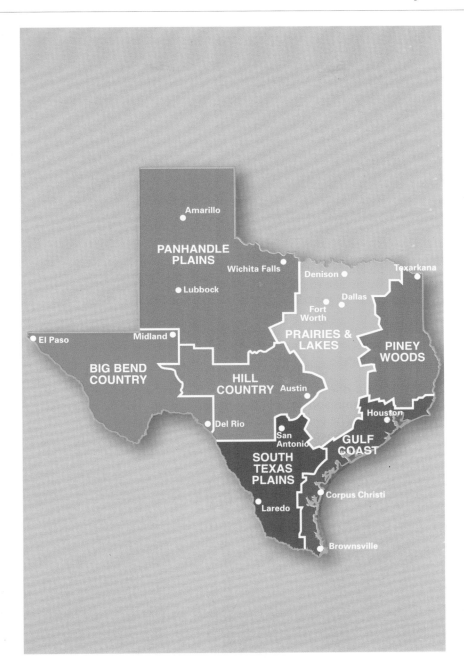

Texas State Parks

We love taking our dogs to the many state parks across Texas so we've included as many parks as possible in this guide. Most of the parks are extremely dog-friendly but share common rules:

- your dog needs to be on a leash no longer than six feet long
- you must pick up your dog's waste and dispose of it properly
- your dog is not permitted in any buildings including screened shelters, cabins, and restrooms
- your dog is not permitted in designated swim areas

Admission fees at state parks vary by park; some parks charge per person and some per carload.

Many of the parks offer camping facilities that range from cabins and shelters to RV and tent sites. However, dogs are not permitted in any buildings at state parks and this includes shelters and cabins. If you would like to overnight at a Texas state park, you'll need to bring an RV or tent. The central reservation number for all Texas state parks is (512) 389–8900, Monday through Friday 8 a.m. to 6 p.m., and Saturday 9 a.m. to noon, or see www.tpwd.state.tx.us for online, mail, and fax reservations. For TDD service, call (512) 389–8915 weekdays.

We have a one-year **Texas State Parks Pass** which we love; it provides admission for our entire car of two- and four-legged passengers. The pass (which we purchased at a state park) costs $70. You can also call (512) 389–8900 to order a pass but it will incur a shipping fee. The park pass also provides discounts on camping and at park stores. For travelers age 65 years or older (or those with at least a 60 percent VA disability), there is the free or discounted (depending on age) Texas Parklands Passport.

Info: (512) 389-4800 or (800) 792-1112; www.tpwd.state.tx.us.

Bringing a Dog into Texas

Traveling from out of state into Texas? If you're driving into Texas, you won't need to show a Certificate of Veterinary Inspection (although it's always a good idea to travel with one). If you fly into Texas, most airlines will require proof of rabies if not a Certificate of Veterinary Inspection. Check with your airline upon booking to see what paperwork you'll need to obtain from your veterinarian.

In accordance with state law, all dogs and cats three months of age or older must be vaccinated against rabies and be accompanied by a rabies vaccination certificate dated and signed by the veterinarian who administered the immunization. To qualify as being currently vaccinated, 30 days must have lapsed since the initial vaccination.

If you're traveling to Texas from Mexico or another country (or if you cross the border during your trip), you'll need to show proof of rabies vaccination. If your dog is a puppy less than three months of age, you'll have to confine him in your home until 30 days after that initial vaccination is administered. Regardless of the animal's age, if the initial vaccination was given less than 30 days prior to arrival, your dog must be confined for the balance of the 30 days.

The Center for Disease Control and Prevention (CDC) may have additional requirements for animals arriving from another country; the CDC's Division of Global Migration and Quarantine may be contacted at (800) 232-4636 or www.cdc.gov/animalimportation for further information. Please keep in mind that, even if the CDC states that dogs or cats under certain circumstances do not need to be vaccinated against rabies for entry into the US, the animal still needs to be vaccinated against rabies in accordance with Texas state law for entry into Texas.

DOG-FRIENDLY HOTELS

Throughout Texas, you'll find many dog-friendly hotels, bed and breakfasts, and campgrounds. *DogTipper's Texas with Dogs* is a selective list created from the thousands of properties that accept dogs. For a comprehensive list of properties, check out our Resources section in the back of this book for great websites that list all the dog-friendly accommodations in Texas and beyond.

Tips for a Tail-Wagging Hotel Stay

Because a hotel is a strange new environment for your dog, it can cause him to become anxious,

and even behave differently than he would at home. It is important to reassure him, make him feel comfortable there, and, of course, to be courteous to the other guests staying there. How your dog behaves will help determine whether the manager of that property continues a pet-friendly policy so consider yourself a pet ambassador!

- When you check in, ask if the hotel has any special amenities for dogs or whether there are any activities nearby you and your dog can enjoy together. We've tried to cover some of the top activities in every city but restaurants change frequently. You might be surprised to learn, for example, that a restaurant down the street has an outdoor patio where dogs are welcome.
- Ask about any insect or ant poisons that the property may use in the rooms or on the grounds, which could be toxic to your dog.
- Consider requesting a ground floor room, to make it easier for you and your dog to enter and exit.
- Many hotels prohibit unattended dogs in a room. And in any case, the hotel's housekeeper will not be able to come in and clean your room if you leave your dog unattended. Inquire when your room is scheduled to be cleaned, and arrange for you and your dog to be out of the room when the maid arrives. *The knock on the door may trigger a barking response in your dog that annoys other guests.*
- When you arrive at your room, immediately set out your dog's bowls (give him fresh water right away, as he may have become dehydrated in the car ride), set out his toys, his bed if you brought that along—anything to make this strange environment seem like home. Play with him soon after you arrive to show him this strange room is a fun place, and you are not leaving him there alone.
- Turn on the TV or the radio to mask the hotel sounds until your dog becomes acclimated. Some reassuring words from you will help him, too.
- Be sure to take your dog on more walks than usual, giving him every opportunity to "do his business." The trip may have taken him out of his normal rhythm, and you want to avoid accidents in the room. Exercise will also result in a calmer dog.
- Check out the hotel exits and if possible find a side or back stairway to take your dog out rather than having to go through the lobby each time. Keep him on a tight leash when

you are on property to make sure he doesn't disturb other guests.

- **Always** clean up after your dog on the hotel grounds, even the parking lot.
- If your dog sleeps on the bed with you, consider bringing a sheet from home to put over the hotel linens, so the hotel does not have to have the blanket and bedspread cleaned after you leave.

Hotel Chain Policies

Most hotels have their own pet policies, even those properties within large hotel chains. (These policies do not apply to service animals.) However, here's a basic rundown of what to expect from hotel chains that have numerous dog-friendly properties:

America's Best Inn and Suites. With several locations around Texas, this budget chain accepts pets at most hotels but check with the property for rates and restrictions. *Info: (800) 237-8466; www.americasbestinn.com.*

Baymont Inn and Suites: Many of the Baymont Inn locations accept pets but policies and fees vary by location. This chain is part of the Wyndham brand. *Info: (800) 337-0550; www.baymontinns.com.*

Best Western: Over 1,600 of the locations in this chain accept pets but policies vary between properties. Up to two dogs, with a maximum weight of 80 pounds each, are permitted in a guest room. According to the corporate site, "There may be a maximum $20 per day charge for each room with a pet or multiple pets or a maximum per week charge of $100. A refundable damage deposit of up to $50 per stay may be required of all guests with a pet." *Info: (800) 780-7234; www.bestwestern.com.*

Candlewood Suites. Pets weighing under 80 pounds are welcome at these properties. The pet fee for a 1- to 6-night stay is up to $75; a stay of seven nights or longer incurs a fee up to $150. Pets may be left unattended in rooms. *Info: (877) CANDLEWOOD; www.candlewoodsuites.com.*

Clarion: This chain is part of the Choice Hotels® brand that offers more than 2,500 pet-friendly properties; rules and fees vary by location. *Info: (877) 424-6423; www.clarionhotel.com.*

Comfort Suites: This chain is part of the Choice Hotels® brand that offers more than 2,500 pet-friendly properties; rules and fees vary by location. *Info: (877) 424-6423; www.comfortsuites.com.*

Courtyard by Marriott: Operated by Marriott, a brand with over 1200 pet-friendly hotels across the dozen brands in their portfolio. *Info: (800) 407-9116; www.marriott.com.*

Days Inn: Part of the Wyndham brand, many properties in this budget-friendly brand accept pets. *Info: (800) 225-3297; www.daysinn.com.*

dogtipper
choice

Drury Hotels: If permitted by law, pets are accepted at all Drury Hotels. There's a maximum of two dogs per room, and dogs cannot go into the public areas of the hotel including dining area, lobby, pool and spa, fitness center, and meeting rooms. Dogs shouldn't be left alone in the guest room for longer than 30 minutes and should be leashed or crated when outside the room. Housekeeping services are not provided when a pet is in the room. Pets are free at all locations, except at the Drury Inn & Suites Flagstaff, Drury Inn & Suites Phoenix Airport and the Drury Inn & Suites Phoenix Happy Valley which charge a daily cleaning fee of $10 per room plus tax. *Info: (800) DRURYINN; druryhotels.com.*

Econo Lodge: This chain is part of the Choice Hotels® brand that offers more than 2,500 pet-friendly properties; rules and fees vary by location. *Info: (877) 424-6423; www.econolodge.com.*

Extended Stay America: This hotel brand permits a maximum of two dogs per guest room. According to the corporate site, "A $25 (+ tax) per day, per pet non-refundable cleaning fee (not to exceed $150 + tax per pet) will be charged the first night of your stay. Weight, size and breed restrictions may apply." *Info: (800) 804-3724; www.extendedstayamerica.com.*

Fairfield Inn and Suites: Operated by Marriott, a brand with over 1200 pet-friendly hotels across the dozen brands in their portfolio although pet policies and rates vary by location. Fairfield is especially popular with business travelers. *Info: (800) 407-9116; www.marriott.com.*

Hawthorn Suites. Suites with fully-equipped kitchens make it easy to prepare you and Fido a meal and give you both plenty of space. Dogs are welcome at most locations. *Info: (800) 337-0202; www.hawthorn.com.*

Holiday Inn and Holiday Inn Express. Numerous hotels within these chains offer pet-friendly accommodations but policies and fees vary by property. *Info: (888) HOLIDAY; www.holidayinn.com and www.hiexpress.com.*

Hotel Indigo. Pet policies vary by location at this chain of boutique hotels that are part of the InterContinental Hotel Group. *Info: (877) 8-INDIGO; www.hotelindigo.com.*

Kimpton Hotels: With locations in Dallas (and, soon, San Antonio), the upscale Kimpton hotels are extremely pet-friendly and welcome any pet, regardless of size, weight, or breed for no additional fees or deposits. *Info: (800) KIMPTON; www.kimptonhotels.com.*

Knights Inn. Many locations of this budget-friendly brand, part of the Wyndham network, accept pets but you'll need to check with the individual property since policies vary. *Info: (800) 477-0629; www.knightsinn.com.*

La Quinta: Two pets per room are welcome at most La Quinta locations with no fee; check the "Special requests" field on the property websites for each location to see any specific restrictions. *Info: (800) SLEEP-LQ; www.lq.com.*

Microtel Inn and Suites. These limited service properties, part of the Wyndham brand, welcome dogs at most locations. Check with the individual property for fees and restrictions. *Info: (800) 337-0050; www.microtelinn.com.*

Motel 6: Unless prohibited by local law, pets stay free at Motel 6. Pets should not be left unattended and rooms cannot be serviced with a dog present. Rooms at this extended-stay chain must be serviced twice per week. *Info: (800) 4-MOTEL6; www.motel6.com.*

Quality Inn. This value brand, part of the Choice Hotels® group witj more than 2,500 pet-friendly properties, accepts pets at many locations. Rules and fees vary. *Info: (877) 424-6423; www.qualityinn.com.*

dogtipper
choice

Red Roof Inn: Unless prohibited by state or local law, Red Roof welcomes one pet per room for no additional fee. You cannot leave your dog unattended in the room and, when your dog goes out with you, he needs to be crated or leashed. Red Roof welcomes all sizes and breeds. *Info: (800) RED-ROOF; www.redroof.com.*

Residence Inn: Operated by Marriott, a brand with over 1200 pet-friendly hotels across the dozen brands in their portfolio, this chain is popular with extended stay travelers. *Info: (800) 407-9116; www.marriott.com.*

Rodeway Inn: Part of the Choice Hotels® brand with over 2,500 pet-friendly locations, the restrictions and fees vary by property. *Info: (877) 424-6423; www.rodewayinn.com.*

Sleep Inn: Another Choice Hotels® brand, restrictions and fees vary by property. *Info: (877) 424-6423; www.sleepinn.com.*

Springhill Suites: This all-suites chain is operated by Marriott, which offers over 1200 pet-friendly hotels across the dozen brands in their portfolio. *Info: (800) 407-9116; www.marriott.com.*

Staybridge Suites: Part of the Intercontinental Hotels Group, this chain of extended stay properties welcomes pets under 50 pounds. Fees vary by property. *Info: (877) 238-8889; www.staybridge.com.*

Studio 6: Unless prohibited by law, Studio 6 welcomes pets for a fee of $10 per day to a maximum of $50 per stay. Pets should not be left unattended and rooms cannot be serviced with a dog present. Rooms at this extended-stay chain must be serviced twice per week. *Info: (888) 897-0202; www.staystudio6.com.*

Super 8: Many of the hotels in this budget-friendly brand accept pets but policies and fees vary. *Info: (800) 454-3213; www.super8.com.*

Travelodge. Part of the Wyndham family, many of the properties in this chain accept pets but policies vary by location. *Info: (800) 525-4055; www.travelodge.com.*

A Visitor's Top 5 Texas Dog Destinations
by Rachel Phelps

*We exhibit and speak at Amazing Pet Expos around Texas with our fellow expo ambassador, Rachel Phelps, publisher of **PrestonSpeaks.com**, a site written from the point of view of her Westie, Preston. Rachel and Preston have flown to Texas from their home base in Kentucky for all the Texas expos so we asked Rachel for her top five Texas dog-friendly destinations.*

With our pet website PrestonSpeaks.com, we travel a lot! Out of all the places we have visited, Texas stands out as one of our favorite states for dog-friendly travel. The Lone Star State has many dog-friendly places to visit. This is great as it keeps us from having to leave our dog Preston behind in the hotel room while we explore the town. I would like to share with you, from a visitor's perspective, some of the most unique and dog-friendly locations we have visited in Texas so far:

River Walk, San Antonio – This charming and very unique gem is a great spot to visit as an out-of-town visitor with their pet. In addition to seeing the famous Alamo and learning about the town's rich history, the River Walk area has many walking paths for you and your pup to enjoy. Preston loved to watch the riverboats pass. We were also able to enjoy a great meal with our dog at one of the restaurants with outdoor seating.

Boneyard Dog Park and Drinkery, Houston – This unique attraction has to be Houston's best-kept local dog park secret. The Boneyard caters to both humans and dogs. The actual fenced-in dog park is over 7,000 square feet with trees for shade, lights at night, and plenty of seating for pet peeps in the park and on a deck that overlooks the play area. There is also an extensive beer and wine selection for the humans. For us, the best part was that the Boneyard is open until midnight almost every night. This meant we could wait for the Texas heat to cool down before taking Preston out to run and play with his new dog friends. Our pup isn't used to the Texas summers!

Galveston Beach, Galveston - We LOVE the ocean and make a point to visit a beach whenever we travel near a coast. We found Galveston Beach to be very dog-friendly (however, dogs need to be on leash). Preston loves to watch the seagulls and play in the waves. People on the beach were very welcoming to sharing the sand with a little dog, and many laughed along with us as Preston tried to catch the waves. Also, several restaurants along the Seawall allow dogs on their outdoor patio.

White Rock Lake Dog Park, Dallas - We have visited a lot of dog parks, but this is one of the few that stands out from the rest. White Rock Lake Dog Park was Dallas's first off-leash dog park. Every time we have visited it has been busy with friendly dogs and pet parents. The park has shade, drinking water, and places for dog lovers to sit and watch over the dogs having fun with their new canine friends. There are also separate areas for big and small dogs. However, what makes this park unique is the doggie beach right beside the fenced in park area. If your dog loves to swim and play in the water, there is a dedicated area just for him!

Fort Worth Stockyards, Fort Worth – You just can't visit Texas without seeing Longhorn cattle up close and personal. This part of Fort Worth has several dog-friendly areas and hotels including the Stockyards Hotel. Also, several restaurants with outdoor seating welcomed us to bring our dog along for a delicious meal.

Overall, as a frequent visitor to Texas with a dog, this state offers many great and unique destinations for you and your four-legged pal! We can't wait to come back soon!

3. Hill Country

The **Texas Hill Country** is one of the most popular vacation areas in the Lone Star State. Austin, the capital city, is the gateway to the region known for its rolling hills dotted with juniper and majestic live oaks and tinted year around with colorful wildflowers. Ranches, wineries, state parks, lakes, and winding rivers tempt canine travelers to break away for a couple of days of country fun.

This portion of the state was shaped by an earthquake roughly 30 million years ago. The convulsion buckled strata of limestone and granite into rugged hills and steep cliffs. The dividing line created by the earthquake, the Balcones Escarpment, zigzags down the state and divides the eastern flat farmland with the western rugged ranchland.

Geographically the Hill Country was shaped by an earthquake but culturally its influences came from many lands. German settlers founded Comfort, Fredericksburg, and New Braunfels and their impact is still seen in the communities' architecture, food, and festivals. Native American, Mexican, and Polish cultures have melded in the dude ranch capital of the world, Bandera.

More recent history is the focal point of Johnson City, birthplace of Lyndon B. Johnson, and nearby Stonewall, where the Texas White House is now part of a state and national park that welcomes four-legged travelers. LBJ was instrumental in the construction of the Highland Lakes, a chain of lakes where Fidos can frolic. State and county parks, lakeshore cottages, and even canoe trips welcome man's best friend.

AUSTIN

Nearby destinations: Bastrop, Cedar Park, Georgetown, San Marcos

dogtipper
choice

Austin consistently ranks as one of the most dog-friendly cities in the nation and with good reason. The city's great dog festivals, pet-friendly hotels, restaurants with pet-friendly patios, a host of

upscale pet boutiques, and progressive attitude toward animal rescue make it the leader of the pack.

Nicknamed the "River City," Austin is home to excellent natural areas, including off-leash parks, hiking trails, urban parks, and wilderness areas on the fringe of the city. The temperate weather makes outdoor recreation possible year around (although the hot summers mean early morning and late evening walks!)

Austin receives its "River City" moniker from the Colorado River that slices through the heart of the city. Once the source of city floods, today the river has been tamed with a series of stair-step lakes, two of which lie within Austin's city limits. Lake Austin flows into Lady Bird Lake (formerly Town Lake) which passes through downtown. North of the lake lie Austin's historic buildings including the granddaddy of them all: the State Capitol. Although the building is off-limits to all but service dogs, the shady grounds are a favorite place to enjoy a dog walk.

Run, Spot, Run

Ann and Roy Butler Hike and Bike Trail. Few metropolitan areas boast more pet-loving, fitness-conscious folks than Austin and that's especially evident along the Ann and Roy Butler Hike and Bike Trail, locally known as the Town Lake Trail. (Lady Bird Lake was previously named Town Lake.) Residents and visitors alike enjoy trails in a range of terrains and difficulty levels, including the dog-friendly 10-mile Ann and Roy Butler Hike and Bike Trail

Getting Around Austin

For one of the most dog-friendly cities in the nation, it's surprising that Austin's Capital Metro Transportation Authority (CapMetro) does not permit pets on board. Only guide and service animals are permitted on the buses and trains. *Info: www.capmetro.org.*

around Lady Bird Lake. The loop includes two pedestrian-only bridges that are great for dogs. *Info: austintexas.gov/page/trail-directory. Free.*

Auditorium Shores. Austin's most popular off-leash area lies on the southern shore of Lady Bird Lake just west of South First Street. This 57-acre area is always packed with dogs enjoying a dip in the lake or a Frisbee game; you'll also find some great photo opportunities here with the city skyline as the backdrop. Currently plans are underway to tempo-rarily close and give this much-used area a multi-million dollar renovation to enhance the off-leash sec-tion and im-prove this landmark for  dog lovers. *Info: 920 W. Riverside Dr.; www.austinparks.org. Free.*

Barton Creek Greenbelt. Stretching from Zilker Park to Westlake, this 7.25-mile trail winds along Barton Creek (which may or may not be flowing, depending on the season). The popular trail passes many scenic spots including limestone cliffs and is a favorite with runners and cyclists. Dogs need to remain on leash. *Info: 2201 Barton Springs Rd. and 3755-B S. Capital of Texas Hwy.; (512) 974-6700; www.austintexas.gov. Free.*

Bat Colony. Austin goes batty for its summer visitors: 1.5 million Mexican free-tailed bats. These tiny guests live beneath the Ann W. Richards Congress Avenue Bridge and exit at sunset to look for dinner (and thankfully feast on the plentiful mosquito population in the region). You and your dog can watch the bats from the hike and bike trail, the bridge, or a free bat viewing area in the parking lot of the Austin American-Statesman at 305 South Congress Avenue. The peak spectator months are July and August. For more on the bats, check out the information kiosks at the Four Seasons Hotel at 98 San Jacinto Boulevard and the Austin American-

Statesman parking lot on the south shore. *Info: Congress Ave. Bridge at Lady Bird Lake. Free.*

Blue Starlight Mini Urban Drive-in. The tradition of the drive-in movie lives on at this in-town theater with 45 drive-in slots as well as numerous walk-in places. Leashed dogs are welcome as long as they're friendly and don't bark during the movie. (No barking film critics here!) The drive-in features all types of older films, from classics to indie movies. *Info: 1901 E. 51st St.; www.bluestarlitedrivein.com. Fee.*

Emma Long Metropolitan Park. Austin's largest park sits on the banks of Lake Austin and offers off-leash fun for Fidos along the 2.5-mile Turkey Creek Trail. The trail crosses the creek numerous times and is a favorite on hot days. The park, which can get congested on summer weekends, includes boat ramps, a nature trail, restrooms, and tent and RV camping. *Info: 1600 City Park Rd.; (512) 346-1831; austinparks.org. Fee.*

French Legation Museum Park. Austin's oldest remaining house served as the French Legation in the days when Texas was a separate country. Today the structure is a museum surrounded by a 2.5-acre park that welcomes you and your dog to enjoy a game of Frisbee or an afternoon picnic during museum hours. Open Tuesday to Sunday afternoons 1 p.m. to 5 p.m. *Info: 802 San Marcos St. with parking at 9th St. and Embassy Dr. (512) 472–8180; www.frenchlegationmuseum.org. Free for use of grounds.*

Hancock Golf Course. This nine-hole course is one of the oldest in Texas, dating back to 1899. Dogs are welcome to come along and will find plenty of shade to enjoy as you test your skills on this course alongside Waller Creek. *Info: 811 E. 41st St.; (512) 453-0276; www.austintexas.gov. Fee.*

McKinney Falls State Park. We'd love this park just a dog bone's throw from the city if it permitted dogs in the water. However, it doesn't, earning a paws-down from our water-loving Irie. If your dog isn't as wild about watersports as ours are, you will find plenty of trails for some excellent dog strolls (on a leash no longer than six feet). Campers can choose from several types of sites. *Info: 5808 McKinney Falls Parkway , 13 miles southeast of downtown Austin off US 183; (512) 243–1643; www.tpwd.state.tx.us. Fee.*

Mount Bonnell. You and Fido will a get a workout climbing the steps up Mount Bonnell, one of the city's highest points and an excellent vantage point to view Lake Austin and the surrounding countryside. The parking area is located 1 mile past the west end of West 35th Street. Closes at 10 p.m. daily. *Info: 3800 Mount Bonnell Rd. Free.*

Norwood Estate Off Leash Park. This large, fenced dog park is located just off the Ann and Roy Butler Hike and Bike Trail (see above) near the intersection of I-35 and Riverside Drive. *Info: 1009 Edgecliff Terrace. Free.*

Peter Pan Mini Golf. Since 1946, this downtown mini golf course has been an Austin tradition. Dogs are welcome at this hillside course (actually two 18-hole courses) near Zilker Park. *Info: 1207 Barton Springs Rd.; (512) 472-1033; peterpanminigolf.com. Fee.*

Red Bud Isle. Located just below where Lake Austin spills into Lady Bird Lake, this 13-acre island offers off-leash fun and frolicking for Fidos. Come early (the parking area isn't large) and explore the off-leash island which includes both quiet and busy spots for dog swimming  and fetching beneath the shady cypress trees. *Info: 3401 Red Bud Trail; www.austinparks.org. Free.*

dogtipper

choice

Spicewood Vineyards. Located west of Austin in the community of Spicewood, this award-winning vineyard welcomes Fidos on leash to its outdoor tables and shady patio. This vineyard offers tours and tastings Wednesday through Sunday. *Info: 1419 Country Rd. 409 Off TX 71, turn on to County Rd. 408 south for .7 mile then right onto County Rd. 409 for 1.5 miles; (830) 693–5328; www.spicewoodvineyards.com. Free admission.*

Starmark Animal Behavior Center. Located north of Austin near the small community of Hutto, Starmark Animal Behavior Center (formerly Triple Crown Dog Academy) is a giant in the world of dogs. This 350-acre ranch is one of the largest canine facilities in the world; along with its huge boarding and training facilities (and a school for dog trainers), it hosts many special dog events, from breed shows to agility trials. *Info: 200 County Rd. 197, (512) 759-2275; www.dogtrainingandboardingaustin.com.*

Sustainable Food Center Farmers' Market. These Austin farmers' markets are run by a local non-profit and comprise the largest certified growers-only farmers' market in the state. Four locations invite you to bring your leashed dog and shop for everything from local produce to dog treats. *Info: Downtown (400 West Guadalupe St. at Republic Square Park, Saturday 9 a.m.–1 p.m.); Sunset Valley (3200 Jones Rd. at Toney Burger Center, Saturday 9 a.m.–1 p.m.); The Triangle (4600 Lamar Blvd. — Triangle Park, Wednesday 3 p.m.-7 p.m.); East (2835 E. Martin Luther King Jr. Blvd., Tuesdays 3 p.m.-7 p.m.); (512) 236-0074; www.sfcfarmersmarket.org.*

Texas Capitol Complex. The iconic Capitol building is the heart of the city, surrounded by shady grounds that invite you and your dog to stroll and enjoy the grounds of the seat of Texas government. The southeast corner of the grounds contains the Capitol Complex Visitor Center, housed in the oldest government office building in the state (once the workplace of short-story writer O. Henry) and today a visitors and information center with statewide coverage. *Info: parking at the Capitol Visitors Parking Garage at 1201 San Jacinto; (512) 463-4630; www.tspb.state.tx.us.*

Zilker Park. This 355-acre park at 2100 Barton Springs Road is Austin's backyard, a popular place to enjoy everything from a shady picnic to a kayak outing on Lady Bird Lake. For a Frisbee game, head to the 47-acre "Great Lawn" off-leash area bounded by Stratford Drive, Barton Springs Road, and Neff Road. Your other dog-friendly options in the park include:

- **Barking Springs.** Just downstream from Barton Springs, a human-only swimming hole that's definitely one of the tops in the country, you'll find what's nicknamed "Barking Springs" for its popularity with four-legged water lovers. People and their pooches can swim together at the spillway for Barton Springs. The 68-degree, crystal-clear water is guaranteed to cool the hottest Austin day. *Info: 2101 Barton Springs Rd.; (512) 867-3080. Free.*

- **Zilker Boat Rentals**. Dogs are welcome at this canoe and kayak rental company that's operated on the shores of the lake since 1969. If you need a doggie life jacket, you'll need to bring your own. *Info: 2100 Barton Springs Rd.; (512) 478-3852; www.zilkerboats.com. Fee.*

- **Zilker Botanical Garden.** Leashed dogs are welcome in the multiple gardens that comprise these botanical gardens. Stroll through the Xeriscape Demonstration Garden to see the native plants that are tolerant of Central Texas's hot, dry summers. Nearby, keep Fido away from the spines at the Cactus and Succulent Garden filled with West Texas cactus and succulents. Blooming cherry trees fill the Isamu Taniguchi Oriental Garden in early spring while the Mabel Davis Rose Garden blooms throughout the spring. Your dog walk can also include the Herb and Fragrance Garden and the Hamilton Parr Memorial Azalea Garden, in bloom during March and April, and the Douglas Blachly Butterfly Trail, lined with local flowers and plants that attract numerous species of Texas butterflies. *Info: 2220 Barton Springs Rd.; (512) 477-8672. Free.*

- **Hartman Prehistoric Garden.** Here's your dog's chance to meet a dinosaur! This 1.5-acre garden welcomes pets on leashes to view the ancient plants of the Cretaceous period, approximately 100 million years ago. The garden features replicas of original dinosaur tracks, two large dinosaur sculptures, limestone cliffs, and more. *Info: 2220 Barton Springs Rd.; www.hartmanprehistoricgarden.com. Free (parking fee on weekends and holidays).*

Fetch This!

Austin Lofty Dog Village Store. Offering Rover-related items ranging from locally-made goods to designer bedding and fashion-forward canine clothing, Lofty Dog has shown its support for the city's pets in need by establishing Animal Lovers of Austin, a non-profit which raises both awareness of and funds for Travis County animal rescue groups. *Info: 2700 W. Anderson Ln.; (512) 451-1858; www.austinloftydog.com.*

Bark 'n Purr Pet Center. For nearly six decades, this store, located one block north of 45th Street, has offered premium pet foods, treats, toys, and travel needs. They also offer free delivery on orders of $20 or more so if Fido runs out of food on your vacation, just call up an order for delivery to your hotel room. *Info: 4604 Burnet Rd.; (512) 452-3883; www.barknpurr.com.*

Dogadillo Dog Boutique. Products for both pampering and play can be found at this Fido-friendly facility, located in the Hill Country Galleria. Doggedly devoted pet parents can also raise their glass to their four-pawed pals at a monthly Yappy Hour event. *Info: 12912 Hill Country Blvd.; (512) 402-9663; dogadillo.com.*

Dogstuff. Featuring a large array of gift items, this store has something to please every dog or dog lover. Many of the accessories like leashes, collars, apparel for both canines and humans and home decor items are available in a variety of specific breed motifs. They will also special order items on request. *Info: 8868 Research Blvd.; (512) 452-2756; www.dogstuff.com.*

Gallery of Pets. In business in the same location for 35 years, this pet emporium on Austin's northwest side has a large selection of premium pet foods. Thanks to their Frequent Buyer policy, every 13th bag or case of pet food is free. The store also sells pet toys and accessories. *Info: 11689 Research Blvd.; (512) 345-8920; www.galleryofpets.com.*

Groovy Dog Bakery. Customers may meet Kayin, official greeter and taste tester at this 'bark'ery, which sells not only canine candies and barbecue-flavored, peanut butter and gourmet veggie treats, but also toys and gifts for both pets and people. For an $8 charge, animal-loving little ones can also don a chef's hat and create their own Groovy Dog Bakery treats in the Kanine Kids Korner. *Info: 4477 S. Lamar Blvd.; (512) 891-7333; www.groovydog.com.*

Mud Puppies. Has your dog been doing too much swimming in Austin and need a doggie bath? This well-respected facility, known for its grooming, training, boarding, and day care, also has a self-serve wash at its two locations. *Info: 12233 FM 620, (512) 249-2498; 2015 E. Riverside Dr., (512) 912-0200; www.mud-puppies.com.*

Tomlinson's. Family-operated since 1946, what began as a chick hatchery and livestock feed store has developed into a small pet product supply chain which carries premium dog (and cat) food, collars, grooming tools and health supplies. *Info: 908 E. 49 1/2 St., (512) 452-1560; 4211 S. Lamar Blvd., (512) 445-4549; 3300 Bee Caves Rd., (512) 306-1121; 5900 W. Slaughter Ln., (512) 276-2057; 7301 RR 620 North, (512) 215-9242; www.tomlinsons.com.*

Woof Gang Bakery. Committed to offering your tail-wagging chum a taste of the good life, the Austin branches of this 'pup'ular franchise—which specializes in handmade gourmet dog treats— also carries a wide selection of toys, bowls, collars, leads, apparel and spa products for Spots. *Info: 1204 North Lamar, 512-391- WOOF (9663); 701 Capital of Texas Hwy. S., 512-329-WOOF; www.woofgangbakeryaustin.com.*

Treats & Eats

Amy's Ice Cream. An Austin institution since 1984, pet parents and their pups can enjoy a tasty treat outside one of the chain's 12 area locations. *Info: 10000 Research Blvd. (The Arboretum), (512) 345- 1006; 1012 West 6th St.; (512) 480-0673; www.amysicecreams.com.*

Austin Terrier. With a name like this, you just know this dog-themed northwest Austin eatery has to be dog-friendly, and it is. Although the patio isn't the largest in Austin, it welcomes you and your dog; the menu is filled with burgers, sandwiches, salads, and pizzas. *Info: 3435 Greystone Dr.; (512) 369-3751; www.austinterrier.com.*

Bow-Wow Chow. Food trucks have really swept the Austin food scene…but this is a food truck especially for dogs! Specializing in all-natural, preservative-free fresh pet treats, this truck is gener- ally found at the area's most popular dog parks. Check the @BowWowChowATX Twitter account for the day's location. *Info: bow-wowchow.com, twitter.com/BowWowChowATX.*

Crown and Anchor Pub. Drink a toast to your tail-wagging chum on the uncovered patio of this Austin institution, which has been serving award-winning beer and some of the best pub grub around for more than a quarter of a century. While you sip on some suds, Spot can lap water from a dog bowl and chow down on a free dog treat, which are made in house. *Info: 2911 San Jacinto Blvd.; (512) 322-9168; crownandanchorpub.com.*

Dirty Martin's Place. A favorite among college students at the University of Texas campus, this hamburger joint—which has offered a menu of Americana meals for the past 80 years—welcomes pet parents and their pooches in the outdoor area. *Info: 2808 Guadalupe St., (512) 477-3173; dirtymartins.com.*

Dog and Duck Pub. Offering a taste of Britain in the form of Bubble and Squeak, Shepherd's Pie and Bangers and Mash along with traditional American fare, this eatery—which consistently wins local pub grub polls—invites pet parents and their four-pawed pals to enjoy the convivial atmosphere on the venue's patio. *Info: 406 West 17th St.; (512) 479- 0598; www.doganddduckpub.com.*

Green Mesquite BBQ. From classic hamburgers and 'cue to Po Boys and Jambalaya, this eatery offers a heaping helping of tasty treats served up with a side order of live blues and bluegrass tunes that provide sustenance for the soul, all of which can be enjoyed with your canine companion on the patio. *Info: 1400 Barton Springs Rd., (512) 479-0485; 9900 South I-35 in Southpark Meadows, (512) 282-7100; wwwgreenmesquite.net.*

Guero's Taco Bar. Enjoy Tex-Mex with your tail-wagging chum on the patio of this taqueria, which has been an Austin staple since 1986. *Info: 1412 South Congress; (512) 447-7688; www.guerostacobar.com.*

Hanover's Draught Haus. Located north of Austin in the suburb of Pflugerville, this casual bar is known for its live music and large beer garden and also serves burgers, bratwust, and fajitas as well as barbecue on Fridays and Saturdays. The 1903 building began its life as a saloon before being converted to a lumberyard. The dog-friendly patio has been the site of pet benefits such as Wag the Dog Canines & Cocktails to benefit Texas Humane Legislation Network. *Info: 108 East Main St.; (512) 670–9617; www.hanoversaustin.com.*

Jasper's. This restaurant at The Domain proves that dog-friendly can go hand-in-paw with upscale dining. Celebrity chef Kent Rathbun (whose clients have ranged from Oprah to Ross Perot) created this restaurant known for its "gourmet backyard cuisine." Dog diners can enjoy the open-air patio of Austin's most dog-friendly (although not budget-friendly) mall. Seafood, dry-aged prime steak, and even pizza create a menu with something for everyone. *Info: 11506 Century Oaks Terrace in The Domain; (512) 834-4111; www.jaspers-restaurant.com.*

Lucy's Retired Surfers Bar and Restaurant. Bringing a splash of Southern California to Texas's capital city, your Spot will be stoked about the chance to chow down at this Fido-friendly eatery, which features a "Yappy Hour" menu complete with a Hot Diggity Dog (a wiener without a bun); a Canine Kahuna (a grilled, boneless and skinless chicken breast); a Surf Dog Delight (a 3-ounce burger patty) and, on Saturdays and Sunday brunch, a Rover Easy (two scrambled eggs). To wash down the delicious dishes, dogs are offered a free bowl of crushed ice. *Info: 506 West Ave.; (512) 236-0083; www.lucysretiredsurfers.com/austin.*

Rudy's BBQ. Rudy's claims to be the home of the "Worst Bar-B-Que in Texas" and always boasts a long line ready to belly-up for brisket, barbecue tacos, and more. The barbecue is smoked in German-style pits where the meat is never in direct contact with the heat or flames, and is served with Rudy's famous "sause" which is now shipped worldwide. Dogs are welcome on the expansive wrap-around patio. *Info: 11570 Research Blvd.; (512) 418-9898; www.rudysbbq.com.*

Sherlock's Baker St. Pub and Grill. One look at the menu—which includes such favorites as Watson's Chicken Tender Platter and Shepherd's Pie—and it's elementary why Austin pet parents love this British-style pub. Dog devotees can enjoy their meal alongside their canine companions on the patio. *Info: 9012 Research Blvd., (512) 380-9443; 3003 South Lamar Blvd., (512) 691-9140; www.sherlockpubco.com.*

Taco Deli. Sit on the patio with Spot and savor a Tex-Mex meal at one of this restaurant chain's three Austin locations. Menu items include Carne Asada, Ceviche Yucatan and Puerco Verde, as well as vegetarian dishes including the Freakin' Vegan (refried black beans, avocado and pico de gallo) and Papadulce. *Info: 1500 Spyglass Drive, (512) 732- 0303; 12001 Burnet Rd., (512) 339-1700; 4200 North Lamar Blvd., (512) 419-1900; www.tacodeli.com.*

Whole Foods Market. Dogs are welcome on the shady outdoor patios of this chain supermarket, which is open seven days a week. *Info: 9607 Research Blvd., (512) 345-5003; 525 North Lamar Blvd., (512) 542-2200; 12601 Hill Country Blvd. (in Bee Cave), (512) 206-2730; 4301 West William Cannon, (512) 358-2460; www.wholefoodsmarket.com.*

Stay, Lie Down

Austin is home to numerous dog-friendly chains including **Baymont Inn & Suites, Best Western, Candlewood Suites, Days Inn, Drury Inn, Econo Lodge, Extended Stay America, Homewood Suites, La Quinta, Red Roof Inn, Residence Inn, Rodeway Inn, Staybridge Suites, Super 8**, and more.

dogtipper choice

Decker Creek Bed and Breakfast and Biscuit. Located on 50 acres on Decker Creek, this dog-centric "B&B&B" just might be a dream dog vacation. Each of the property's two cabins has its own screened porch and fenced yard plus you'll find acres and acres to explore, a creek for a doggie dip, and even agility equipment. Stays include a full country breakfast as well as homemade dog biscuits; you also don't need to worry about packing dog towels, beds, or crates if you need them. *Info: 16029 Decker Laker Rd., Manor; (512) 743-8835 or (512) 743-8090; deckercreek.com.*

The Driskill Hotel. Built in 1886 by cattle baron Jesse Driskill, The Driskill is Austin's oldest hotel. Within easy walking distance of the State Capitol and right in the Sixth Street entertainment district, this elegant hotel welcomes small dogs but has some restrictions. Up to two dogs per room are permitted but only for dogs 35 pounds or less. At the time of check-in, you'll need to show proof of bordetella and rabies vaccinations within the past 12 months. Dogs may not be left in guest rooms and, except for check in and departure, can't be in the lobby or other public areas. Also, dogs aren't permitted on the bed covers or other furnishings. *Info: 112 E. Sixth St.; (800) 252–9367 or (512) 474–5911; www.driskillhotel.com.*

Hotel San José. The "Keep Austin Weird" vibe for which the city is known takes center stage at this downtown hotel known for its cool atmosphere and clientele. The South Congress (SoCo, to the trendy) former motor court is just a few blocks from the lake and is within walking distance of several restaurants, including dog-friendly Jo's, located right in the parking lot. The rooms, with their concrete floors and minimalist style, are a favorite with dog lovers. *Info: 1316 South Congress Ave.; (512) 852-2360 or (800) 574-8897; www.sanjosehotel.com.*

Lake Austin Spa Resort. Frequently lauded as one of the best spas in North America, the spa, available to day visitors, and adjoining 40-room resort lie on the shores of Lake Austin, a narrow swath of water that begins at the foot of the Hill Country and flows through the western part of the city. The resort is especially known for its 25,000-square-foot LakeHouse Spa, a two-story, Texas-sized structure resembling many Hill Country farmhouses with its limestone exterior and screened upstairs porch. With 30 treatment areas staffed by over 80 therapists, the facility features many signature treatments created with products grown right on the resort grounds such as prickly pear, rosemary, and lemon verbena. Dogs aren't permitted in the spa (or other guest areas including the dining room, pool, gardens, or boat docks). Only the freestanding cottages are dog-friendly. This posh spa charges an equally posh pet fee: $300. *Info: 1705 South Quinlan Park Rd.; (800) 847–5637 or (512) 372–7300; lakeaustin.com.*

Lakeway Resort and Spa. Whether you're looking for a weekend of spa pampering, boating, tennis, or golf, this quiet resort has plenty to offer. Dogs under 30 pounds are welcome. There is a $35 non-refundable pet fee, per pet and dogs cannot be left unattended in rooms. Rooms have private patios, many with great views of the lake; pet guests are restricted to the first floor of the hotel. *Info: 101 Lakeway Drive (18 miles west of Austin on FM 620, off TX 71 on Lake Travis); (512) 261-6600; www.lakewayresortandspa.com.*

Mansion at Judges' Hill. Tucked on the southern edge of the University of Texas campus, this elegant hotel is a historic landmark. The 1900 home in Classical Revival style offers a pampering downtown getaway for you and your dog. You'll enjoy his and hers bathrobes while your dog naps on an embroidered bed and will dine (and drink) from porcelain bowls. The hotel charges a $50 cleaning fee per stay but there are no size restrictions for canine guests. *Info: 1900 Rio Grande St.; (512) 495–1800 or (800) 311–1619; www.mansionatjudgeshill.com.*

dogtipper
choice

W Hotel Austin. If you're looking for a stylish downtown stay with your dog, check out the signature Pets Are Welcome (P.A.W.)

program at the W Austin hotel. The hotel welcomes dogs (and cats) under 40 pounds for a $25 fee above the room rate charge plus a non-refundable $100 cleaning fee. At check in, you'll receive a welcome letter with information about special pet services available through the concierge as well as a list of items available through the hotel's Whatever/Whenever® including food, wee pads, pet first aid kits and more. You'll also receive a pet toy, W Hotels pet tag, and clean-up bags. In your room, you'll find a custom W pet bed, food and water bowl with a floor mat, (litter box, litter and scoop, you're traveling with a cat), a "pet in room" sign for your door, and a special pet treat at turndown. Need more? The concierge can arrange for dog sitting ·or walk, a veterinarian, groomer, and even a birthday cake for bowser! *Info: 200 Lavaca St.; (512) 542-3600 or (866) 961-3327; www.whotelaustin.com.*

Pawty Time

dogtipper
choice

April: Mighty Texas Dog Walk and Festival. Every spring, Austinites take to the streets with their pooches for the annual Mighty Texas Dog Walk and Festival, a fundraiser for Service Dogs, Inc. Each year, the event attempts to return the Guinness World Record title for "World's Largest Dog Walk" to the Capital City. (Austin was the scene of two previous records.) Besides a Texas-sized dog walk, the day of fun includes other record-breaking attempts, exhibitions, booths, and more all along the shores of Lady Bird Lake. *Info: www.servicedogs.org.*

April: Buda Weiner Dog Races. Held in Buda, a small town south of Austin on I-35, these annual races have earned the town the name "The Weiner Dog Capital of Texas." Contestants and onlookers come not only from across Texas but from neighboring states who come to watch these petite racers give it their all as some charge to the finish line, others head off to sniff a trail, and some show more interest in their motivating squeaky toys rather than the finish line. Two days of races are accompanied by fun competitions like Best Dressed Weiner Dog and plenty of vendor booths. The event is held in City

Park; parking is so tight that shuttles transport attendees from Cabela's parking lot. *Info: www.budalionsclub.com.*

August: Austin Pet Expo. Held at Palmer Auditorium, this annual event features vendors, adoptable pets from local rescues and shelters, demonstrations, and more. *Info: www.AustinPetExpo.com.*

September: Barkitecture. For nearly 10 years, this annual event presented by Animal Lovers of Austin, Inc. has showcased the work of innovative architects and designers that create unique dog houses for auction. Along with the doghouse fun, the event features numerous adoptable dogs as well as a dog "Spaw." *Info: Triangle Park, www.austinbarkitecture.com.*

October: DogToberfest. This is a time for putting on the dog—the dog costume, that is. This annual event which benefits Austin dog rescues includes not only canine costume contests but pet portraits, wiener dog races, live music and more in The Domain. *Info: dogtoberfestaustin.org.*

Sniff Out More Information
Austin Convention and Visitors Bureau; (866) GO-AUSTIN or (512) 474-5171; www.austintexas.org.

No-Kill Austin

The manner in which a city treats its homeless animals is a peek into the attitude it has toward all pets. Whether pet households want to go the adoption route or not for their next furry family member, it's important to consider how a community handles its homeless animals for two reasons: in case your own pets should become lost and, as a responsible pet lover, to help make sure homeless animals are well-treated and that every effort is made to find them forever homes.

In 2010, the Austin City Council voted to make Austin a no-kill city and several great organizations work to adopt all healthy and treatable animals.

BANDERA

Ready to visit the Cowboy Capital of Texas? Grab your cowboy hat and your dog's bandana and head to this town known for its rodeos, Western stores, dude ranches and all-around Wild West atmosphere.

Run, Spot, Run!

Bandera City Park. This 77-acre day use park is located on the banks of the Medina River. The park includes barbecue pits, fishing, and river swimming for you and your dog. *Info: Main St. at Maple St. Free on weekdays; fee on weekends.*

Hill Country State Natural Area. Originally geared to equestrian travelers looking for 40 miles of horseback riding trails, this park is also a favorite with dog lovers (if you know that your dog is not reactive to horses). Spanning 5,400 acres of rolling Hill Country, this park, located 12 miles southwest of Bandera, also offers walk-in campsites and backpack camping areas. Cool off with a dip in West Verde Creek or fish for catfish, perch, and largemouth bass. As at all state parks, dogs must be on a leash no longer than six feet long and are not allowed in any buildings. *Info: 10600 Bandera Creek Rd.; (830) 796–4413; www.tpwd.state.tx.us. Fee.*

Historical Walking Tours. Turn your dog walk into a history tour by downloading a list of 29 historic stops on a Bandera County CVB walking tour. These buildings have witnessed Bandera's evolution from a frontier town to a vacation destination and include the county courthouse, the old jail, Bandera's first theater, and many homes that date back to the community's earliest days. *Info: www.banderacow boycapital.com.*

Medina Lake Park. This day use lake park welcomes dogs on leash for a day of swimming, boating, fishing, and picnicking. Note: At press time, this park was closed due to low lake levels in the ongoing drought from which Texas is suffering. *Info: Park 37 off FM 1283; (830) 460-1654; www.banderacounty.org. Fee.*

Medina River. The beautiful, cypress-lined Medina River fills with swimmers, canoeists, and -tubers during the summer months. You and your dog can find public access to the river from the TX 16 bridge in town. If the water level is high, however, be extra cautious of submerged trees. *Info: TX 16, east of town.*

Stay, Lie Down

2E RV Guest Ranch Resort. Adjacent to the Twin Elm Guest Ranch, this pet-friendly RV park offers guests use of many of the facilities of the 200-acre dude ranch on the Medina River. Campfires at night and swimming in the dude ranch pool or in the river are available without charge; for a small fee, you can enjoy horseback riding by the hour, a hayride, and tubing on the river. *Info: Just a half mile off FM 470 from TX 16 (4 miles from Bandera); (888) 567–3049 or (830) 796–3628; www.twinelmranch.com.*

River Front Motel. Located across from the Medina River and Bandera City Park, the 11 no-frills cabins at this property welcome pets for a one-time fee of $15. (Pets aren't permitted in the proper-

ty's Bandera Bunkhouse or Carriage House Inn.) Each free-standing cabin includes a furnished kitchenette (perfect for making
Fido's dinner), private bath with shower, daily maid service, ceiling
fans, cable TV, heat and air-conditioning. When you're ready for
fun, just grab the leash, step and stroll through the park to the
Medina River! *Info: 1103 Maple St.; (800) 870-5671;
www.theriverfrontmotel.com.*

Fetch More Information
*Bandera County Convention and Visitors Bureau; (800) 364-3833;
www.banderacowboycapital.com.*

BOERNE
Because of its proximity to San Antonio, quiet Boerne has boomed
in recent years. The town (pronounced burr-knee) still recalls its
German heritage around every street corner, including the bilin-
gual German-style street signs along the *Hauptstrasse* (Main
Street).

Run, Spot, Run!
Guadalupe River State Park. Located 13 miles east of Boerne off TX
46, this park's big draw, especially for dog lovers, is the river. The
park boasts four miles of frontage along the cold, clear river; although dogs aren't allowed in the designated swimming beach area
(or adjacent areas), they can enjoy the rest of the river. *Info: 3350
Park Rd. 31 in Spring Branch; (830) 438–2656; www.tpwd.state.tx.us.
Fee.*

Old No. 9 Trail. Part of the Rails-to-Trails Conservancy, this path-
way was first used by Native Americans to cross the Hill Country
before eventually becoming part of the San Antonio and Aransas
Pass Railway Company and finally TX 9. When the highway was
rerouted, this trail once again became a foot trail and now offers
a 1.4-mile stroll for you and Rover on a crushed stone surface.
Water fountains (and a mister near the trailhead) make this
wheelchair-accessible route cooler for two- and four-legged visitors during the hot summer months. *Info: 358 Esser Rd.;
www.railstotrails.org. Free.*

Sister Creek Vineyards. Located north of Boerne between the East
and West Sister Creeks in "downtown" Sisterdale, this winery

welcomes dogs on the grounds although not in the tasting room (which is housed in a restored cotton gin). Open daily. *Info: 1142 Sisterdale Rd. (830) 324-6704; www.sistercreekvineyards.com. Free grounds.*

Treats and Eats
Peach Tree Cafe. You and your dog can sit outside this casual eatery and enjoy everything from pecan-crusted chicken to chicken-fried steak. Be sure to save room for the peach cobbler! *Info: 448 South Main St.; (830) 249–8583.*

Sniff Out More Information
Greater Boerne Convention and Visitors Bureau; (888) 842–8080 or (830) 249-7277; www.visitboerne.org.

BUCHANAN DAM
The biggest of the Highland Lake chain, Lake Buchanan is formed by Buchanan Dam, the largest multiarch dam in the world. A favorite with anglers, the northeast side of the lake offers one of the best opportunities to spot the American bald eagle from November through March.

Run, Spot, Run!
Black Rock Park. This Lower Colorado River Authority park offers overnight accommodations for pet families (see below) but it's also popular as a day-use park. Bring your fishing gear, swimming shoes, or birding binoculars to enjoy a day of fun on the shores of the expansive lake. Dogs are welcome on leash throughout the park. *Info: 3400 RR 261; 512-369-4774 or 800-776-LCRA, ext. 4774; www.lcra.org.*

Fall Creek Vineyards. In nearby Tow, dogs are permitted on the grounds of this award-winning winery often lauded as one of Texas's best. Located right on the shores of Lake Buchanan, the vineyards here span sixty-five acres. *Info: 1820 County Rd. 222; (325) 379-5361; www.fcv.com.*

Stay, Lie Down

ogtipper

choice

Black Rock Park. This Lower Colorado River Authority (LCRA) park offers pet-friendly waterfront guest cabins that welcome two dogs! Five of the cabins welcome dog travelers; the cabins each

include two sets of bunk beds. The cabins feature electricity, an outside water spigot, heat and air-conditioning, a ceiling fan, a front porch, a picnic table and a grill. A restroom with showers is located nearby and the area also includes Wi-Fi access. From the cabins, you can walk your dog down to the lake shore for a swim. *Info: 3400 RR 261; (512) 369-4774 or 800-776-LCRA, ext. 4774; www.lcra.org.*

Sniff Out More Information
Lake Buchanan Chamber of Commerce; (512) 793–2803; buchanan-inks.com.

BURNET
Burnet is one of those Texas towns that separates the residents from the visitors. To sound like a local, say "BURN-it"…and it's the closest town of any size to Lake Buchanan, pronounced "BUCK-an-an." Got that?

Run, Spot, Run!
Canyon of the Eagles Lodge and Nature Park. This 900-acre park serves as an ecotourism destination for all types of travelers, both two- and four-legged, whether it's strolling on marked nature trails, birding, butterfly watching, fishing, kayaking, or even enjoying the stars at an observatory. *Info: 16942 RR 2341; (512) 334-2070 or (800) 977–0081; www.canyonoftheeagles.com. Fee.*

Hamilton Creek Park. Tucked in a residential area, this quiet park lines both sides of Hamilton Creek. Wide sidewalks along the creek make this a nice place for a dog walk (but be aware that there are usually numerous ducks in the creek if your dog is particularly reactive). *Info: one block west of US 281 on Jackson St. Free.*

Highland Lakes Air Museum. Located at the Burnet Municipal Airport off US 281 just south of Burnet, you and your dog can stroll the grounds of this museum for a look at World War II airplanes, tanks, and more. Operated by the Highland Lakes Squadron of the Commemorative Air Force. *Info: 2402 S. Water St.; (512) 756–2226; www.highlandlakessquadron.com. Free for grounds only.*

Inks Lake State Park. Our dogs just love this state park for one special reason: the lake. With its crushed granite floor, the lake waters are, for this part of the state, very clear. Irie and Tiki love wading in the shallow waters, swimming in the deep waters, and just hanging out in the peaceful park (which can get busy in peak times). The 1,200-acre park offers camping, lakeside picnicking, and plenty of wildlife viewing opportunities. *Info: 3630 Park Rd. 4 West; (512) 793-2223; www.tpwd.state.tx.us. Fee.*

Longhorn Cavern State Park. Although dogs aren't permitted in the cavern itself or in park buildings, this small park still makes a nice stop for a stroll or a picnic. We especially enjoyed our visit during spring bluebonnet season. There's no admission fee for just visiting the park (only for cave entry). *Info: Six miles west of US 281 on Park Rd. 4 at 6211 Park Rd. 4 South. (877) 441–CAVE or (830) 598–CAVE; www.tpwd.state.tx.us or www.longhorncaverns.com. No fee for just coming in park (only for taking cave tour or camping).*

Stay, Lie Down

Canyon of the Eagles Resort. Tucked in a 940-acre private nature park owned by the Lower Colorado River Authority, this lodge offers a whole menu of outdoor fun for you and your dog, from long walks on 14 miles of hiking trails to a game of Frisbee to water-front fun (including dog-friendly canoe-ing). The resort of-fers guest rooms in

buildings designed after 1920s-style Hill Country homes, each with porches and rocking chairs. The rooms include plenty of niceties but don't look for a television set; the lodge knows that guests come here for the natural surroundings and outdoor fun. Guests also can visit the Eagle Eye Observatory, which is open several evenings per week for sky viewings. Dogs are welcomed for a $20 per night fee for the first pet and $10 per night for the second pet; dogs need to be leashed at all times and, if left alone in the room, crated. Dogs are not allowed in the pool. *Info: 16942 RR 2341; (512) 334-2070 or (800) 977-0081; www.canyonoftheeagles.com.*

Canyon of the Eagles RV Park and Campsites. Along with the beautiful resort, the Canyon of the Eagles Park also offers an RV park with 23 sites (back-in sites only) as well as three camping areas. Dogs are welcome on leash no longer than six feet long. *Info: 16942 RR 2341; (512) 334-2070 or (800) 977–0081; www.canyonoftheeagles.com.*

Sniff Out More Information
Burnet Chamber of Commerce; (512) 756–4297; www.burnetcham ber.org.

Blue Lacy, State Dog of Texas

Burnet County was the birthplace of the Blue Lacy, the breed of dog developed by the four Lacy brothers in the mid 1800s. The Lacy brothers noted that the breed originated with a cross of Greyhound, scenthound, and coyote. Today the Blue Lacy, named for its gunmetal blue fur, is known as a family pet and working dog that is highly intelligent and sensitive. In 2005, the Blue Lacy was named the "Official Dog Breed of Texas."

CEDAR PARK
Nearby destinations: Austin, Georgetown, Lago Vista

Located on the northwest outskirts of Austin, Cedar Park was once a separate community, one named for the "cedar choppers" that cut local juniper trees for fence posts.

Run, Spot, Run!
Austin Steam Train. You and Fido can take a ride on the historic Austin Steam Train which offers a two-hour run from Cedar Park to Burnet for a stop for lunch before returning; a shorter run to

Bertram has only a 15-minute stop. Dogs are permitted on the train but must remain in their crate or carrier the entire journey. Once you get to Burnet, the two of you can walk into town. (See the Burnet section for dog-friendly stops.) *Info: 401 E. Whitestone Blvd.; (512) 477–8468; www.austinsteamtrain.org. Fee.*

Brushy Creek Regional Trail. This trail, recently expanded to a length of nearly seven miles, is one of our dogs' favorite thanks to its water fun and wide trails. Although the park may get busy in the areas of the splash pads and playgrounds, the dog-friendly trail winds along the water and offers plenty of entry points for a doggie swim, picnics, and photo sessions in wildflower fields. The trail itself is wide and easily shared by dogs and bicycles. The trail winds alongside several parks including Twin Lakes Park off US 183 (a busy park with swimming and sports facilities), Creekside Park off Parmer Lane (our dogs' favorite with lake swimming as well as fishing and picnicking), and easternmost Champion Park (on Brushy Creek). *Info: parks.wilco.org. Free.*

Cedar Bark. Our Irie and Tiki are in love with this large fenced dog park. Three separate sections—small dog (under 30 pounds), large dog, and large dog swimming area offer a variety of fun. The swimming area is definitely our dogs' favorite thanks to a large pond with a fountain as well as a dock for those dock diving dogs. Along with benches and fountains for both four- and two-legged visitors, the park also includes a separate fenced dog shower area for rinsing off rovers after a swim. *Info: 2525 W. New Hope Dr.; (512) 401-5500; www.cedarparktx.us. Free.*

dog**tipper**

choice

Fetch This!
Doggie Deli. All-natural treats, high quality foods including many holistic lines, and cute accessories fill this shop which also features a self-serve doggie wash. *Info: 2051 Cypress Creek Rd., (512) 249-8300; www.doggiedeliboutique.com.*

Petco Cedar Park. Located near Lakeline Mall on US 183, this store features food, treats, and travel needs. *Info: 14010 North US 183; (512) 331-5874; www.petco.com.*

PetSmart Austin Lakeline. Located near Lakeline Mall near US 183 and RR 620, this PetSmart features veterinary services. (And it's where our Irie went to training classes!) *Info: 11066 Pecan Park Blvd., (512) 996-8605; www.petsmart.com.*

Tomlinson's. Like its Austin branches, this family-owned store specializes in premium foods and treats as well as health supplies and accessories. *Info: 2800 E. Whitestone Blvd. (HEB shopping center); (512) 260-8566; www.tomlinsons.com.*

Woof Gang Bakery & Grooming Cedar Park. Baked goods lure four-legged customers in this store which also includes accessories, grooming and a self-serve dog wash. *Info: 11521 N. RR 620; (512) 335-9663; woofgangbakery.com.*

Treats and Eats

dogtipper

choice

Dog House Drinkery & Dog Park. Put one bar together with one dog park and you have the Dog House Drinkery and Dog Park. A large, fenced dog park out back invites your dog to play while you enjoy a beverage and talk with friends. Although food isn't served, food trucks often stop by on Sundays when the park features live music. *Info: 3800 County Rd. 175, Leander; (512) 630-5699; doghousedrinkerydogpark.com.*

The Dig Pub. The dog-friendly patio at this casual eatery welcomes doggie diners as their two-legged companions enjoy the craft beer for which this pub is known. More than pub grub, the select menu features flatbread pizzas and grilled sandwiches to dig into including the South by Southwest with ham, green chilies, pepper jack cheese and more. *Info: 401 Cypress Creek Rd.; (512) 996-9900; thedigpub.com.*

Stay, Lie Down

Cedar Park is home to pet-friendly **Candlewood Suites, Comfort Suites,** and **La Quinta** properties.

Rio Bonito Cabin Resort and RV Park Campground. Located alongside the North San Gabriel River north of Cedar Park, this pet-friendly facility has full-service cabins and RV sites. For cabin rentals, there's a $50 per pet fee. Sadly, Pit Bulls and Pit Bull mixes, Rottweilers and Dobermans are not allowed at the park. Dogs are not permitted on the beds or furniture in the cabins. There is a dog run and you and your dog can enjoy river access, too. *Info: 1095 County Rd. 256, Liberty Hill; (512) 922-3933; www.rbcabinresort.com.*

Sniff Out More Information
Cedar Park Convention and Visitors Bureau; (512) 260–7800; www.cedarparkfun.com.

CONCAN
Word has it that this town is named for *con quién*, a Mexican gambling game. Today it's a sure bet for outdoor recreation from swimming to camping.

Run, Spot, Run!
Garner State Park. One of Texas's most popular parks, especially in the summer, the focal point of this getaway is the Frio River. This beautiful park, named for former U.S. Vice-President John Nance Garner, is located on the chilly, spring-fed waters of the river (frio means "cold" in Spanish), promising a cool dip even on the hottest summer day. You and your dog will find a full list of fun here both on the river and off; you'll find camping and over 12 miles of trails built by the Civilian Conservation Corps during the 1930s. The park is one of the state's busiest so plan your trip accordingly. *Info: 234 RR 1050; (830) 232–6132; www.tpwd.state.tx.us. Fee.*

Stay, Lie Down
Neals Lodges. Since 1926, this riverside resort has been a family favorite. Through the years, the resort has grown and now includes cabins, condominiums, lodges, and RV sites; only the cabins and RV sites are pet-friendly. There's a $25 per pet fee for your stay (not per night). Cabins include linens, refrigerator, microwave, and coffeepot as well as dishes and utensils. *Info: 20970 TX 127; (830) 232-6118; nealslodges.com.*

dog**tipper**

choice

Sniff Out More Information
Frio Canyon Chamber of Commerce; (830) 232-5222; www.frio canyonchamber.com.

FREDERICKSBURG
Nearby destinations:: Johnson City

This Hill Country community is one of our favorite getaways with our dogs thanks to its proximity to great natural attractions, a fun, historic atmosphere, and numerous dog-friendly accommodations in this capital of the Texas bed and breakfast world.

Run, Spot, Run!

Becker Vineyards. This beautiful vineyard and winery, filled with forty-six acres of French vinifera vines, is also home to a lavender farm that's in bloom April and May. Leashed pets can stroll the grounds and you're welcome to have a picnic (but no alcohol). *Info: 464 Becker Farms Rd. (10 miles east of Fredericksburg off US 290). 830–644–2681; www.beckervineyards.com. Free for grounds.*

Chisholm Trail Winery. Bring your dog to enjoy the grounds of this unassuming winery located 9 miles west of Fredericksburg and known for its Western saloon atmosphere. The winery's covered patio overlooks Spring Creek Vineyards. If you're hungry, check out the Oval Oven Pizzeria (below). *Info: 2367 Usener Rd.; (830) 990-2675; www.chisholmtrailwinery.com. Free for grounds.*

Lady Bird Johnson Municipal Park. Located just southwest of Fredericksburg on TX 16, this 150-acre park features a nature trail, picnicking, and camping; it's also adjacent to an RV park. *Info: TX 16 S; three miles south of Fredericksburg; www.fbgtx.org. Free.*

Luckenbach. Waylon Jennings's country song made this tiny burg a Texas institution. Quiet except during evening dances, Luckenbach makes a fun photo stop with your dog. The town consists of a shop or two and a small general store serving as a post office, dance hall, beer joint, a bust of Luckenbach founder Hondo Crouch, and general gathering place. *Info: from US 290, turn south on FM 1376 and continue for about 4.25 miles; (888) 311–8990; www.luckenbachtexas.com. Free.*

dogtipper choice **Enchanted Rock State Natural Area.** This 640-acre granite outcropping is one of our dogs' favorite stops in the Lone Star State. Second in size only to Georgia's Stone Mountain, Enchanted Rock

is the largest stone formation in the West. Named for the creaking sounds that the Native Americans heard from the rock as it cooled during the night, Enchanted Rock offers plenty of fun for dogs of all activity levels, from picnicking and a base trail around the rock to gentle hikes up the main formation to more difficult climbs on the smaller formations. In the warm weather months of April through October, it's best to get out here early before the granite heats up (or bring booties for your dog's paws). On weekends and holidays, the park limits the number of visitors. You'll find both primitive and walk-in campsites but bring supplies from nearby Fredericksburg. *Info: 16710 Ranch Rd. 965, (830) 685-3636 or (800) 792-1112; www.tpwd.state.tx.us. Fee.*

South Llano River State Park. It's over an hour's drive from Fredericksburg to Junction but this state park makes a fun day trip if you're staying in Fredericksburg for several days, especially if you, like us, have a dog that loves water. Situated on the Llano River, this park offers not just tubing for you and your dog but canoeing, swimming and fishing fun, as well as miles of trails to explore. Your dog is welcome everywhere but in buildings; you'll also find RV and tent campsites. *Info: 1927 Park Rd. 73, Junction; (325) 446-3994; www.tpwd.state.tx.us. Fee.*

Fetch This!

Fredericksburg's many specialty shops offer antiques, linens, Texana, art, and collectibles. Most stores are in historic buildings along Main Street.

Dogologie. Located in the heart of the town's shopping district, this fun boutique sells goodies for dogs and dog lovers ranging from apparel and bedding to toys and treats (as well as fun baked goods). *Info: 148 E. Main St.; (830) 997-5855; www.dogologie.com.*

Treats and Eats

Altdorf German Biergarten and Restaurant. Whenever we're in Fredericksburg, this restaurant is our first choice for an al fresco lunch in the shady beer garden that welcomes dogs. German fare is tops (we never miss the wiener schnitzel) but they also offer sandwiches, Mexican fare, steaks and burgers. Closed Tuesdays. *Info: 301 West Main St.; (830) 997–7865; www.altdorfbiergarten-fbg.com.*

Ausländer Biergarten and Restaurant. A large beer garden behind this longtime restaurant welcomes dogs. You'll find traditional bratwurst, Wiener schnitzel, Jager schnitzel, and even Texas schnitzel, topped with a spicy ranchero sauce. The beer garden features an extensive selection of beverages accompanied by live music. Closed Wednesdays. *Info: 323 East Main St.; (830) 997–7714; www.theauslander.com.*

Hondo's on Main. Named for Hondo Crouch, the late owner and "mayor" of Luckenbach, this popular eatery and live music venue  welcomes dogs to its large patio and shaded garden to enjoy enchiladas, Frito pie, tortilla soup, or Donut Burgers, with Angus beef shaped like a doughnut. (Try the Chili Cheese Burger with the doughnut hole filled with Terlingua beef chili!) Open Wednesday through Sunday. *Info: 312 W. Main St.; (830) 997-1633; www.hondosonmain.com.*

Oval Oven Restaurant. Located at Chisholm Trail Winery outside of town, this pizzeria creates its magic in a hand-built brick oven using many local ingredients. A patio welcomes you and your dog; try the Meat Lover's Pizza which includes quail sausage or get traditional with the Italian Sausage pizza then pair it with a Chisholm Trail vintage. Open Friday through Sunday. *Info: 2367 Usener Rd.; (830) 990-2675; www.chisholmtrailwinery.com.*

Stay, Lie Down

Fredericksburg is the capital city of Texas bed-and-breakfast inns, with accommodations in everything from Sunday houses to local farmhouses to residences just off Main Street. Several reservation services provide information on properties throughout the area.

dogtipper
choice
The All Seasons Collection. This extensive collection of B&B accommodations are all pet-friendly! Each charges a per visit pet fee of $30 and, while pets are welcome, two-legged children under age 17 are not. These properties each feature luxury linens and the

amenities of a fine ho-
tel. Properties range
from log cabins to tra-
ditional houses. *Info:*
(800)   685-6110;
www.fredericksburgtx
bedandbreakfasts.com.

Gastehaus Schmidt.
This service represents
numerous bed-and-
breakfast accommodations, including cottages, log cabins, and
traditional homes; many properties are pet-friendly. The rules and
fees at each property vary but you'll find a handy form on the
website to search for pet-friendly B&Bs. *Info: 231 W. Main St.*
(866) 427-8374; www.fbglodging.com.

Sniff Out More Information
Fredericksburg Convention and Visitors Bureau; (888) 997–3600
or (830) 997–6523; www.fredericksburg-texas.com.

Old Tunnel State Park
Unlike most Texas state parks, dogs are NOT permitted in the
Fredericksburg-area Old Tunnel State Park. The rule is designed to protect the population of bats that reside in the
tunnel. *Info: www.tpwd.state.tx.us*

GEORGETOWN
Nearby destinations: Austin, Cedar Park

Start with a small Texas county seat. Add a sprinkling of cultural
attractions, a pinch of recreational sites, a dash of locally-owned
businesses and a heaping helping of restored historic buildings and
what do you have? The perfect recipe for one charming town
that's a favorite with dog lovers.

Today visitors and their dogs can stroll along an award-winning
downtown square to get a feel for the small-town atmosphere that
makes Georgetown so special. Just as it was over a century ago, the

courthouse square still thrives as the heart of the Georgetown business community.

North of the courthouse square, San Gabriel Park has served for centuries as a gathering site. Today, park lovers and pets enjoy shady picnics under the oak and pecan trees. Crystal-clear springs bubble up at three sites on the park grounds, and often you can watch these little "salt and pepper" springs spew up chilly water. Dogs can enjoy a dip in the river on leash. Upstream, west of Georgetown, the North San Gabriel River has been controlled to create Lake Georgetown, a reservoir popular with dogs (for off-leash swimming), campers, hikers, and bird lovers.

Run, Spot, Run!

Bark Park. This beautiful dog park, nestled beneath tall pecan trees, features small and large dog sections with plenty of room to run. *Info: 151 Holly St. near San Gabriel Park; (512) 930-3595; parks.georgetown.org/bark-park. Free.*

Blue Hole. West of the park at Blue Hole, where river waters reflect limestone cliffs, a revitalization has made this beautiful spot again a place to be appreciated by residents and visitors. At Blue Hole, walkers and joggers journey along the wide paths that wind beside waters as green as fresh spring leaves. On quiet mornings anglers try their luck with just the sound of an occasional cardinal singing its friendly song in the distance. *Info: Austin Ave. at Second St. Free.*

Inner Space Cavern. Georgetown's most famous visitor attraction isn't dog-friendly but does offer free kennels where your dog can enjoy a nap as you take a guided tour of this underground cavern. Discovered during the construction of the interstate highway, Inner Space features beautiful formations: "The Warriors," two stalagmites that have grown together, the "Flowing Stone of Time" in the Outer Cathedral, and "Ivory Falls," a flow of white stalactites. When you meet up with Fido again, you'll be able to tell him about the special effects you saw in the grand finale of the tour: a show at the "Lake of the Moon." *Info: I–35 at exit 259; (512) 931–CAVE; www.myinnerspacecavern.com. Fee.*

Lake Georgetown. Built on the north fork of the San Gabriel River, this 1,310-acre lake is home to three public parks that offer off-leash fun for Fidos including lake swimming (although not at the improved beach) as well as fishing, boating, camping, and hiking. Public facilities include Jim Hogg Park with overnight camping, electric and water hookups, and boat ramp; Cedar Breaks Park with picnic facilities and campsites with electric hookups; Russell Park for picnicking and camping; and Tejas Park for picnics and hikes along oak-shaded trails. Stretching nearly 17 miles, the Good Water Trail traces the lake and can be accessed at the different parks. Although your dog is allowed off-leash on the trail, he needs to be under voice control and should remain on leash during both hunting season (when deer hunting may be taking place in the area) and nesting season for the protected golden-cheeked warbler and black-capped vireo. Along with the protected birds, these parks are also home to white-tailed deer, coyote, skunk, raccoon, ringtail, armadillo, and opossum. *Info: FM 2338, 3.5 miles west of town; (512) 930–5253. Fee.*

San Gabriel Park. This park, just south of the junction of the North and South San Gabriel Rivers, includes picnic sites and walking trails; below the dam, dogs will appreciate a dip in the shallow water. (Leashes no longer than 6 feet are required.) *Info: Off Austin Ave.; (512) 930–3595. Open daily. Free.*

Fetch This!

PetSmart Georgetown. Located in Wolf Ranch, this PetSmart includes veterinary services as well as food, treat and travel needs. *Info: 1013 W University Ave. (512) 868-2288; www.petsmart.com.*

Tail Waggins Dog Bakery. For over a decade, this bakery and boutique has been serving up food and treats for healthy hounds. Featured on *Texas Country Reporter*, this extensive bakery offers everything from scones and biscotti to special occasion goodies like the Birthday Bone. And, if your dog needs a little freshening up on your trip, you'll also find both a full-service and self-service dog wash here. *Info: 2102 N. Austin Ave.; (512) 868-0047. www.tailwagginsbakery.com. Open Tuesday through Saturday.*

dogtipper

choice

Treats and Eats

Duke's BBQ Smokehouse. Located just off I-35, this easy-to-access restaurant welcomes Fido on the expansive covered patio. Brisket, slow-cooked for fifteen hours over mesquite and oak, is tops here, but don't miss the sausage as well, prepared by Slovachek Sausage in Snook. *Info: 408 West Morrow St., east of I–35 at exit 261A. (512) 930–2877; www.dukesbbq.com Open for breakfast, lunch, and dinner daily.*

Stay, Lie Down

Georgetown is home to several dog-friendly hotels (most along the I-35 corridor) including **Candlewood Suites, La Quinta, Quality Inn**, and more.

Pawty Time

February: San Gabriel Mardi Paws. Help the four-legged residents of Georgetown's Animal Shelter at this Mardi Gras event. Put on your pooch's best costume and get ready to parade through San Gabriel Park. After the walk, the event features contests for the biggest dog, smallest dog, cutest dog, best dog/person look-alike, best dog costume, and ugliest dog. *Info: georgetown.org.*

Sniff Out More Information

Georgetown Convention and Visitors Information Center; (800) GEO–TOWN or (512) 930–3545; www.visitgeorgetown.com.

INGRAM

This small community on the banks of the Guadalupe River started in what's now known as "Old Ingram," a popular stop with visitors thanks to its art galleries.

Run, Spot, Run!

Canine Camp. Every spring, Ingram is home to a three-night Canine Camp that invites dog lovers and dogs to vacation together in a canine version of summer camp. Conducted by

The Canine Center for Training and Behavior in Austin, the camp features basic obedience, canine sports, Canine Good Citizen and Therapy Dog seminars and more, all conducted by trainers and dog professionals. The all-inclusive camp is conducted on a 725-acre private ranch with a full schedule of training and educational sessions as well as fun and free time. *Info: (512) 721-8496; morefunthandirt.com/event/canine-camp. Fee.*

Stonehenge II and Easter Island Statues. OK, it's not every day you get the free opportunity to pose your dog at Stonehenge or with an Easter Island statue but here's your chance. Stonehenge II is 90 percent as tall and 60 percent as wide as the UK original and, having seen both, we have to say it's pretty darn impressive. Originally in Hunt, Texas, the installation was moved to the Hill Country Arts Foundation in Ingram and is now available for touring anytime. Alongside Stonehenge II, you'll find two 13-foot Easter Island heads. *Info: 120 Point Theatre Rd. S.; (830) 367-5121; www.hcaf.com. Free.*

Sniff Out More Information
West Kerr County Chamber of Commerce; (830) 367–4322; www.wkcc.com.

JOHNSON CITY
Nearby destinations: Fredericksburg

You might think that Johnson City is named for President Lyndon Baines Johnson—but you'd be wrong. Although it's the center of many of the Hill Country historic attractions associated with him, the town was actually founded in the late 1870s by James Polk Johnson, a second cousin to the former U.S. president.

Run, Spot, Run!

The Exotic Resort Zoo. It's unusual for dogs to be permitted in wildlife parks but this private park will permit well-behaved pooches aboard the safari trucks. (Be honest with yourself when you're considering this one. There's no way we could take our two dogs on the open-air trams with all these strange and wonderful animals around.) The 137-acre ranch is viewed on guided tours for a look at 80 different species. The 500 animals seen from the open-air safari trams include camel, buffalo, deer, and more. Open daily 9 a.m.-6 p.m. *Info: 235 Zoo Trail four miles north of Johnson City on US 281; (830) 868–4357; www.zooexotics.com. Fee.*

LBJ National and State Historic Parks. Located between Johnson City and Fredericksburg, these combined parks span 700 acres and comprise LBJ's Ranch (often called the "Texas White House" during his term) as well as historic areas. Dogs on fixed leashes no longer than six feet are permitted on the LBJ Ranch as well as on the walking trails at the LBJ State Park and Historic Site; they are not permitted inside buildings. You can also take a self-guided driving tour of the ranch, a great way to see a real, working Texas cattle ranch. You'll also find picnic areas for a stop for you and Fido. *Info: US 290 14 miles west of Johnson City; (830) 868-7128; www.nps.gov. Free; there's a fee if you and your travel partner want to take turns and join in the ranger-led tours of Johnson's home.*

LBJ National Historic Park. This downtown park contains the LBJ Boyhood Home and the Johnson Settlement, rustic cabins and buildings that once belonged to LBJ's grandfather, a cattle driver, and give visitors a look at the beginnings of the Johnson legacy. Although your dog cannot enter any of the buildings, the two of you are welcome to walk (on a fixed leash no longer than six feet) along the Settlement Trail, a circular trail just under a mile long that winds among the buildings. *Info: South of US 290 at Ninth St.; (830) 868-7128; www.nps.gov. Free.*

dogtipper

choice

Pedernales Falls State Park. This state park is one of our all-time favorite getaways with our dogs. Although dogs (and people) are not permitted on the cascading falls for which the park is named, you'll find plenty of downstream fun beneath the cypress trees. Enjoy a day of swimming and wading with your dog as well as picnicking, camping, and hiking. Note: this park can experience dangerous flash floods. If you notice even a slight rise in the river, you should get to higher ground immediately. The park has sirens to warn of an approaching flash flood but stay alert to changing conditions. *Info: 2585 Park Rd. 6026; (830) 868-7304; www.tpwd.state.tx.us. Fee.*

Sniff Out More Information
Johnson City Convention and Visitors Bureau; (830) 868–7684; www.johnsoncity-texas.com.

KERRVILLE
Back in the 1800s, Kerrville was known as a health center thanks to its unpolluted environment and low humidity. Today those same features draw many travelers to this Hill Country town, including many Winter Texans who opt to stop here with their RVs and dogs rather than continuing further south.

Run, Spot, Run!
Kerrville-Schreiner Park. Formerly a state park, this city-owned park offers 7 miles of hiking trails, as well as fishing and swimming in the Guadalupe River. Your leashed dog is welcome everywhere except in buildings and at the designated beach. During summer months, canoes are for rent for a river excursion. The park includes 120 campsites. *Info: 2385 Bandera Hwy.; 830-257-7300; www.kerrville.org. Fee.*

Louise Hays City Park. Bring a picnic lunch for you and Fido and enjoy this 63-acre park on the Guadalupe River. The day-use park includes trails, barbecue pits, picnicking, and river access. *Info: Off TX 16 to Thompson Drive; (830) 792–8386. Free.*

Stay, Lie Down
Because of its popularity with Winter Texans, Kerrville is home to many RV parks. For a listing, contact the Kerrville Convention and

Visitors Center; (800) 221–7958; www.kerrvilletexascvb.com. Kerrville also has several dog-friendly chain hotels including **America's Best Value Inn, Comfort Inn, Days Inn, La Quinta, Motel 6, Super 8,** and more.

Escondida Resort. Created by "Texas Country Reporter" star Bob Phillips, this 10-room resort (Spanish for "hidden") is filled with elegant hardwood and iron furniture and subtle Mexican tile accents. The resort welcomes dogs for $25 per day for pets under 25 pounds but please note: pets are required to sleep in their own beds. You'll be charged $150 per day if your pet gets in your bed, and there will be a minimum charge of $75 for cleanup and/or damage. You'll need to provide advance notice if you are bringing your small dog with you. Info: *23670 TX 16 N., Medina; (888) 589-7507 or (830) 589-7507; wwww.escondidaresort.com.*

Y. O. Ranch Resort Hotel and Conference Center. This 200-room hotel salutes the Y. O. Ranch, one of Texas's most famous ranches, about half an hour away. The lobby is filled with reminders of the area's major industries—cattle and hunting. Dogs of any size are welcome for a fee of $10 per stay; if your stay is over three days, there's a flat fee of $25 per stay. *Info: 2033 Sidney Baker; (830) 257–4440; www.yoresort.com.*

Sniff Out More Information

Kerrville Convention and Visitors Bureau; (800) 221-7958 or (830) 792-3535; www.kerrvilletexascvb.com.

LAGO VISTA
Nearby destinations: Cedar Park, Marble Falls

With a name that translates as "Lake View," it's no surprise that much of Lago Vista boasts a view of Lake Travis. This sprawling lake offers anglers, boaters, and swimmers innumerable coves and quiet stretches. LCRA operates many public parks in this region. Lago Vista is called the gateway to the Balcones Canyonlands National Wildlife Refuge, a preserve that protects two endangered species but does not welcome canine visitors.

Run, Spot, Run!

Flat Creek Estate Vineyard and Winery. You and your dog are welcome to visit this country winery tucked in a quiet Hill Country valley. The winery's tasting room was renamed Trooper's Den in 2012 in honor of the owners' Red Doberman, and official "vineyard dog"; when he passed away, Trooper's ashes were spread over the 2012 planting of Montepulcian in Trooper's Block. Don't miss the winery's Bistro (see Treats and Eats, below.) *Info: 24912 Singleton Bend East Rd. (between Marble Falls and Lago Vista); (512) 267–6310; www.flatcreekestate.com. Free for grounds.*

dogtipper
choice

Treats and Eats

The Bistro at Flat Creek Estate. You and your dog can dine outside while you enjoy a multi-course wine-paired menus prepared by Executive Chef Sean Fulford. Rustic lunch specials, served Tuesday through Sunday 11 a.m.-4 p.m., include wood-fired

pizzas, the Flat Creek Angus burger, roasted chicken and more. Weekend brunch is offered 11 a.m.-1 p.m. and ranges from Flat Creek Eggs Benedict to barbacoa tacos. Reservations required. *Info: 24912 Singleton Bend East Rd.; (512) 267-6310; www.flatcreekestate.com.*

Sniff Out More Information

Lago Vista Area Chamber of Commerce and Visitors Bureau; (512) 267–7952 and (888) 328-5846; www.lagovista.org.

MARBLE FALLS
Nearby destinations: Burnet, Lago Vista

Although the falls for which the city is named for are hidden by Lake Marble Falls, this city still has a link to its marble heritage thanks to Quarry Mountain. This quarry provided the granite used in the construction of the Texas State Capitol building and continues to be a source of granite today.

Run, Spot, Run!

Lakeside Park. Every August, this park is packed for the Lakefest Drag Boat Races , one of the largest drag boat races in the nation, but the rest of the year it's a relaxing place for you to enjoy a dog walk or a picnic with your pooch. *Info: 307 Buena Vista; (830) 693-1769; www.marblefalls.org. Free.*

Shaffer Bend Recreation Area. One of the largest parks on Lake Travis and one of the top LCRA parks, Shaffer welcomes dog lovers looking for an undeveloped site that offers good lake views, plenty of wildlife, and various kinds of vegetation. The 523-acre park has no potable water so bring some for you and your dog. A mile-long swimming area offers a chance to cool off after hiking. *Info: 9 miles east of Marble Falls at 706 County Rd. 343A; (512) 473-3366; www.lcra.org. Fee.*

Fetch This!

Pottery Ranch. Located halfway between Burnet and Marble Falls, this Texas-sized store welcomes you and your dog to shop for everything from pottery to patio furniture, Texana to teak. *Info: 6000 US 281 N. at Rodeo Town, Marble Falls; (830) 693-0100; www.hillcountryteak.com.*

Stay, Lie Down

Paseo Vacation Apartments at the Horseshoe Bay Resort . Horseshoe Bay, located on Lake LBJ, is one of the premier resorts in Central Texas. Especially known for its golf, the resort also features a spa, gardens, a yacht club and more. Dogs are welcome in these apartments with a $75 non-refundable cleaning fee.
Info: 200 Hi Circle North off FM 2147, southwest of Marble Falls. 877-611-0112; hsbresort.com.

Sniff Out More Information

Marble Falls Chamber Visitors Center; 830-693-4449 or (877) MF-TEXAS; www.marblefalls.org.

NEW BRAUNFELS

Nearby destinations: San Antonio, San Marcos

Founded by German immigrants that were attracted by the Comal and Guadalupe Rivers, New Braunfels still draws many travelers

Old Yeller

The Texas Hill Country community of **Mason** was the hometown of the late Fred Gipson, author of *Old Yeller*. Today a statue of Old Yeller stands outside in front of the Mason County M. Beven Eckert Memorial Library and makes a great photo op with your devoted dog. Although your own Old Yeller can't enter the building, you and your travel companion can take turns visiting the library to see the display of memorabilia about Fred Gipson and what just might be the saddest dog movie of all time. *Info: 410 Post Hill Rd.; (325) 347-5446 or (325) 347-5232. Free.*

for the two-mile-long Comal (the world's shortest river) and the Guadalupe River. Its crystal-clear waters begin with the springs in downtown Landa Park, eventually merging with the Guadalupe River, home to many local outfitters. Located on the scenic drive called River Road, the outfitters provide equipment and transportation for inner-tubers—and their dogs—to enjoy a float down the cypress-shaded waters.

Run, Spot, Run!

Canyon Lake. Think of Canyon Lake and you might just think of summer fun on the lake...but the good times at this lake and surrounding community take place all year. The community nicknamed "the water recreation capital of Texas" offers you and your dog everything from bird watching to lakeside strolls. Canyon Lake is located about half an hour northwest of New Braunfels.

Comal River Tubing. Take a float down the Comal River with your dog. Chuck's Tubes rents inner tubes to four-legged visitors, too. There's a $25 charge if your dog punctures his tube or loses it and there's no refund if your dog decided he'd hates tubing and would rather just dog paddle. Also, a Comal County ordinance requires all dogs to be on a leash; there's a $500 fine for letting your dog run loose. *Info: 493 N Market St.; (830) 625-3991; chuckstubes.com. Fee.*

Guadalupe River Tubing. Go tubing with your dog on the Guadalupe River! River Sports Tubes permits dogs in the tubes as well as on the shuttles buses. If you'd like your dog to wear a life jacket, you'll need to bring it yourself (although they have human jackets for rent). Your dog will need to be leashed so please consider the safety issues with your dog before booking. Tubes rent for $15 and they offer some tubes with bottoms for dogs. *Info: 12034 FM 306; (830) 964-2450; www.riversportstubes.com. Fee.*

Landa Park. This day-use park named for New Braunfels's first millionaire is a family favorite thanks to its miniature train, glass-bottom boat cruise, a golf course, and a one-and-a-half-acre spring-fed swimming pool. Unfortunately, dogs are not permitted in any waterway in the park; they may walk in the park on leash and accompany you for a picnic, however. *Info: Landa and San Antonio Sts.; (830) 221-4000; www.nbtexas.org. Free.*

Fetch This!
Buc-cee's. Like the location in Bastrop, this convenience store is so much more. Along with hot food and innumerable soft drink fountains (not to mention countless restrooms), the store serves as a large gift store filled with Texas souvenirs and even dog accessories. *Info: 2760 I-35 N.; www.bucees.com.*

Stay, Lie Down
Along with some riverfront cabins that are available for rent (check with the New Braunfels Chamber, below), you'll also find some budget-friendly brands that welcome your dog: **Days Inn, La Quinta, Motel 6, Red Roof, Rodeway Inn, Super 8,** and more.

Sniff Out More Information
New Braunfels Convention and Visitors Bureau; (800) 572–2626 or (830) 625–2385; www.nbjumpin.com.

Water Safety

Please take special care tubing with your dog. Leashes are required but remember that it's easy for leashes to snag on branches or beneath rocks as you float down the river. Please use your best judgment to keep your dog safe. It is always safest to put a life vest on your dog for water activities.

SAN MARCOS

Nearby destinations: Austin, New Braunfels

South of Austin on I-35, this university town is home to the crystal-clear Aquarena Springs that feed the San Marcos River which has been used by humans for more than 13,000 years. The river flows through town, offering some beautiful swimming spots.

Run, Spot, Run!

Aquarena Center. Although dogs can't go on the glass-bottom boats for which this park is known, the staff will watch your dog for you and you're welcome to walk Fido on the beautiful grounds of this resort that dates to 1928, when A. B. Rogers purchased 125 acres at the headwaters of the San Marcos to create a grand hotel. The centerpiece of the resort was — and still is — Spring Lake, fed by more than 200 springs that produce 150 million gallons of water daily. This 98-percent-pure water is home to many fish (including white albino catfish) and various types of plant life. After its days as a hotel, the property became a family amusement park but today Aquarena Center focuses on ecotourism, with exhibits and activities aimed at introducing visitors of all ages to the natural history and attractions of this region. *Info: 921 Aquarena Springs Drive; (512)245–7570; www.aquarena.txstate.edu. Free admission (fee for boats).*

dog**tipper**

choice

Dog Park. This regional dog park spans two acres and offers shaded areas, benches, a water fountain, and pet mitts. *Info: 250 Charles Austin Dr.; www.ci.san-marcos.tx.us. Free.*

Fetch This!
PetSmart San Marcos. This full-service pet supply store also includes a Banfield Pet Hospital. *Info: 1050 McKinley Place Dr.; (512) 392-5959; www.petsmart.com.*

Stay, Lie Down
With its large college population and location right on busy I-35, it's not surprising that the city is home to many hotel chains including many that welcome dogs: **Days Inn**, **Econo Lodge**, **Embassy Suites**, **La Quinta**, **Motel 6**, **Ramada**, **Red Roof**, **Super 8**, **Travelodge**, and more.

Crystal River Inn. Designated rooms at this 1883 Victorian inn are available for guests traveling with pets for a $50 pet fee; call before booking. The owners here offer a wide selection of special packages and can help point you in the right direction regardless of what you and Fido would enjoy doing, whether that's tubing on the river or shopping downtown. Breakfasts at the inn are often lauded as some of the best in the region and range from Eggs Benedict to Bananas Foster crepes to raspberry French toast. *Info: 326 West Hopkins St.; (888) 396–3739 or (512) 396–3739; www.crystalriverinn.com.*

Pawty Time
October: Pet Fest. A Texas-size list of activities creates a full day of furry fun at Pet Fest. Three stages showcase a variety of activities including Blessing of the Animals, K9 police demonstrations, dancing dogs, parade of pets, and more. *Info: www.preventalitter.com/pet-fest.*

Sniff Out More Information
San Marcos Convention and Visitors Bureau; (888) 200–5620 or (512) 393–5900; www.toursanmarcos.com.

VANDERPOOL

Vanderpool is a quiet getaway in all but the fall months. Tucked into the hills surrounding the Sabinal River, this small town is a center for sheep and goat ranching.

Run, Spot, Run!

Lost Maples State Natural Area. When you think of Texas, you probably don't picture fall color but this state park will show you that, yes, you can do some leaf peeping in the Lone Star State. Heavily visited in October and November when the bigtooth maples provide some of the best color in the state, this park can limit weekend visitors to 250 cars to keep the park from getting overcrowded. You and your dog will be happiest during an autumn visit with a weekday trip, if you can, when you can walk your dog on the miles of trails, camp, and photograph the fall colors. As at all state parks, dogs must remain on a leash no longer than six feet and are not permitted in buildings. *Info: 37221 FM 187; (830) 966-3413; www.tpwd.state.tx.us. Fee.*

Stay, Lie Down

Foxfire Log Cabins. Many of the cabins at this resort along the Sabinal River are dog-friendly, charging a $10 per pet, per night fee along with a $50 deposit for damages. Located just a mile from Lost Maples State Park, the resort makes a convenient home base for your trip although, with a look at the beautiful swimming hole at this property, it might be tough to pull yourself away! Each cabin has two bedrooms, one bath and also a furnished kitchen (no microwave). You'll also find a wood-burning fireplace as well as a fire ring outdoors (although don't worry that you'll have to snuggle with Fido to stay warm; the cabins also have window unit heaters). *Info: 117 Olsen Ranch Rd., Vanderpool; (830) 966-2200 or (877) 966-8200; www.foxfirecabins.com.*

dogtipper
choice

4. South Texas Plains

Texas's top vacation destination is San Antonio, a city that Will Rogers once described as one of only three unique cities in the country. (Wonder what the other two were? San Francisco and New Orleans.)

The Alamo City is also the gateway to the South Texas Plains, a region that extends to the Mexico border and south to the Rio Grande Valley, a region filled with miles of citrus groves and coastal flats dotted with birds from throughout North America.

GOLIAD

Goliad has always had a special place in Texas history, much like the Alamo and the Battle of San Jacinto. The third oldest city in the state, the Spaniards moved their Mission Espíritu Santo and its royal protector, Presidio La Bahia (Fort of the Bay), to this location in 1749 to protect their route to the Gulf.

During the Texas Revolution, 390 soldiers surrendered at the Battle of Coleto and were marched back to the presidio. All but the physicians and mechanics were executed with only a handful escaping to share the tale. The largest loss of life during the fight for independence, soon "Remember Goliad" soon became a cry alongside "Remember the Alamo."

Run, Spot, Run!

Angel of Goliad Hike and Bike Nature Trail. Bring your dog to explore this two-mile-long trail that extends from downtown then follows the San Antonio River by the Presidio La Bahia, Goliad State Park, and more historic sites. Along with historic sites, you'll also learn more about the native vegetation through trail markers. *Info: www.texastrails.org. Free.*

Coleto Creek Park and Reservoir. This 3,100-acre reservoir, fed by four creeks, is surrounded by a 190-acre park that's especially popular with Winter Texans. You and your dog can camp here (both RV and tent camping is available), enjoy water fun, or take a long dog walk on the nature trail. *Info: 15 miles northeast of Goliad on US 59; (361) 575–6366; www.coletocreekpark.com. Fee.*

Goliad State Park & Historic Site. The focal point of this 178-acre park is the reconstruction of the Mission Nuestra Senora del Espíritu Santo de Zuniga, better known as Mission Espíritu Santo. This reconstruction was done by the Civilian Conservation Corps in the 1930s; dogs cannot enter the grounds of the mission (the demarcation is clearly marked). You and your dog will be able to enjoy plenty of other activities in the park including hiking (including trails along the San Antonio River), picnicking, and tent and RV camping. *Info: US 183 at 108 Park Rd. 6; (361) 645-3405; www.tpwd.state.tx.us. Fee.*

Goliad Paddling Trail. Your dog won't have to dog paddle on this state-designated canoe paddling trail, a 6.6-mile excursion that travels from US 59 to Goliad State Park on the San Antonio River. The leisurely trip can be started at several points including Goliad State Park, US 59, and Ferry Street. *Info: Numerous entry points; www.riverrec.org and www.canoetrailgoliad.com. Free.*

Presidio La Bahia. Near Goliad State Park, this historic presidio is the oldest fort in the West, one of few sites west of the Mississippi that was active in the American Revolution, the only fully restored Spanish presidio, and the only Texas Revolution site with its original appearance intact. Although your dog can't go inside, it's worth a photo stop. *Info: US 183, south of the San Antonio River; (361) 645–3752; www.presidiolabahia.org. Fee to enter; free to see front grounds. Fee.*

Sniff Out More Information
Goliad Chamber of Commerce; (361) 645-3563; www.goliadcc.org.

Border Safety

For years, the towns just across the Mexico border were great tourist destinations that we frequently enjoyed for shopping and dining. Sadly, because of drug cartel violence that is currently plaguing the Mexican border communities, we no longer recommend travelers cross the border. Although violence has not been aimed at travelers, street shootings have been frequent and the safety situation remains fluid. Crossing the border with your dog requires a Certificate of Veterinary Inspection. Check with the Mexican Embassy (mexico.embassy.gov) well before your trip if you think you may want to cross the border with Bowser.

MCALLEN

One of the most popular spots in the Rio Grande Valley, McAllen, located just eight miles from the Mexican city of Reynosa, is a favorite with travelers looking to enjoy some ecotourism fun, especially birding. About 16 miles southeast of the city, the Santa Ana National Wildlife Refuge challenges birders with many rare species. McAllen also welcomes thousands of Winter Texans every year who come—many with pets—to enjoy the region's semi-tropical climate in local RV parks.

Run, Spot, Run!

Bentsen-Rio Grande Valley State Park. Located west of McAllen near the town of Mission, this park (part of the World Birding Center) is especially popular with birders who come from around the globe for the chance to spot the 340 species that have been sighted here. (Didn't pack binoculars? No worries; the park store rents them.) Your dog is permitted throughout the park except in buildings. Although the park no longer permits camping to reduce the environmental impact of visitors, you'll find nature trails. (Watch out for javelinas). *Info: 2800 S. Bentsen Palm Drive, Mission; (956) 584-9156; www.tpwd.state.tx.us. Fee.*

Estero Llano Grande State Park. East of McAllen in Weslaco, this 230-acre state park is part of the World Birding Center network. Over 200 species of birds have been reported in the park, which features wetlands, woodlands, and more, a diverse habitat that brings in many species. Keep an eye out for the toothy residents of Alligator Lake when you walk your dog! Closed Monday and Tuesday from July through October. *Info: 3301 S. International Blvd. (FM 1015), Weslaco; (956) 565-3919; www.theworldbirdingcenter.com. Fee.*

Falcon State Park. Seventy miles northwest of McAllen, this state park sits on the shores of Falcon Lake and the US-Mexico border. Falcon has long had a national reputation as a top bass lake but you and your dog will find plenty of other fun here as well including swimming, hiking on several trails, and picnicking. However, several piracy incidents and murders in recent years on Falcon Lake lead us to ask you and your dog to take precautions if boating on the lake. Please check on the current safety conditions before planning your trip. *Info: 146 Park Road 46, Falcon Heights; (956) 848-5327; www.tpwd.state.tx.us. Fee.*

McAllen Dog Park. This off-leash dog park is the first in McAllen and has separate sections for small and large dogs as well as a trail for you and your dog to take around the park. The park does have lighting for evening visits. *Info: Tamarack Ave. and 5th St.; mcallendogpark.ning.com. Free.*

Santa Ana National Wildlife Refuge. This refuge challenges over 100,000 birders annually with many rare species. Pets are prohibited south of the canal road but you'll find plenty of additional areas to explore with your leashed dog. Birders have the chance to see green jays as well as rare species and feathered visitors indigenous to Mexico—about 388 species in all which have been identified here. *Info: 7 miles south of Alamo, Texas, on FM 907 about 1/4 mile east on US 281; (956) 784-7500; www.fws.gov. Fee.*

Stay, Lie Down

McAllen is home to numerous budget hotel chains including **Drury Inn**, **La Quinta**, **Motel 6**, **Staybridge Suites**, **Studio 6**, **Super 8** and more. The McAllen area is also home to numerous RV parks due to its large population of Winter Texans that call this area home from November through March or April.

Mission Bell RV Resort. Aimed exclusively at travelers age 55 and up, this resort accepts up to two dogs per RV site. This RV park has a dog walk and a dog run but only accepts dogs under 50 pounds; the property's insurance policy also prohibits Pit Bulls, Chows, Mastiffs, Wolf-mixes and Malamutes. *Info: 1711 East Business US 83; (877) 598-5041; www.missionbellrvresort.com.*

Oleander Acres. This very pet-friendly RV park has its own dog park with both small and large dog sections. The resort also has grassy trails that welcome you and Fido to explore. Three sizes of sites are available for daily, weekly, or seasonal stays. *Info: 2421 S. Conway Ave.; (956) 585-9093; www.oleanderacres.com.*

Sniff Out More Information
McAllen Convention and Visitors Bureau; (877) MCALLEN; mcallencvb.com.

SAN ANTONIO
Nearby destinations: New Braunfels, Seguin

San Antonio has the reputation of a fun-loving town including many Fido-loving locations and events. Located 80 miles south of Austin on I–35, the city always has something going on to attract visitors. No matter when you choose to visit, you can bet that somebody, somewhere, is hosting a festival. Perhaps it has something to do with the sunshine or the fresh air. Whatever it is, you can feel it. It sizzles up like fajitas in a city that abounds with colorful traditions and vivid memories.

Run, Spot, Run!
The Alamo. Located in the very heart of San Antonio, the Alamo,

the "Cradle of Texas Liberty," is probably the most famous spot in Texas. Established in 1718 as the Mission San Antonio de Valero, it plunged into history on March 6, 1836, when 188 men died after being attacked by Santa Anna's Mexican forces. Among the most famous defenders were Jim Bowie, William B. Travis, and Davy Crockett. Dogs can only stand on Alamo grounds no closer than the start of the wide grassy area that lies in front of the building. (Basically they'll need to remain on the sidewalk near the street but you'll still be able to get a nice photo with the Alamo as a backdrop.) *Info: 300 Alamo Plaza, between Houston and Crockett Sts.; (210) 225–1391; www.thealamo.org. Free.*

Brackenridge Park. Located two miles north of downtown, if you have time for only one park visit during your stay in San Antonio, this is the one. The sprawling 343-acre facility offers a variety of trails to explore, and mutt mitts are available for scooping the poop. In the park, don't miss the Japanese Tea Garden. Dogs on leash are welcome at this lush garden where climbing vines and tall palms provide a shady walk even on summer days and koi-filled ponds add to the tranquil ambiance. *Info: in Brackenridge Park, 3800 North St. Mary's St.; (210) 212-4814; www.saparksfoundation.org. Free.*

La Villita. This area on the east bank of the San Antonio River was developed in the mid-to-late 18th century by Mexican settlers who

lived, without land title, on the outskirts of the Alamo mission. Today La Villita is San Antonio's finest crafts area, filled with weavers, glassblowers, sculptors, and even boot makers. The historic area at the River Walk makes a nice place for a stroll with your dog. Within the restored buildings, shops sell everything from woven wall hangings to silver jewelry, and the historic Little Church is often the site of weddings. Most shops open daily. *Info: on River Walk South Alamo at Nueva or River Walk at the Arneson Theatre; (210) 207-8614; lavillita.com. Free.*

Market Square. Originally a market dating back to the early 1800s, a century ago Market Square earned its place in the history books as the birthplace of chili con carne, the state dish of Texas. The "chili queens" that sold the spicy dish are long gone but today Market Square is home to a festive atmosphere with open-air restaurants, a large indoor Mexican marketplace, outdoor kiosks selling imports, and, frequently, live music. You and your dog can stroll the busy area styled after a typical Mexican market. El Mercado's fifty shops sell a profusion of goods, from silver jewelry, Mexican dresses, and piñatas to onyx chess sets, leather goods, and much more. Prices are slightly higher than in the Mexican markets, and you can't bargain with the vendors like you can south of the border. Open daily. *Info: 514 West Commerce St.; (210) 207–8600; www.sanantonio.gov. Free.*

Madison Square Park. Since 2010 Rovers have romped in this .65-acre area, which offers a drinking fountain for dogs, mutt mitts for picking up poo, and plenty of benches for pet parents. *Info: 400 Lexington Ave.; (210) 207-7275; www.sanantonio.gov. Free.*

McAllister Park. Fire hydrants, play features, and canine-level

water fountains dot the 1.5-acre McAllister Park dog park. The two fenced areas are open seven days a week from 5 a.m. until 11 p.m. *Info: 13102 Jones-Maltsberger Rd.; www.sanantonio.gov. Free.*

Pearsall Park Dog Park. This 1.5-acre park is festive with bright green, red and yellow colors and includes picnic tables and play areas. Open from 5 a.m. until 11 p.m. (no lighting). *Info: 4700 Old Pearsall Rd.; www.sanantonio.gov. Free.*

Phil Hardberger Dog Park. Offering a total of 1.8 acres of adventure for your four-legged family members, pet parents with small dogs can relax at one of the picnic tables as they watch their tiny tail-wagger play in a two-story doghouse in the small dog area. There is a separate area for large dogs, and a water fountain is available. *Info: West–8400 NW Military Highway, (210) 207-3284; East–13203 Blanco Road, (210) 207-3284; www.philhardbergerpark.org. Free.*

River Walk or Paseo del Rio. The Paseo del Rio, as it's also called, is a European-style river walk that lies below street level and ranks as one of our favorite destinations in the state. If your dog is not afraid of crowds, you'll find that the River Walk, with its many

outdoor dining options, is incredibly dog-friendly. Part of an urban renovation project decades ago, the River Walk's winding sidewalks, which follow an arm of the San Antonio River, are lined with two-story specialty shops, sidewalk cafes, luxury hotels, art galleries, and bars. (You'll

also see open-air barges touring the river; sadly these are not dog-friendly.) Like New Orleans's Bourbon Street, this area of San Antonio has an atmosphere all its own. Arched bridges connect the two sides of the walk, so visitors never have to venture up to street level. One of the busiest sections of the Paseo del Rio extends from the Hyatt Regency Riverwalk at Crockett Street to the Hilton Palacio del Rio Hotel at Market Street. This stretch of walk boasts most of the sidewalk restaurants and shops. A new extension offers the chance to stroll with your dog all the way to the old Pearl Brewery. *Info: www.thesanantonioriverwalk.com. Free.*

San Antonio Missions National Historical Park. The national park, which stretches for 9 miles along the San Antonio River, is comprised of four remaining missions (outside the Alamo) that were constructed by the Franciscan friars in the 18th century. Although canines cannot walk inside any park buildings or the four churches, Spots can see the sites as they stroll the grounds on a leash or are carried by their pet parent. The Yanaguana Nature trail at Mission San Juan, however, is off limits to pets in order to protect the wildlife in the area. Instead, you and your dog are welcome on the Missions Hike and Bike Trail which connects the sites, following the San Antonio River, although swimming is not permitted.

- **Mission San José.** The most complete structure in the tour, Mission San José was built in 1720. It has beautiful carvings, a restored mill with waterwheel, and what may be the only complete mission fort in existence. Make this mission your first stop; it is also home to the Visitors Information Center. *Info: 6701 San José Drive; (210) 932–1001; www.nps.gov/saan. Free.*

- **Mission Concepción.** Built in 1731, this mission has earned the distinction of being the oldest unrestored stone church in the country. *Info: 807 Mission Road; (210) 534–1540; www.nps.gov/saan. Free.*
- **Mission San Juan Capistrano.** Relocated here from East Texas, this mission was never completed. *Info: 9102 Graff Road; (210) 534–0749; www.nps.gov/saan. Free.*
- **Mission San Francisco de la Espada.** Established in 1731, its original chapel was in ruins by 1778 and the building was reconstructed around 1868. *Info: 10040 Espada Rd.; (210) 627–2021; www.nps.gov/saan. Free.*

Tom Slick Dog Park. A fun place to take your pack, this one-acre area features separate sections for large and small dogs, watering stations, fountains, and hoses to clean off your canine companion after his romp. *Info: 7400 TX 151; (210) 207-7275. Free.*

Fetch This!

Bass Pro Shop Outdoor World. Dogs on leash are welcome inside this expansive store that sells outdoor goods including camping supplies. *Info: 17907 I-10 W.; (210) 253-8800; www.basspro.com.*

Fifi & Fidos Pet Boutique. Each Monday through Saturday pet parents and their pups can say "Hi" to the proprietor's pup Chica as they mull over merchandise for their barking buddy. The store not only stocks travel equipment for canines, including car seats, carriers and strollers, but also tasty treats, toys and grooming accessories. *Info: 5120 Broadway; (210) 822-2525; www.fifiandfidos.com.*

Petco. You'll find several Petco stores in San Antonio but this location is convenient for downtown vacationers. *Info: 3143 SE Military Drive; (210) 337-9185; www.petco.com.*

PetSmart North San Antonio. San Antonio has numerous PetSmart locations but this facility is located within a short driving distance of Phil Hardberger Dog Park. This expansive store includes a full-service Banfield pet hospital as well as doggie day care, boarding, and more. *Info:* 12960 Park Central; (210) 545-6875; *www.petsmart.com.*

Treats and Eats

Casa Rio. We've dined at this River Walk eatery for many years. The restaurant dates back to 1946, when it was built by Alfred F. Beyer on land first granted title in 1777 by the King of Spain. A hacienda was built here during the city's Spanish colonial period, and today it remains the core of the restaurant; cedar doors, cedar window lintels, a fireplace, and thick limestone walls are evidence of that early dwelling. We dined here with Preston, the Westie from PrestonSpeaks.com who was appearing with us at the San Antonio Pet Expo, and the service was excellent. Even on a busy weekend, we were given a riverside seat and the waitstaff brought Preston some water while we dined on enchiladas. Rover can watch river boats float past on the patio of this historic eatery as diners chow down on such south of the border fare as fajitas, quesadillas, chili relleno and enchiladas. *Info:* 430 E. Commerce St.; (210) 225-6718; www.casa-rio.com.

Charlie Wants a Burger. Take your barking buddy for a bite to eat at The Alamo City's new hot spot for families and their Fidos. A member of the Paesanos Restaurant Group, the restaurant offers Charlie's Burgers Good Boy biscuits and peanut butter biscuits for its four-pawed patrons, who can enjoy their meal and the scenery of the San Antonio River Walk on the outdoor patio. The sports bar also offers food for the soul, as 10 per cent of the proceeds from the restaurant's gift shop will benefit The San Antonio Humane Society. *Info:* 223 Losoya St.; (210) 227.0864; charliewantsaburger.com.

The Friendly Spot. Sit back with your four-pawed pal and sip some suds at this outdoor establishment where 180 brews and 25 drafts are on tap. *Info:* 943 S. Alamo St., (210) 224-BEER (2337); *www.thefriendlyspot.com.*

La Margarita. This establishment also is owned by Mi Tierra and is best known for its excellent fajitas, which are brought to your table in cast-iron skillets. Open for lunch and dinner. *Info: 120 Produce Row; (210) 227–7140; www.lamargarita.com.*

Los Patios. The proud recipient of San Antonio's first ever dog-friendly restaurant permit, patrons and their pups can enjoy the serene ambiance of the tree-shaded front courtyard patio at Gazebo Restaurant at Los Patios, a 20-acre haven from the hustle and bustle of city life. Diners with dogs will receive a flyer detailing the do's and don'ts of Spot's stay. Open for lunch and Sunday brunch, the refined eatery offers a mouth-watering menu that includes grilled rainbow trout, enchiladas, soft meat tacos and Gazebo burgers. After lunch, pet parents can enjoy a constitutional with their canine along the venue's nature trail. *Info: 2015 NE Interstate 410 Loop; (210)655-6171; www.lospatios.com.*

Mi Tierra. This is the place to head for an unbeatable Tex-Mex meal that includes homemade tortillas, enchiladas, and chiliquiles, a spicy egg-and-corn tortilla breakfast dish served with refried beans. Decorated year-round with Christmas ornaments, this San Antonio institution is open 24 hours a day, 365 days a year. *Info: 218 Produce Row; (210) 225–1262; www.mitierracafe.com.*

Rita's on the River. Enjoy a taste of the good life alongside your tail-wagging chum as you sit on the patio, tap your feet to the beat of live Mariachi music and watch the river boats float by. The restaurant's Tex-Mex menu includes carne guisada, pork tacos and chalupas, or you can order such 'gringo grub' as a Texas-style chicken fried steak, grilled chicken sandwich or a turkey burger. *Info: 245 E. Commerce; (210) 227-7482; www.ritasontheriver.com.*

Vegeria. Offering Tex-Mex and American cuisine created with compassion for all creatures great and small, the city's first vegan and gluten free restaurant welcomes Rovers. *Info: 8407 Broadway; myvegeria.com.*

Stay, Lie Down

San Antonio is home to numerous budget and bowser-friendly hotel chains including **Baymont Inn and Suites, Days Inn, Holiday Inn, Howard Johnson, La Quinta, Motel 6, Ramada, Red Roof Inn, Staybridge, Studio 6, Travelodge**, and more. Many budget properties are located along I-35, I-10, or along the loops that circle the city (Loop 410 and Loop 1604).

Admiralty RV Resort Park. A peaceful retreat for those traveling by RV, this site offers two playgrounds just for pooches. Pets are not allowed in the human playground, at the pool or in any of the buildings, and must be accompanied at all times and on a leash no more than 6 feet long. Two-legged patrons can enjoy the RV resort's junior Olympic size heated swimming pool and fitness center. *Info: 1485 North Ellison Drive, off Loop 1604; (877) 236–4715 or (210) 647–7878; www.admiraltyrvresort.com.*

Crockett Hotel. Travelers with two canine companions who each weigh 60 pounds or less can check in for an additional $60 per pet, then check out this hotel with a proud history. Situated on grounds that were once part of the Alamo battlefield, Davy Crockett was said to have defended the southeast palisade, and the hotel is named in his honor. Today the 138-room hotel has been faithfully restored to its turn-of-the-20th-century grandeur. *Info: 320 Bonham St.; (210) 225-6500 or (800) 292-1050; www.crocketthotel.com.*

Drury Inn & Suites Riverwalk. For no pet fee, dog parents can check in with two tail-wagging chums of any size at this historic landmark hotel. Constructed in the early 1920s, the property still retains touches of Gatsby-era glamour as it caters to the 21st century needs of its patrons. The hotel is tucked in a quiet arm of the River Walk but within easy walking distance of the bustling restaurant and bar area. *Info: 201 N. St. Mary's St.; (201) 212-5200 or (800) DRURY-INN; www.druryhotels.com.*

The Emily Morgan Hotel. Named after the woman known in Lone Star lore and lyrics as "The Yellow Rose of Texas," the Emily Morgan—which is located literally next door to the Alamo—welcomes tail-wagging travelers when guests register their pet and pay a $50 non-refundable pet fee per guest room. Pups will acquire a taste for the good life as they chow down on items ordered from a special pet menu created by the hotel's Executive Chef, while two-legged patrons can dine at The Oro Restaurant. *Info: 705 E. Houston St.; (210) 225-5100 or (800) 824-6674; www.emilymorganhotel.com.*

The Fairmount. For a non-refundable fee of $75 dogs that weigh less than 35 pounds are welcome to stay at the Guinness Book of World Record-holding hotel that calls itself "San Antonio's Little Jewel." Four-pawed guests must be well groomed as well as well behaved, and must be on a leash or carried while on the property. Canines cannot be unattended in the room unless in a kennel or carrier, and the cost of any doggie damages caused by a pet is the responsibility of the pet parent. *Info: 401 S. Alamo St.; (210) 224-8800 or (877) 229-8808; www.thefairmounthotel-sanantonio.com.*

Hotel Havana. If you are traveling with your pack of pooches, the Hotel Havana is a cozy place to call your temporary home during your stay in San Antonio. Two dogs, no matter their size, can relax in a room with their pet parent for an additional fee of $25 per day. A state and national landmark listed on the National Register of Historical Places, this 1914 retreat is a portal to the past, with antiques and artifacts decorating the 27 rooms, which also offer such contemporary comforts as flat screen TVs, iPod connections for music and movies and free wireless Internet service. *Info: 1015 Navarro St.; (210) 222-2008; www.havanasanantonio.com.*

Hotel Indigo San Antonio Riverwalk. For a one-time, non-refundable $25 pet deposit, your sightseeing Spot can stay with you in one of the 149 stylish guest rooms or five suites offered at this boutique retreat, which is located on a quiet stretch of the River Walk known as the Museum Reach. For two-legged travelers, there's an on-site health and fitness center, an outdoor pool, business center and the Bridges Bar & Bistro. *Info: 830 N. St. Mary's St.; (210) 527-1900 or (887) 846-3446; www.hotelindigo.com.*

Hyatt Regency San Antonio. We love this River Walk hotel with its

soaring atrium and a segment of the river that's diverted right into the hotel lobby. The hotel is very centrally located right in the heart of the River Walk action or follow the steps up the water gardens and you'll find yourself facing the Alamo.

Up to two pets under 70 pounds are permitted in guest rooms. There is a $35 pet fee per dog, per night. *Info: 123 Losoya St.; (210) 222-1234 or (800) 233-1234; www.hyatt.com.*

Menger Hotel. Located next door to the Alamo, this historic hotel has welcomed such famous guests as playwright Oscar Wilde, Civil War generals Robert E. Lee and William Sherman, author William Sydney Porter (better known as O. Henry) and Mount Rushmore sculptor Gutzon Borglum since opening its doors in 1859. Your four-pawed pal can follow in their footsteps. For a pet fee of $100 per pet, per stay, a dog weighing under 25 pounds can check in with a human parent. *Info: 204 Alamo Plaza; (210) 223-4361 or (800) 345-9285; mengerhotel.com.*

Mokara Hotel & Spa. When we stayed at this property, it was the Watermark but today the luxury hotel and spa is known as the Mokara. Located right on the River Walk, the hotel welcomes dogs (up to two per room) weighing less than 25 pounds each for a $50 fee. This 96-room, four-star retreat tempts pet parents  with the hotel's on-site Mokara Spa, where guests can unwind with massages, scrubs, soaks and other therapies and be pampered at the hair and nail salon, which caters to both genders. The Mokara also features world-class dining at Ostra, offering fresh seafood and an oyster bar set on an exquisite terrace along the river. *Info: 212 W. Crockett St.; (210) 396–5800 or (866) 605–1212; www.mokarahotels.com.*

Omni La Mansion Del Rio. Four-legged travelers weighing less than 25 pounds are welcome at this River Walk four-star retreat for a $50 non-refundable deposit. An elegant Spanish Colonial–style structure, today this former university facility teaches lessons in living the good life including music from a Mariachi troupe on Friday afternoons. *Info: 112 College St.; (210) 518-1000; www.omnihotels.com.*

Plaza San Antonio Marriott. For a non-refundable $100 sanitation fee pets are permitted at this elegant resort, which is located just two blocks from the River Walk. Human guests can enjoy the hotel's fitness center, outdoor heated pool and dining at the poolside bar, Palm Terrace lounge or Anaqua Restaurant & Grille. *Info: 555 S. Alamo St.; (210) 229-1000 or (800) 421-1172; www.marriott.com.*

St. Anthony Riverwalk Wyndham Hotel. Prince Rainier and Princess Grace of Monaco, Judy Garland, Fred Astaire, John Wayne, Bruce Willis, George Clooney—the list of luminaries who have lodged at this historic property during their stays in the Alamo City goes on an on, and your Spot can feel like a star at the St. Anthony thanks to the retreat's pet policy, which allows for dogs up to 75 pounds with payment of a non-refundable $75 pet deposit. Just a short stroll from the River Walk, the Alamo, the Henry B. Gonzales Convention Center, La Villita, the Alamodome, San Antonio Children's Museum, and HemisFair Park, the hotel offers a 24-hour business center and fine dining at The Madrid Room. *Info: 300 E. Travis St.; (210) 227-4392 or (877) 999-3223; www.wyndham.com.*

Sheraton Gunter. Dogs weighing 50 pounds or less are welcome at this turn of the 20th Century sanctuary, provided that guests notify the hotel of their request to bring their Rover at the time of the booking. While dogs who are attended at all times are allowed in the room, pets are not permitted in Club Level rooms or the Club Lounge. *Info: 205 E. Houston St.; (210) 227-3241 or (800) 325-3535; gunterhotel.com.*

The Westin Riverwalk. The welcome mat is out at the 473-room Westin Riverwalk for Fidos up to 40 pounds, and dogs over the determined weight may still be able to stay at the hotel's discretion. Upon arrival Rovers receive a pet welcome kit, food bowls, and the use of a Westin Heavenly Dog Bed. Guests checking in with a tail-wagging chum must sign a pet waiver, and a guest's credit card may be charged for any additional cleaning or canine-caused damage. *Info: 420 W. Market St.; (210) 224-6500 or (888) 627-8396; www.westinriverwalksanantonio.com.*

Pawty Time
January: Pucks and Paws. Giving dogs in need an assist, the San Antonio Rampage hockey team invites sports fans and their Fidos

to enjoy watching a game together, with proceeds from dog ticket sales benefiting AAPAW (Alamo Area Partners for Animal Welfare). *Info: www.sarampage.com.*

March: Bark in the Park/Perrito Grito. People with a passion for pets gather at Woodlawn Lake Park for a day of play with a purpose complete with celebrity-judged best dressed, mutt strut, best trick and look-a-like contests; toe-tapping (and tail-wagging) music; pet adoptions and spay/neuter clinics. *Info: talkaboutitsa.wix.com.*

March: Kite Festival and Dog Fair. Go fly a kite with your canine companion in McAllister Park at an annual celebration of spring produced by the San Antonio Friends of the Parks. Dogs of all sizes are invited to promenade alongside their pet parents in a pooch parade (which includes a prize awarded to the canine with the best costume) and romp in the 1 1/2-acre fenced dog park. Attendees can also mull over pet-related merchandise at vendor booths. *Info: www.saparksfoundation.org/fest_of_tails.html.*

March: Paws in the Park. For this event, the San Antonio Botanical Garden invites four-legged visitors to stroll the gardens and see the plants awaken from winter's chill. This event benefits local animal welfare groups and permits a stroll through the 38-acre gardens. *Info: www.sabot.org.*

March: San Antonio Pet Expo. San Antonio's slogan is "Something to remember," and families with Fidos can create memories together at this annual event with pet contests, discounted vaccinations and microchipping, celebrity guest speakers and adorable adoptables from area rescue organizations. *Info: www.sanantoniopetexpo.com.*

April: Pooch Parade. Promenade with your pup for a paws cause at the annual Pooch Parade, a stroll through the streets of Alamo Heights to help Therapy Animals of San Antonio, Inc. *Info: www.therapyanimalssa.org.*

August: Dog Days of Summer at the San Antonio Botanical Gardens. Enjoy two days of dogged devotion which include canine contests, dog training demonstrations, educational booths, pet adoptions and much more. Plastic pools of water will be available for tail-wagging attendees, and "mutt mitts" will be on hand so pet

San Antonio's Theme Parks

Only two-legged visitors are permitted at San Antonio's theme parks (with the exception of service animals) but both parks do provide complimentary dog kennels. You'll need to bring a bed or blanket for your dog to lie on.

At **Six Flags Fiesta Texas**, you'll find the free kennels just to the right of the Guest Relations desk (where you purchase your tickets). To get assistance dropping off or picking up your dog, use the phone located by the door to call security; they'll come over to assist you. Your dog must have current vaccinations and registration tags. The kennels are not air-conditioned but do have roofs so they have shade; the kennels also have fans. Reservations are not needed and you can pick up your dog any time during the day to walk him on the grassy area in front of the kennels. *Info: 17000 I-10 West, 15 miles northwest of downtown; (800) 473–4378 or (210) 697–5050; www.sixflags.com.*

SeaWorld San Antonio, home of Shamu, also offers free, unattended outdoor kennels. Kennels are located off the main guest parking lot. Upon entering the parking lot, take either the first or second road to the right; the kennels are located to the far left. Locks and keys are provided for the kennels, and the park asks that you check on your dog periodically throughout the day. The kennels are not air-conditioned but are covered and open-air. *Info: 10500 SeaWorld Drive; (800) 700–7786; www.seaworldparks.com.*

parents can pick up after their pooch. *Info: 555 Funston Place; (210) 207-3250; www.sabot.org.*

August: Hoops and Hounds. A slam dunk with basketball enthusiasts and their barking buddies, the WNBA team the Silver Stars invites fans and their four-legged friends to cheer them on as they take on an opposing team in a game where the real winners are San Antonio's animals, as bedding, leashes collars and toys are collected for Alamo Area Partners for Animal Welfare. *Info: www.wnba.com/silverstars.*

December: Blessing of the Animals. For more than a quarter of a century families have brought their fur babies to Market Square for prayers and a benediction. The free day of dogged devotion also includes tasty treats and arts and crafts vendors. *Info: www.marketsquaresa.com.*

Sniff Out More Information
San Antonio Convention and Visitors Bureau; (800) 447-3372; www.visitsanantonio.com.

Choke Canyon State Park
The star of the show at this park, located near the community of Three Rivers between San Antonio and Corpus Christi, is the 26,000-acre Choke Canyon reservoir, a lake well-known for its fishing opportunities. This state park consists of two units: South Shore, a day-use only park, and the larger Calliham Unit. Calliham sprawls over 1,100 acres and includes camping as well as hiking trails. The 385-acre South Shore park offers you and your dog the chance to camp, boat, hike, or enjoy some water fun. Both parks are filled with wildlife, ranging from the Rio Grande turkey to fox to the American alligator (so keep an eye on Fido and remember that here, like other state parks, he must be on a leash no longer than six feet). *Info: Calliham is three and a half miles west of Three Rivers on TX 72; South Shore is 12 miles west of Three Rivers on TX 72 to Tilden; (361) 786–3868; www.tpwd.state.tx.us. Fee.*

5. Piney Woods

The eastern portion of Texas is known for its dense forests perfect for long, shady dog walks. An especially popular getaway during the fall as well as spring during azalea and dogwood seasons, the region offers plenty of opportunities for weekend camping among a cushion of pine needles, enjoying small town festivals that celebrate the changing season, and cruising the countryside to see color displays.

CLEVELAND

Long a timber shipping point, Cleveland is one of the oldest communities in Texas. To the north of the small town sits the Sam Houston National Forest, a favorite destination with dog lovers.

Run, Spot, Run!

Big Creek Scenic Area. Spanning 1,420 acres in the Sam Houston National Forest, this park is sliced by the Lone Star Hiking Trail (see below). Camping is prohibited but you and your four-legged companion can enjoy a day of quiet hiking. *Info: 394 FM 1375 W., New Waverly; (936) 344-6205; www.fs.fed.us. Free.*

Double Lake Recreation Area. This expansive park is tucked between the small Double Lake and endless pine forest, offering campers and hikers plenty of great options (including canoeing with your dog). Dogs on leash are also permitted on the many multi-use trails that wind through the park beneath the towering pines. You can extend your stay by camping in the many sites for both tents and RVs. *Info: 301 FM 2025, Coldspring; (936) 344-6205; www.recreation.gov. Fee.*

dogtipper **Lone Star Hiking Trail.** You and Fido might not choose to hike the entire 128 miles of this trail in the Sam Houston National Forest but you'll find plenty of options on this shady trail beneath towering pines. Some portions of the trail (which can be accessed from **choice** five points) have campgrounds; others don't even have drinking water. During deer hunting season (November and December), wear bright colors and consider a safety vest or at least an orange collar for your dog since hunting is permitted in the forest. Access points near Cleveland include The Winters Bayou/Tarkington Creek section which begins northwest of Cleveland on FM 1725; another entrance can be found about 4 miles northwest of Magnolia on FM 945. *Info: (936) 537-3570; fs.fed.us. Free.*

Wolf Creek Park. You won't have to worry about wolves but you and your canine can enjoy camping, walking and swimming at Lake Livingston. Fishing is a popular option here thanks to the park's boat ramps and fishing piers; you'll also find a small grocery store here in this park operated by the Trinity River Authority of Texas. Dogs on leash are permitted throughout the park except in designated picnic and swimming areas and in the playground area. *Info: 21 Wolf Creek Park Rd. (FM 224 at Park Rd. 60), Coldspring; (936) 653-4312; trinityra.org. Fee.*

Stay, Lie Down
Along with pet-friendly campgrounds in several of the above parks, Cleveland is also home to several pet-friendly chains including **Best Western, La Quinta, Motel 6,** and **Super 8.**

Sniff Out More Information
Cleveland Convention and Visitors Bureau; (281) 592-2395; visitclevelandtexas.com.

CONROE
Nearby destinations: Houston, Montgomery

Located 40 miles north of Houston, this community is a favorite weekend getaway for many big city residents. The city's 21,000-acre Lake Conroe, the man-made lake is a watersports capital although the primary park, Lake Conroe Park, is *not* dog-friendly.

Run, Spot, Run!
Moorhead's Blueberry Farm. Dogs are allowed on leash at this 20-acre blueberry farm that offers you the opportunity to pick 20 varieties of blueberries, all grown without pesticides. This farm holds the title as the oldest pick-your-own blueberry farm in the state. The farm is open daily during the season, usually late May through July. *Info: 19531 Moorhead Rd.; (281) 572-1265 or (888)*

702-0622; www.moorheadsblueberryfarm.com. Free admission, fee for berries.

Southern Star Brewing Company. Since 2008, this brewery has been producing Pine Belt Pale Ale and has now expanded to several other beers. On Saturdays, you and your dog (on leash) are welcome to visit the brewery for a free tour and (for you) a tasting. Food trucks are stationed at the brewery on many Saturdays but you're also welcome to bring a picnic lunch. *Info: 1207 N. FM 3083 East; (936) 441-2739; southernstarbrewery.com. Free.*

W. Goodrich Jones State Forest. This 1722-acre forest is often lauded for its birding with a special management area set aside for the Red Cockaded Woodpecker. The day-use park offers two small lakes as well as picnic areas (no campfires) and hiking trails. *Info: 1328 FM 1488; (936) 273-2261; texasforestservice.tamu.edu. Free.*

Wiggins Village Park. This eight-acre park didn't begin as an off-leash park but as a water retention area doing double duty as practice fields. A few years ago, two of the fields were transformed into a dog park. Largely undeveloped, you'll want to bring your own water for you and Fido during a visit to this park. *Info: 565 Bryant Rd.; www.cityofconroe.org. Free.*

Fetch This!
Conroe is home to **PetSmart Conroe** (2900 I-45; 936-494-2500) which includes a Banfield Pet Hospital and a **Petco** (1410 North Loop 336 West; 936-441-4700).

Stay, Lie Down
You'll find several dog-friendly hotel chains in Conroe including **Baymont**, **La Quinta**, **Motel 6**, and **Ramada**.

Sniff Out More Information
Conroe Convention and Visitors Bureau; (936) 522-3500; www.conroecvb.net.

DAINGERFIELD
This petite town of just over 2,500 residents, with its historic

downtown that just says "small town Texas," is the gateway to the Daingerfield State Park.

Run, Spot, Run!
Daingerfield State Park. This 500-acre park is one of the oldest in Texas, created by the Civilian Conservation Corp in the 1930s. Surrounded by pine and hardwood forests, the park offers you  and your dog plenty of great options for long, shady walks on the nature trails as well as water fun on the 80-acre lake. Campers can choose from 40 campsites with full hookups, water and electricity, and 12 water-only tent sites. *Info: 455 Park Rd. 17; (903) 645-2921; www.tpwd.state.tx.us. Fee.*

Sniff Out More Information
Daingerfield Chamber of Commerce; (903) 645-2646; www.daingerfieldtx.net.

HUNTSVILLE
Many Texans know Huntsville as the home of the headquarters of the Texas prison system but you don't have to be sentenced here to want to visit—and stay—in this picturesque and historic community. The adopted home of General Sam Houston, the leader of the Texas Revolution is remembered here with a 67-foot-tall statue (7600 TX 75 S.) that's the world's tallest statue of an American hero.

Run, Spot, Run!
Fort Boggy State Park. Located northwest of Huntsville near the community of Centerville, this park was the location of a fort in the 1840s; today it primarily provides protection against urban burnout. The park on Boggy Creek as well as a small lake offers 3-1/2 miles of trails, swimming for you and your dog, free paddleboats, and

birding. And even the park ranger warns to bring bug spray during spring months when Fort Boggy becomes Fort Buggy! This day-use park is open Wednesday through Sunday. *Info: 4994 TX 75 S., Centerville; (903) 344-1116; www.tpwd.state.tx.us. Free.*

Huntsville State Park. Located 6 miles southwest of Huntsville, this 2,000-plus-acre park adjoins Sam Houston National Forest so expect plenty of shady trails for you and Fido to explore. Hiking, camping, canoeing on Lake Raven, and fishing are top activities. Your dog will find plenty of paddling options but dogs are not permitted in the designated swimming area. The Lone Star Hiking Trail (see Cleveland) comes through here and travels to Sam Houston National Forest. Other trails in the park great for canine exploration are Chinquapin Trail along Big Chinquapin Creek (with a boardwalk), Dogwood Trail and Loblolly Trail. Keep an eye out for horses on some trails; you and your dog should always yield the trail to equestrians. *Info: State Park Rd. 40; (936) 295-5644; www.tpwd.state.tx.us. Fee.*

Lake Livingston State Park. Located east of Huntsville about a mile southwest of Livingston, this park offers 635 acres of recreational opportunities along Lake Livingston. It's a great place to camp, swim, picnic, boat, and fish for crappie, catfish, perch, and bass. There are also trails through the forests for hiking, horseback riding, and mountain biking. *Info: 300 State Park Rd. 65, off US 59; (936) 365-2201; tpwd.state.tx.us. Fee.*

Pineview Dog Park. Near Sam Houston State University, this fenced park is usually a quiet place to let your dog exercise; drinking fountains and benches are available. *Info: 2335 23rd St. Free.*

Sam Houston Statue and Visitors Center. This 67-foot tall statue (on a 10-foot base) sculpted by artist David Adickes is the world's tallest statue of an American hero. On the path to the statue, your dog can pose next to a 3-D model of the statue's head. The site is also home to the city visitors center. *Info: 7600 TX 75 S. (exit 109 or 112 off I-45); (936) 291-9726. Free.*

Stay, Lie Down
Huntsville is home to several dog-friendly budget chains including **Best Western, Econo Lodge, La Quinta, Motel 6** and more.

Pawty Time
April: Family Fun DOG Show. All dogs are encouraged to enter this fun competition for titles that range from best tail wagger to best newspaper retriever. Proceeds go to animal welfare organizations; organized by Huntsville Walker County Pet Organization. *Info: www.facebook.com/HWCPO.*

Sniff Out More Information
City of Huntsville; (936) 291-9726; www.huntsvilletexas.com.

JEFFERSON
Nearby destinations: Marshall

Over a century ago, Jefferson was known as the "Riverport to the Southwest." In the 1840s, the town was established as a port city on the Big Cypress Bayou, linking northeast Texas with Shreveport and the Red River. Steamers brought supplies and people to Jefferson and left stocked with the area's richest crop—cotton. At its peak, Jefferson was the second largest port city in the state. When the natural log jam on the Red River broke and the water from Cypress Bayou drained, the city's steamboat commerce ended.

Although it never returned to its earlier status, Jefferson now enjoys a new role: that of the tourist capital of East Texas. Tucked beneath tall pines and moss-draped cypress trees, this town now lets visitors step back in time to the heyday of river travel. Jefferson is home to many bed and breakfast facilities and antiques shops.

Run, Spot, Run!
Caddo Lake State Park. *See Marshall, Texas.*

dogtipper **The Graceful Ghost.** This popular tourist boat welcomes dogs on leash to explore Caddo Lake in a replica 1800s paddlewheel steamboat that's one of the last wood-burning, steam-powered stern paddle wheelers in the world. Tours require a minimum of six guests

choice

and aren't scheduled for Sundays and Mondays. The Coast Guard-approved vessel provides a 75-minute narrated tour of this historic area. *Info: 510 Cypress Drive, Uncertain; (903) 789-2238; gracefulghost.com. Fee.*

Lake o' the Pines. Fishing, boating, water skiing, and swimming are available at Lake o' the Pines. Camping with your dog is also an option. *Info: From Jefferson, 4 miles west on TX 49, then 4 miles west on FM 729, then 2 miles west on FM 726; (903) 665-2336; www.tpwd.state.tx.us. Fee.*

Stay, Lie Down
The Carriage House Bed and Breakfast. Built in 1920, this historic inn welcomes pet travelers (including those with cats) to its rooms in the cottages behind the inn. The most pet-friendly room is the Jay Gould Room which includes its own private fenced yard! The Western-themed room, named for a railroad baron, features a queen bed and full bath. The inn's insurance policy prohibits stays by pit bulls, Dobermans, Rottweilers, German Shepherds, and Chows but there's no weight restriction. You may have up to two dogs in a room for a per stay fee of $50. *Info: 401 N. Polk St.; (903) 665-9511; carriagehousejefferson.com.*

Steamboat Inn. Four rooms, each with a private bath and fireplace, welcome pet travelers in this B&B located just one block from downtown. *Info: 114 N. Marshall St.; (903) 926-7741; www.steamboatinntx.com.*

Sniff Out More Information
Jefferson Tourism; (903) 665-3733; www.visitjeffersontexas.com.

KOUNTZE
Nearby destinations: Beaumont

Kountze is the gateway to one of Texas' most unique parks: Big Thicket National Preserve. The park is divided into several units with multiple entrance points but most visitors stop by the Turkey Creek Unit for the Visitors Information Station.

Run, Spot, Run!
Big Thicket National Preserve. We love this dense thicket but we're going to warn you: regardless of where you and Fido hike in the park, be prepared for mosquitoes (as well as heat and humidity during the summer months). Dog-safe mosquito repellent is a must-have on your packing list and please be sure your dog is current on heartworm preventative! Once safely protected from those pesky skeeters, you and your dog can enjoy all the trails at Big Thicket (on a leash no longer than six feet long). The two of you will find plenty of hikes to enjoy together thanks to 40 miles of hiking trails. Near the Big Thicket Information Center lies the Kirby Nature Trail, a good choice for those visiting the park for the first time. The trail makes three loops. The inside loop is 1.7 miles long and you can pick up a booklet for a self-guided tour of the cypress-shaded region. *Info: 6102 FM 420; (409) 951-6700; www.nps.gov/bith. Fee.*

Stay, Lie Down
You'll find a wide selection of dog-friendly chain hotels in Beaumont, about 30 miles from the park.

Indian Springs Camp and RV Park. Whether you'd like to tent or RV camp, this park is located just across the road from the Big Thicket Information Center. The 200-acre camp is somewhat dog-friendly; however, they specify "Pit Bull and other large dogs are not allowed due to safety concerns." (Since most pitties are about half the size of our dogs, we didn't even try this park with our Irie and Tiki.) The park has miles of nature trails, canoeing opportunities, fishing, and more. Dogs must be on leash at all times. *Info: 6106*

Park Precautions

Big Thicket is an untamed park and you and your dog should be sure to take additional precautions in this area. During hunting season, please be sure your dog is wearing an orange collar (and always have your dog on leash regardless of the season).

Feral hogs are another danger in the park. Feral hogs generally run from people but if they have young, these creatures will defend and become aggressive. It is very important to never allow your dog to approach a piglet. Mountain lions are increasing in number in the park, perhaps because of the growing number of feral hogs. The park keeps track of hog and lion sightings so report your experiences at the Information Station or at trail registers found on the trailheads.

Holland Cemetery Rd., just east of US 69; (409) 246-2508; indianspringscamp.net.

Sniff Out More Information
Kountze Chamber of Commerce; (866) 456-8689; www.kountze chamber.com.

LUFKIN
Nearby destinations: Huntsville, Nacogdoches

This East Texas community is surrounded by pine forests. Vacationers will find that Lufkin, a capital of the lumber industry, is a good access point to the Sam Rayburn Reservoir, the largest lake entirely in Texas, as well as the Angelina and Davy Crockett national forests.

Run, Spot, Run!
Angelina National Forest. The Lufkin area is home to some of the state's best forests, tall stands of trees known as the piney woods (primarily Longleaf Pine in the southern portion of the forest and Loblolly and Shortleaf Pine in the northern portion, just in case your dog asks!) Angelina National Forest includes Bouton Lake,

Boykin Springs, Sandy Creek, and the Caney Creek recreation areas and several hiking trails including the 5.5-mile Sawmill Hiking Trail. Dogs on leash are permitted in the park including the campground and on the trails but not in the beach and swimming areas. *Info: Located off TX 63; (936) 897-1068; www.fs.usda.gov. Fee.*

Davy Crockett National Forest. The 160,000-acre Davy Crockett Park includes the Big Slough Canoe Trail and Wilderness Area, the 4-C's Hiking Trail with its 19 miles of marked trail, and several other recreation areas; your dog is welcome on-leash. *Info: (936) 655-2299; www.fs.usda.gov. Fee.*

Lake Sam Rayburn. The largest man-made lake entirely in the state, this truly Texas-sized lake spans 114,400 acres. The lake is lined with cabins as well as RV parks and campgrounds. You and your dog can also enjoy boating or fishing at this lake known for its population of largemouth bass. *Info: east on TX 103; (409) 384-5716; www.swf-wc.usace.army.mil/samray. Free.*

Ratcliff Lake Recreation Area. Located in the Davy Crockett National Forest, this lake welcomes pets on leash (anywhere except the beach). You'll find a campground here and can take off on the nearly 20-mile-long Four C Hiking Trail all the way to the Neches Bluff overlook. *Info: west on TX 103 to TX 7 then west for 12 miles; (936) 655-2299; www.fs.usda.gov. Fee.*

Stay, Lie Down
Lufkin is home to numerous dog-friendly budget chains including **Best Western**, **La Quinta**, **Motel 6**, **Quality Inn**, and more.

Sniff Out More Information
Lufkin Convention and Visitors Bureau; (936) 633-0349; visitlufkin.com.

MARSHALL
Nearby destinations: Jefferson

This East Texas town is best known for its pottery, produced by several pottery companies in town. The town is sometimes called the Pottery Capital of the US. Here potters have been mining clay from east Texas's rolling hills for more than a century, now turning out more than a million pots each year. Marshall is especially popular during spring and fall months for its brilliant blooms and colors.

Run, Spot, Run!

Caddo Lake National Wildlife Refuge. Established in 2000, this 8,500-acre park welcomes your leashed dog for a day of hiking, photography, and wildlife viewing. A former railroad right of way is now a nine-mile-long nature trail, and several other trails invite you to explore the park. Be sure to bring mosquito repellant! *Info: 15600 FM 134; (903) 679-9144; www.fws.gov/refuge/caddo_lake. Free.*

Caddo Lake Paddling Trails. It's a little faster than dog paddling, and canoe travel makes a great way for you and your dog to explore the swamps and bayous of this region. There are 10 designated paddling trails in the area; check with the Marshall CVB for information and, if needed, information on canoe liveries in the area. *Info: (903) 702-7777; www.visitmarshalltexas.org. Free.*

Caddo Lake State Park. Located 15 miles northeast of Marshall near the community of Karnack, Caddo Lake is the only natural lake of

 any size in the state of Texas. The lake was created by the "Great Raft of the Red River," a mass of trees and debris that through years of floods created a dam. Today the lake is held in place by a modern dam but the lake retains a swampy, bayou feel with tall, moss-draped cypress trees and an endless maze of watery corridors to explore by boat or canoe. On land, you and Fido can find hiking trails, picnic areas, and campgrounds. Warning: keep an eye out for alligators! *Info: 245 Park Rd. 2, Karnack; (903) 679-3351; www.tpwd.state.tx.us. Fee.*

The Graceful Ghost. See Jefferson for details on this dog-friendly steam paddlewheeler.

Martin Creek Lake State Park. Located 25 miles southwest of Marshall, this state park is best known for its water fun: fishing, (unsupervised) swimming, and boating. Dogs aren't permitted in the designated swimming area but you will find plenty of lake frontage for a dip. You'll find plenty of hiking opportunities, too, and your dog just might spot a nutria, gopher or swamp rabbit. Campsites welcome dogs except in the cabin and screened shelter areas. *Info: 9515 County Rd. 2181D, Tatum; (903) 836-4336; www.tpwd.state.tx.us. Fee.*

Stay, Lie Down
Marshall is home to several dog-friendly chain hotels including **Days Inn, Holiday Inn**, La Quinta, **Motel 6**, and more.

Sniff Out More Information
Marshall Convention and Visitors Bureau; (903) 702-7777; www.visitmarshalltexas.org.

MONTGOMERY
Nearby destinations: Conroe, Houston

One of the oldest towns in Texas, the community of Montgomery is called the "Birthplace of the Lone Star Flag" due to its role as the location where the first Republic of Texas flag was designed. Today the town, located on the southwest edge of the Sam Houston National Forest, is home to many dog-friendly parks (but please note that Lake Conroe Park is NOT open to four-legged guests.)

Run, Spot, Run!
Cedar Brake Park. Designed to be fully-accessible for physically challenged travelers, this park has wide paths that also make it great for a morning dog walk. *Info: Eva St. (TX 105) at Houston Rd. Free.*

Memory Park. Filled with many native plants donated in the name of loved ones, this quiet park provides tranquility for dog walks by duck nesting areas, a Shakespeare Garden, fountains, bridges, and more. *Info: located behind the Charles B. Stewart Library at 202 Bessie Price Owen Drive. Free.*

Montgomery County Nature Preserve. Located behind the recycling center, this 71-acre greenway offers a quiet place for a dog walk with your leashed Lassie. The park is filled with native plants including many that attract butterflies; official butterfly counts are conducted here every year. Open daily. *Info: 1122 Pruitt Rd.; (281) 367-3977. Free.*

Stay, Lie Down

Montgomery is home to several dog-friendly chain hotels including **America's Best Inn and Suites, Drury Inn, Econo Lodge, Embassy Suites, Extended Stay America, La Quinta, Red Roof Inn, Residence Inn, Staybridge Suites** and others.

La Torretta Del Lago Resort and Spa. This pampering resort on the shores of Lake Conroe welcomes dogs under 30 pounds in the golf  cottages. The resort, which spans 300 acres, is home to an entire array of activities including an 18-hole golf course, spa, tennis courts, miniature golf course, a beach, kayaking, and more. Dog travelers pay a $250 deposit with $50 going towards the cleaning fee upon checkout. When in the room alone, dogs need to be crated. *Info: 600 La Torretta Blvd., just off TX 105; (936) 448-4400; latorrettalakeresort.com.*

Sniff Out More Information
City of Montgomery; (936) 597-6434; www.montgomerytexas.gov.

NACOGDOCHES
Nearby destinations: Lufkin

Nacogdoches, the oldest town in Texas, began as a Native American settlement. Legend has it that this east Texas community was named for the son of a Caddo family who lived on the Sabine River. The young man was sent to walk three days toward the setting sun; his twin brother was instructed to walk three days toward the rising sun. And their new homes? Each was named for the twin who settled there: Nacogdoches to the west and Natchitoches, to the east in Louisiana. The brothers each settled in their newfound region but frequently visited each other along a route that legend says became the eastern end of the Camino Real.

Run, Spot, Run!

Caddo Mounds State Historic Site. Located 25 miles west of Nacogdoches near Alto, this 397-acre park welcomes dogs on leashes (and they even have a golf cart they'll loan you to go out and see the mounds if Fido's tired!) The site was the southwestern-most ceremonial center for the great Mound Builder culture which for 2,500 years dominated the woodlands. The mounds were constructed by the Hasinai, a group of Caddo Indians, about 1,200 years ago. Two temple mounds are found here; you and your dog can stroll the trails on a self-guided tour of the site. *Info: 1649 TX 21 West, Alto; (936) 858-3218; www.visitcaddomounds.com. Fee.*

Gayla Mize Garden. The newest of the four gardens at Stephen F. Austin University, this garden welcomes you and your leashed dog to relax and stroll among the flowers that were planted to honor a pioneer in Nacogdoches gardening. *Info: Parking on Starr Ave. at University Dr.; sfagardens.sfasu.edu. Free.*

Lanana Creek Trail. The shady trail, originally a Native American footpath, today runs through the campus of Stephen F. Austin State University. Mostly asphalt surface, the trail offers you and Rover a look at seasonal blooms including paw-paw, dogwood and buckeye. *Info: E. Main St. between Lanana St. and University Dr. Free.*

Mission Tejas State Historical Park. This park, located just west of Caddo Mounds State Historic Site, recalls the first Spanish mission built in East Texas in 1690. (Dogs are not permitted inside the building or in any other building in a state park.) You and Fido will find plenty of options for hiking. Today the park offers camping among the pine trees as well as picnicking and pond fishing. *Info: 120 State Park Rd. 44, Grapeland; (936) 687-2394; www.tpwd.state.tx.us. Fee.*

Pineywoods Native Plant Center. Local plants take center stage at this 40-acre garden. Your dog will enjoy the shady walk through the native bottomland hardwood forest on the two-mile-long

Tucker Woods Trail or check out the blooms of East Texas wild-flowers at the Lady Bird Johnson Wildflower Demonstration Garden. The Lanana Creek Trail connects the center to the other gardens on the university campus. *Info: 2900 Raguet St.; sfagardens.sfasu.edu. Free.*

dogtipper

choice

Ruby M. Mize Azalea Garden. Over 500 varieties of azaleas fill this garden, the largest azalea garden in Texas. Although best known for its azaleas in bloom from March through May, don't miss the fragrant smell of gardenias and hydrangeas from May through August or the beautiful Japanese maples and camellias from October through February. You and Fido can combine a visit to this garden with a stroll through the adjoining SFA Mast Arboretum and the nearby Pineywoods Native Plant Center. *Info: 2107 University Dr.; sfagardens.sfasu.edu. Free.*

SFA Mast Arboretum. This 18-acre garden was the first arboretum at a university in Texas and boasts over 7,500 varieties of plants. Your dog will enjoy strolling through 20 themed gardens and you can extend your walk by crossing the bridge to the Ruby M. Mize Azalea Garden as well. *Info: Wilson Dr.; sfagardens.sfasu.edu. Free.*

Stay, Lie Down
Nacogdoches is home to several dog-friendly discount hotel chains including **Days Inn**, **Holiday Inn**, **La Quinta**, **Super 8**, and more.

Sniff Out More Information
Nacogdoches County Chamber of Commerce; (936) 560-5533; www.nacogdoches.org.

RUSK
Rusk is best-known as the home of the Texas State Railroad steam train (which, sadly, isn't dog-friendly with the exception of service dogs) but you and Fido will find several other reasons to visit this

town named after one of the signers of the Texas Declaration of Independence.

Run, Spot, Run!

Jim Hogg Memorial Park. Formerly a state park, today the city of Rusk operates this historic park named for Jim Hogg, the first state-born governor of Texas. The park includes a replica of Hogg's birthplace and, of special interest to dog travelers, nature trails that wind through the woods and, at one point along the trail, overlook an iron ore strip mining field from the 1880s. *Info: two miles east of Rusk off US 84 East and Fire Tower Rd., then to Park Rd. 50; www.rusktx.org. Free.*

Rusk Footbridge and Garden Park. Believed to be the longest footbridge in the country at 546 feet, this bridge was built to span a valley that sometimes flooded so citizens could walk into town. First constructed in 1861 then rebuilt in 1889, today the bridge provides a fun photo opportunity for you and your pooch. *Info: West 6th and Main Sts.; (903) 683-4242; www.rusktx.org. Free.*

Stay, Lie Down

Weston Inn and Suites. This two-story hotel, with rooms that open onto outdoor walkways, offers a picnic area as well as free continental breakfast and high-speed Internet access. Some rooms include kitchenettes. Dogs are permitted for just $5 per pet per night with up to three pets per room. *Info: 590 N. Dickinson Dr.; (903) 683 – 8383; westoninntexas.com.*

Sniff Out More Information

Rusk Chamber of Commerce; (903) 683-4242; www.ruskchamber.com.

TEXARKANA

Your dog has the opportunity to have his photo taken with paws in two states in this city that sits on the state line between Texas and Arkansas.

Run, Spot, Run!

Atlanta State Park. Located southwest of Texarkana on Wright Patman Lake, this 1500-acre park is a favorite with anglers, campers, and boaters but also popular for its nature trail and hiking trail. You and your dog can stroll beneath the tall pines in this area that was once home to Caddo Indians. *Info: 927 Park Rd. 42, Atlanta; (903) 796-6476; www.tpwd.state.tx.us. Fee.*

PetSafe JefFURson Dog Park. This park, which was constructed after winning PetSafe's annual Bark For Your Park contest, is located on the Arkansas side of Texarkana in Jefferson Park and, at press time, is scheduled to open in fall 2013. The community beat out over 1,000 other cities to win $100,000 for the spectacular park. *Info: East 12th and Jefferson Ave., Texarkana, Arkansas. Free.*

Rocky Point Park. Located at the 30,000-acre Wright Patman Dam and Lake on the Sulphur River, this dog-friendly park offers hiking trails, fishing, and camping with 124 campsites. Dogs are welcome on leash and are prohibited from designated swimming areas. *Info: Located south of the dam. Turn west off US 59 and follow the signs; (903) 838-8781; www.reserveamerica.com. Fee.*

State Line Post Office and Photographer's Island. Mail home a postcard from the only post office located in two states! The post office has two separate zip codes for the Texas and Arkansas mail. Directly in front of the post office, you and your dog can have your photo snapped on Photographer's Island. Here a sign marks the state line. *Info: 500 State Line Ave.; (903) 794-8561. Free.*

Fetch This!

PetSmart Texarkana. Conveniently located just off I-30, this store offers quality foods, treats, and travel needs. *Info: 117 Richmond Ranch Rd.; (903) 832-0244; www.petsmart.com.*

RV Art Gallery. Although not specifically for pets, we know that 64 percent of RVers travel with pets (largely dogs) so we had to include the nation's only art gallery for RVers! Shop for travel trailer charms, RV birdhouses, home furnishings for your home on wheels, and books on RV lifestyle and history. The store is located at the KOA Texarkana. *Info: 500 W. 53rd St.; (800) 467-5521; www.rvartgallery.com.*

Stay, Lie Down

Texarkana, Texas and adjacent Texarkana, Arkansas are home to numerous dog-friendly hotel chains including **Baymont Inn and Suites, Candlewood Suites, Clarion, La Quinta, Motel 6, Rodeway Inn, Super 8**, and more.

Sniff Out More Information

Texarkana Chamber of Commerce; (903) 792-7191; www.texarkana.org.

TYLER

Tyler may be known as the Rose Capital of the World, but each spring the city celebrates another natural beauty during the Tyler Azalea and Spring Flower Trails. Whenever you visit, you and Fido have plenty of options for outdoor fun.

Run, Spot, Run!

Rose Rudman Park Trail. This 2.5-mile concrete trail winds through the city and welcomes dogs on leash. *Info: 450 Shiloh Rd. Free.*

Tyler State Park (*see photo on next page*). Lake fun for Fidos ranges from nature walks to swimming and boating at this forested park on a peaceful 64-acre lake. Both tent and RV camping options are available in this park including some beautiful lakeside RV spots; RVers must bring and use jack pads in these sites. *Info: 789 Park Rd. 16; (903) 597-5338; www.tpwd.state.tx.us. Fee.*

Fetch This!

PetSmart Tyler. Along with food, treats, and travel supplies, this store includes a full-service Banfield veterinary clinic. *Info: 5610 S. Broadway; (903) 534-5261; www.petsmart.com.*

Stay, Lie Down

Tyler is home to several dog-friendly budget hotels including **America's Best Value Inn, Baymont Inn and Suites, Candlewood Suites, Days Inn, Holiday Inn, La Quinta, Motel 6**, and more.

Sniff Out More Information

Tyler Convention and Visitors Bureau; (800) 235-5712; www.visit-tyler.com.

6. Prairies and Lakes

One of the most expansive sections of Texas, the Prairies and Lakes region starts in the prairies that give away to the Gulf coastal plains and works its way all the way up to a large expanse of North Central Texas best known as the home of the Dallas-Fort Worth Metroplex. The cities of Dallas and Fort Worth have long been touted as the city slicker and the country cousin, two destinations that share a geographic area but boast very different atmospheres.

South along I-35 lie many historic communities such as Waco, home to Baylor University and Temple and Belton with their nearby lakes. East of I-35 lie Brenham and College Station as well as small Texas towns Lockhart, and Luling, well known among barbecue buffs.

ATHENS

Your dog may perk up those ears when you mention that Athens is known as "The Home of the Original Hamburger." The city says that the all-American favorite was first created downtown by Fletcher Davis or Uncle "Fletch"; the hamburger was so well-loved that the townspeople pooled their money and sent him to the World's Fair in St. Louis in 1904 to introduce his creation to the world. The rest is history. Three cities now lay claim to the "first hamburger" but McDonald's University has acknowledged Athens as the home of the original hamburger, a title also bestowed on the town by the Texas State Legislature.

Run, Spot, Run!

East Texas Arboretum and Botanical Society. This pet-friendly botanical garden welcomes dogs on leashes to enjoy its formal gardens, demonstration windmill, and two miles of hiking trails. Enjoy a dog walk among huckleberry, grapevines, honeysuckle, dogwood, dewberry and more. You and your dog will negotiate a suspension foot bridge as you cross an old beaver pond. *Info: 1601 Patterson Road; (903) 675-5630; www.eastexasarboretum.org. Fee.*

Historic Walk. If you'd like to transform your dog walk into a historic stroll, visit the City of Athens website to download a map of a 6.5-mile hike past numerous historic markers in the city. The 10K course is sanctioned by the American Volkssport Association and is a fun, free way for you and your dog to take a walk back in history. *Info: www.athenstx.org. Free.*

Purtis Creek State Recreation Area. Located in the historic region that was once home to Wichita and Caddo Indians, this lakeside park is a favorite with anglers and campers. The 1,582-acre park is located on the Cedar Creek Reservoir which limits activity to just 50 boats at a time, maintaining the peaceful atmosphere of the park. Activities include camping, fishing, boating, hiking and picnicking. As at other state parks, dogs are required to be on a leash no longer than six feet and are not permitted in any buildings. *Info: 14225 FM 316, Eustace (from Athens, travel 12 miles west on US 175 to Eustace, turn north on FM 316 for 3.5 miles to park); (903) 425-2332; www.tpwd.state.tx.us. Fee.*

Sniff Out More Information
City of Athens; (888) 294-2847; athenstx.org.

BASTROP
Nearby destinations: Austin, Smithville

The home of the "Lost Pines," the westernmost stand of loblolly pines in America, sadly Bastrop was in the headlines in 2011 as the site of the most destructive wildfire in Texas history. Nearly 1,700 homes were destroyed in this devastating wildfire which heavily impacted the pine forest. Some regions remain intact and planting of new seedlings promises to eventually return the area to its previous beauty.

Run, Spot, Run!
Bastrop Bark Park. Located across from the Police Department, this park is open for four-legged visitors 7:00 a.m. to dusk. *Info: 104 Grady Tuck Lane; (512) 321-3957. Free.*

Bastrop State Park. The piney woods were a huge draw in this park and some areas of pine forest remain in this part that includes an eighteen-hole golf course, campsites, and a ten-acre fishing lake.

The park is home to 1930s-built stone and cedar CCC cabins but these are not dog-friendly. Hiking with your dog is an option at this park which offers several trails. As at all state parks, your dog must be on a leash no  longer than six feet. It's especially important for your dog to remain close to you in this park and for you to remain on your toes as you watch for falling trees, a real danger with the numerous dead, burned trees in the park. *Info: 100 Park Road 1A, 1.5 miles east of Bastrop; (512) 321–2101 or (512) 389–8900; www.tpwd.state.tx.us. Fee.*

Lake Bastrop Parks. The Lower Colorado River Authority (LCRA) administers two lake parks on 900-acre Lake Bastrop: North Shore Park and South Shore Park and both welcome dogs. The North Shore Park offers camping (tent and RV), hiking, birding, and a fishing dock. The South Shore Park also offers camping as well as mini-cabins with bunk beds; several of the cabins are pet-friendly. *Info: FM 1441 (North Shore); County Road 352/South Shore Road (South Shore; (512) 498-1922; www.lcra.org. Fee.*

McKinney Roughs Nature Park. Leashed dogs are permitted on most of the trails of this day-use park operated by the Lower Colorado River Authority. The 1,100-acre park with lots of Colorado River frontage is a favorite with equestrians so make sure your dog is comfortable moving over on the trail to give right of way to horses. *Info: 1884 TX 71 West, Cedar Creek; (512) 303–5073; www.lcra.org. Fee.*

Riverwalk. You and your dog can enjoy this nature walk along the banks of the Colorado River. Opened in 1998, the one-mile trail features a variety of trees, native plants, and wildflowers. It is accessible from either Fisherman's Park or Ferry Park. *Info: 904 Main St. Free.*

Fetch This!

Buc-cee's. This Texas-sized gas station/convenience store/gift shop is an attraction in itself due to its sheer size. Dogs can't enter the store but, if you take turns with your human travel companion, you'll find a dog accessory section (even Buc-cee's dog toys), Texana gifts, and hot food. Outside, dog relief areas include pet mitts. *Info: 1700 Highway 71 E.; www.bucees.com.*

Petco Bastrop. This Petco, besides offering food, treats, and travel supplies, is home to one of Petco's Information Resource Centers where you can go in and get free, uninterrupted time with a Pet Specialist. *Info: 739 TX 71 W.; (512) 321-5800; www.petco.com.*

Treats and Eats

dogtipper

choice

Bastrop Brewhouse. Look for this brewery's pooch mascot, Barleywine "Half Pint" Peters, at this spot known for live music, local cuisine, and handcrafted ales. The menu includes burgers made with Bastrop-raised beef, Texas trout, and Brewhouse Ale battered fish and chips. *Info: 601 Chestnut St.; (512) 321-1144; www.bastropbrewhouse.com.*

Stay, Lie Down

Bastrop is home to several dog-friendly budget hotels including **Comfort Suites** and **Quality Inn**; you'll also find numerous chains near the Austin-Bergstrom International Airport a short drive west.

Hyatt Regency Lost Pines Resort and Spa. Opened in 2006, this luxury resort is known for its distinctive central Texas atmosphere.

The hotel, located adjacent to the McKinney Roughs Nature Park, spans over 400 acres and offers an equestrian center, an Arthur Hills–designed golf course, rafting on the Colorado River, a full-service spa, and more. Pets incur a fee of $150 for stays of up to six nights. (An additional $150 fee is charged for stays of seven to 30 nights.) Dogs under 75 pounds (or two dogs whose combined weight does not exceed 75 pounds) are welcome. Canine guests receive use of a branded Hyatt pet bed, water and food bowls, and a pet amenity. *Info: 575 Hyatt Lost Pines Rd., Cedar Creek; (512) 308–1234; lostpines.hyatt.com.*

Sniff Out More Information
Bastrop Visitor Center; (512) 303-0904; www.visitbastroptx.com.

BRENHAM
Across Texas, Brenham is known as the home of Blue Bell ice cream (and, yes, we treat our dogs with a spoonful of vanilla now and then!) The town is rich with dog-friendly options as well, from a historic downtown to surrounding parks.

Run, Spot, Run!
Animal Friends Dog Park. Open 7:30 a.m. until dusk, this off-leash park includes separate small (under 20 pounds) and large dog areas. The park includes ponds, an agility area, water stations, a washing station, and shaded seating. *Info: 3901 TX 36 N.; (979) 277-0400; animalfriendstexas.org. Free.*

Lake Somerville State Park and Trailway. Whether your dog is a water pup or a landlubber, he'll find plenty of fun at this state park that's divided between two units. Both the Birch Creek Unit and the Nails Creek Unit offer rental canoes, camping, picnicking, and plenty of lake fun. The two units are connected by the Lake Somerville Trailway which extends for 13 miles, a great hike for you and your dog to share on the western edge of the reservoir. *Info: Birch Unit, 14222 Park Road 57, Somerville, (979) 535-7763; Nails Creek Unit, 6280 FM 180, Ledbetter, (979) 289-2392; www.tpwd.state.tx.us. Fee.*

Pleasant Hill Winery. Dogs are welcome outdoors at this winery that's housed inside a reconstructed hilltop barn. Open Saturday 11 a.m. to 6 p.m. and Sunday noon to 5 p.m. *Info: Salem Road, just south of US 290 and TX 36 intersection; (979) 830–VINE; www.pleasanthillwinery.com. Fee for tours.*

Washington-on-the-Brazos State Historic Site. You and Fido will be taking a step back in Texas history at this park located between

Brenham and Navasota. Located on the banks of the Brazos, this quiet park is shaded by acres of walnut and pecan trees. Washington is known as the birthplace of Texas, the place where, on a cold March day in 1836, founders gathered and signed the Declaration of Independence, establishing Texas as a sovereign nation. From 1842 to 1845, Washington served as the capital of the Republic, also gradually becoming a commerce center on the busy Brazos, one that eventually dwindled with the growth of the railroads.

The history of this special site is kept alive at Washington-on-the-Brazos State Historic Site, a park with numerous interpretive  trails. Although dogs are not permitted inside buildings (including the Star of the Republic Museum, built in the shape of a star: see photo on left), you can stroll the interpretive trail from Independence Hall—a replica of the original building where the signing of the Texas Declaration of Independence took place—to the historic Washington town site. *Info: from Brenham, take TX 105 east 14 miles and turn right on FM 912 to Washington-on-the-Brazos State Historic Site; (936) 878-2214; www.tpwd.state.tx.us. Free.*

Stay, Lie Down

Brenham is well-known for its historic bed and breakfast inns, although most don't court the dog traveler (unlike Fredericksburg, which has several B&B booking agencies with many dog-friendly properties.) If your heart is set on a B&B, call the Brenham–Washington County Convention and Visitor Bureau for recommendations in the area at (888) BRENHAM. We did find one property, Country Cabins, www.cedarscabins.com, that accepts pets but they have to be boarded in kennels on property. That's not really our idea of a dog-friendly vacation.

You will find several hotel chains that welcome four-legged travelers including **Best Western**, **Comfort Suites**, **La Quinta**, **Rodeway Inn**, **Super 8**, and more.

Sniff Out More Information
Brenham/Washington County Convention and Visitors Bureau; (888) BRENHAM; www.visitbrenhamtexas.com.

BRYAN-COLLEGE STATION
If you watch college football, then you're no doubt familiar with the adjoining communities of Bryan-College Station. Home to Texas A&M University (and the state's veterinary school), the region is strongly linked with the dog world.

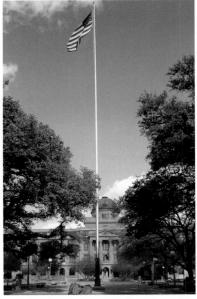

Run, Spot, Run!
Canine Station – University Dog Park. Four acres of University Park are designated for the off-leash park and include swimming ponds for pooches, agility equipment, and open space to play. The fenced park contains separate small dog and large dog areas. *Info: 300 Park Rd., College Station; www.cstx.gov. Free.*

Graves of Reveille. The mascot of Texas A&M University is Reveille, a dog whose tradition dates back to 1931. The first Reveille was a mixed breed stray taken in by students; the dog barked whenever the bugler played "Reveille." Each dog continues the Reveille name although the dog's breed was changed to Rough Collie with Reveille III. Every mascot has always been buried at the college's Kyle Field in a grave facing the south end zone and the scoreboard. An expansion of the field meant that the scoreboard was blocked so all the graves were moved to the stadium's north entrance where a special electronic scoreboard was added so that the graves would always face the scoreboard. Look for the brick plaza by the stadium where a brass plaque recalls the faithful mascots seen at every Aggie football game: "Reveille I, and the Reveilles that follow her, will always have a special place in an Aggie's heart and symbolize the undying spirit of Texas A&M."

Info: Joe Routt Blvd., College Station; (979) 845-5851; www.tamu.edu. Free.

Lick Creek Park Off Leash Area. This unfenced park permits dogs to be off-leash as long as they're under good voice control. Spanning 515 acres, this park features miles of trails for you and your dog to explore. *Info: 13600 East Rock Prairie Road, College Station; www.cstx.gov. Free.*

Messina Hof Winery and Resort. This award-winning winery, one of the best-known names in the state's booming wine industry, welcomes dogs on property. Pop in and get some turtle food then stroll down to feed the turtles with Fido! Started in 1983, the winery includes forty-five acres of vineyards. *Info: 4545 Old Reliance Road, Bryan; (979) 778–9463; www.messinahof.com. Free for visiting grounds.*

Steeplechase Dog Park. This off-leash park (it was the first in College Station) is heavily wooded making this a favorite on hot summer days. The park, located in nine-acre Steeplechase Park, is situated along a tributary of Bee Creek. Rose bushes along the fence line provide seasonal beauty. *Info: 301 Westridge Dr., College Station; www.cstx.gov. Free.*

Fetch This!

Petco. This Petco offers vaccinations as well as dog food, treats, and travel needs. *Info: 1901 S. Texas Ave., College Station; (979) 694-9958; www.petco.com.*

PetSmart College Station. This large PetSmart includes a full-service Banfield pet hospital. *Info: 1505 University Drive E.; (979) 260-4134; www.petsmart.com.*

Treats and Eats

Genghis Grill. The dog-friendly patio invites you to dine with Rover; you'll enjoy a build your own bowl of goodies that range from Thai chicken to chicken sausage to sweet and sour pork. *Info: 700 University Dr. E., College Station; (979) 260-6800; www.genghisgrill.com.*

Stay, Lie Down

With its many students and football visitors, it's not surprising that Bryan-College Station has numerous pet-friendly chains including **Econo Lodge, Hawthorn Suites, Holiday Inn, Homewood Suites, Howard Johnson, Knights Inn, La Quinta, Motel 6, Travelodge**, and more.

Hilton College Station & Conference Center. Welcoming dogs up to 75 pounds for no fee, this hotel is located less than two miles from the Texas A&M campus. *Info: 801 University Drive East, College Station; (979) 693–7500; www.hiltoncs.com.*

Pawty Time

March-April: Texas A&M College of Veterinary Medicine & Biomedical Sciences Open House. Every year, the veterinary school welcomes the public for a day of behind the scenes fun including tours of the large and small animal hospitals, Teddy Bear Surgery, pictures with Reveille, and more. *Info: vetmed.tamu.edu/openhouse.*

Sniff Out More Information

Bryan–College Station Convention and Visitors Bureau; (800) 777–8292 or (979) 260–9898; www.bryan-collegestation.org.

DALLAS

For many visitors, this is the land of icons that symbolize Texas—from J.R. to the Dallas Cowboys. Everything's bigger in the Lone Star State and the "Big D" holds a special place in the hearts of Texans. Surrounded by a Metroplex that covers 12 counties and spans nearly 9,000 square miles, Dallas lives up to its new tourism slogan: "Live Large. Think Big."

Getting Around

Dallas' DART buses and trains permit dogs if they are in a crate or carrier. (This restriction doesn't apply to service animals.) According to the DART site, "Non-service animals are allowed on DART vehicles when carried in an appropriate, securely latched cage or container." *Info: (214) 979-1111; www.dart.org.*

Run, Spot, Run!

Bark Park Central. Located downtown, this park is literally beneath the overpasses of the Central Expressway – a plus when it comes to shade, a negative if you have dogs that worry about traffic noise. Evening lighting makes this park accessible after dark and you'll find a dog wash station here as well. *Info: 2530 Commerce St. Free.*

Cedar Hill State Park. Although it's located just minutes from Dallas, this park is world's away in terms of tranquility. Situated on the 7,500-acre Joe Pool Reservoir, the 1,800-acre park is home to boat rentals, hiking trails, camping and even the reconstructed Penn Farm Agricultural History Center. (As at other state parks, dogs are not permitted in any buildings.) *Info: 1570 West FM 1382, Cedar Hill; (972) 291-3900; www.tpwd.state.tx.us. Fee.*

City of Irving Dog Park. Both small (25 pounds and under) and large dog sections promise plenty of four-legged fun at this popular park. The park offers shaded benches as well as casual seating on large boulders, water fountains, and even free Wi-Fi hotspots. The Dog Park is part of the Irving Animal Care Campus. *Info: 4140 Valley View Lane, Irving; www.cityofirving.org/ parks-and-recreation/Irving Dog Park.asp. Free.*

Coppell Dog Park. Under construction at press time in the suburb of Coppell, the city's first dog park will offer two and a half acres for four-legged fun. Benches in the fenced area will be available. *Info: In MacArthur Park, 400 S. MacArthur Blvd., Coppell. Free.*

Dallas Heritage Village. Formerly known as Old City Park, this collection of historic homes and structures welcomes dogs on leashes on the 20-acre grounds. The structures, the largest collection of its kind in Texas, represent Dallas in the 1840-1910 period.

The 1860s Living Farmstead has costumed docents who also reenact farm chores. *Info: 1515 South Harwood St.; (214) 413-3679; www.dallasheritagevillage.org. Fee. Closed January and August.*

Grand Prairie Dog Park. Located in adjacent Grand Prairie, this three-acre dog park invites your dog to join in off-leash fun. You'll find the park north of the Prairie Paws Adoption Center in Veterans Park. The park features three distinct areas: small dogs, large dogs and a rotation field to keep the grass growing. Both you and Fido will find water fountains and you can hang out on a bench in the shade while your dog burns off some of that travel energy. This special park honors thousands of dogs and dog handlers that have served and given their lives for America in times of war and peace. *Info: 2222 W. Warrior Trail, Grand Prairie; (972) 237-8575; www.gptx.org. Free.*

Klyde Warren Park. Adjacent to the Arts District, this park is home to My Best Friend's Park (below) but so much more. Open from 6 a.m. to 11 p.m. daily, this park hosts four or five events every day as well as food trucks at midday. The dog-friendly park includes a botanic garden with native plants, reading and games courtyard, a 25-foot-wide granite walkway shaded by red oaks, and even free Wi-Fi. *Info: 2012 Woodall Rodgers Freeway; www.klydewarrenpark.org. Free.*

Lake Tawakoni State Park. Located 50 miles east of Dallas, this state park is a popular day trip from Dallas (so popular, in fact, that the park has to restrict access during peak times to prevent overcrowding). Although dogs aren't permitted at the designated swim beach, you and Fido will find that the park has five miles of lake shoreline for a swim. You can head off for a long dog walk down the trails as well. *Info: 10822 FM 2475, Wills Point; (903) 560-7123; www.tpwd.state.tx.us. Fee.*

Main Street Garden. Adjacent to Hotel Indigo (see below), this downtown greenspace is also home to a dog run. Although the park is green, the off-leash dog run is primarily concrete although the dogs were certainly having plenty of fun regardless. Dogs are welcome on-leash on the lawn that's bordered by Main Street, St. Paul, Commerce and Harwood. (Be prepared for the park to close for corporate events and concerts on occasion.) *Info: Main, St.*

Paul, Commerce and Harwood Sts.; www.mainstreetgarden.org. Free.

McKinney's Dog Park at Bonnie Wenk. Opened in 2013, this two-acre off-leash park has a splash pad for dogs as well as separate small and large dog sections. The park is lighted and is open until 11 p.m. daily. *Info: 2996 W. Virginia Pkwy., McKinney; www.mckinneytexas.org. Free.*

My Best Friend's Park. Located in Klyde Warren Park between Uptown and Downtown Dallas, this dog park includes some fun fountains where your dog can splash on a hot Dallas day. All of Klyde Warren Park (see above) makes a fun destination. *Info: 2012 Woodall Rodgers Freeway; www.klydewarrenpark.org. Free.*

NorthBark Park. Dallas's newest dog park is open from sunrise to sunset every day except Tuesdays. The park features three separate areas: small dogs, large, dogs, and wet dogs! The beach area is a favorite for many dogs but the two of you can also enjoy walking trails or hanging out in the shaded areas and just watching the fun. *Info: 4899 Gramercy Oaks Drive; (214) 670-1589; www.dallasparks.org. Free.*

Plano's Jack Carter Dog Park. Divided into a large and small dog area, this two-acre park is closed on the first and third Tuesdays of each month for maintenance. *Info: 2601 Pleasant Valley Dr., Plano; (972) 941-BARK; www.jackcarterdogpark.com. Free.*

Redding Trail Dog Park. Located north of Dallas in the suburb of Addison, this dog park offers a half-acre for off-leash fun. Divided into small and large dog sections, the park includes benches and water fountains. *Info: 14677 Midway Rd., Addison; (972) 450-7100; reddingtrail.dfwdogs.com. Free.*

Ruff Range Dog Park-Frisco. Located in the suburb of Frisco, this park includes small and large dog areas. The park closes on Thursdays for maintenance. *Info: at B.F. Phillips Community Park, 5335 4th Army Memorial Dr., Frisco; (972) 292-6506; www.ruffrange.com or www.friscofun.org. Free.*

Tails 'n Trails Dog Park. Open during daylight hours, this park spans nearly six acres and is divided into small dog (under 30 pounds) and large dog sections. You'll find shaded areas, benches, and walking nature trails to enjoy with your dog. *Info: 950 S.E. Green Oaks Blvd., Arlington; 817-459-5898; www.arlingtontx.gov. Free.*

White Rock Lake Dog Park. The first time we visited this dog park,

we were in Dallas for the funeral of a dog-loving friend. We arrived in the city a bit early and the church was not far from this park so

we decided to cheer ourselves up with a visit. Our friend had loved Dachshunds so, when we saw a Doxie running through the park, ears flying, our spirits lifted. Since then, we've returned to the park several times and always have a good time at what was Dallas's first off-leash dog park (opened in 2001 by Texas Ranger Nolan Ryan). The park includes small and large dog sections and is located right on the shores of White Rock Lake, making it a favorite with water-loving pooches. Closed Mondays. *Info: 8000 E. Mockingbird Lane; www.whiterockdogpark.org. Free.*

Fetch This!

Downtown Pawz. All-natural pet foods are the focal point of this centrally-located store which also offers grooming and dog walking. Run out of dog food on your vacation? If you're staying at a downtown hotel, they'll deliver for free! *Info: 1623 Main St.; (214) 760-PAWZ; downtownpawz.com.*

Lucca Bella Doggie Spa and Boutique. This Uptown-area boutique for discerning doggies features everything from all-natural treats and doggie couture to jewelry and furnishings for dog parents. *Info: 2512 Oak Lawn Avenue (between Maple Ave. and Congress Ave.); (214) 559-0855; luccabella.com.*

Petco University Park. Dallas has numerous Petco stores in the city and surrounding communities; this Lovers Lane store is the most central. *Info: 4325 Lovers Lane; (214) 522-4893; www.petco.com.*

PetSmart Dallas (University Park). The Dallas area has numerous PetSmart stores (many with Banfield pet hospitals) but this property is the most centrally located. The store has a Banfield hospital, grooming, day care, and more. *Info: 5500 Greenville Ave.; (469) 232-2030; www.petsmart.com.*

The Pooch Patio. The Pooch Patio has a little bit of everything: a boutique with all kinds of dog goodies, from apparel to treats (and even a line of Pooch Patio gear). There's also doggie daycare, grooming and a self-service bath here as well as a bar for patrons (see *Treats and Eats*, below). *Info: 3811 Fairmount St.; (214) 252-1550; www.thepoochpatio.com.*

Treats and Eats

Bruster's Real Ice Cream. Your dog will get a free doggie sundae at Bruster's (topped with a treat!) Now the hard part: choosing what to order for you. The choices include shakes, banana splits, waffle cones and flavors ranging from Butter Pecan to Peach. *Info: 6301 South Cooper St., Arlington; (817) 419-7000; www.brusters.com.*

Lee Harvey's. Located between Deep Ellum and the heart of downtown, this bar and restaurant isn't anything fancy but many Dallasites give it a big paws up for its dog-friendly fun and food. Fried shrimp, steak tacos, burgers and paninis fill the menu at lunch and dinner times. The real fun is out back, though, with a large dog-friendly patio filled with picnic tables that often features live music. *Info: 1807 Gould St.; (214) 428-1555; leeharveys.com.*

dogtipper  **Mutts Canine Cantina.** This new eatery in Uptown Dallas consists of both a restaurant and bar alongside a private (day passes are available) two-acre dog park. Open for breakfast, lunch and dinner, this casual restaurant invites dog lovers (with or without their dogs) to enjoy the open-air atmosphere and menu that includes burgers, gourmet hot dogs, brunch, and Dallas-brewed beer — and even a doggie vanilla custard with peanut butter. The dog park has big and small dog sections and is manned by professional poop scoopers!

choice

Info: 2889 Cityplace West Blvd.; (214) 377-8723; www.muttscantina.com.

The Pooch Patio. An off-leash front deck and a back patio welcome dog lovers at The Pooch Patio. Yappy hour is celebrated every day from 4-7 p.m. with espresso, wine and beer. *Info: 3811 Fairmount St.; (214) 252-1550; www.thepoochpatio.com.*

The Rusty Taco. Located near the Main Street Garden dog run, this fun eatery serves (you guessed it!) tacos of all descriptions, from traditional to exotic. Order the Rusty Taco with achiote marinated shredded pork, and topped with pineapple, onion and cilantro or go Texan with a barbecue taco. Your dog is welcome on the patio and they even sell Frisbees to take to the park. *Info: Main St. at St. Paul; www.therustytaco.com.*

Spiral Diner and Bakery. Start your day with migas or a breakfast quesadilla (breakfast is served all day) or check out the salads, soups, wraps, sandwiches and hot plates such as soy meatballs, red coconut curry noodles, or grilled Portobello quesadillas. A portion of the proceeds is donated to animal, human and environmental organizations. The eatery (which also has a Fort Worth location) includes an outdoor dining area for you and your dog. Closed Mondays. *Info: 1101 N. Beckley; (214) 948-4747; www.spiraldiner.com.*

Stay, Lie Down
Dallas has just about every dog-friendly hotel chain you could imagine but the city is also home to some special properties we wanted to point out:

The Adolphus. Home to an eclectic mix of treasures ranging from early Flemish tapestries to a Victorian Steinway once owned by the Guggenheims, this antiques-filled 1912 hotel also welcomes treasured furry friends who weigh 30 pounds or less. Pets must be attended at all times and are not allowed on any hotel furniture, including guest room beds. Pet parents will be billed

for any damage to the room and will be required to pay for any room rate adjustments to neighboring guest rooms due to an unruly Rover. *Info: 1321 Commerce St.; (214) 742-8200; www.hoteladolphus.com.*

Aloft Dallas Downtown. The "arf" program offers visiting pups who weigh less than 40 pounds the VIP treatment , complete with an Aloft Hotels brand dog bed, in-room water bowl, complimentary treats and dog toys—all at no additional charge. The property is conveniently close to a doggie day care, a grooming center, and both the Belo Garden—which allows dogs on leashes—and Main Street Garden, which features a dog run. *Info: 1033 Young St.; (214) 761-0000 or (866) 716-8143; www.aloftdallasdowntown.com.*

The Fairmont. A Big D hotel with a big heart when it comes to our barking buddies, The Fairmont welcomes canines weighing less than 100 pounds for an additional $25 per night. *Info: 1717 N. Akard St.; (214) 720-2020; www.fairmont.com/dallas.*

Hotel Indigo. For a one-time, non-refundable fee of $75, two dogs (or a dog weighing less than 75 pounds) can relax as their pet parent unpacks in one of the 170 rooms at this downtown hotel, which is housed in a building deemed a National Historic Landmark. *Info: 1933 Main St.; (214) 741-7700; www.ihg.com.*

Hotel Lumen. This Kimpton Hotel, conveniently located near Snider Plaza and Highland Park Village, does not place a limit on the number, size or weight of their four-legged guests who stay at no additional charge. Guardians are asked to fill out a pet registration form, which includes the options of a dog sitter, doggie day care and a dog walker (all of which may require a service fee.) *Info: 6101 Hillcrest Ave.; (214) 219-2400; www.hotellumen.com.*

dogtipper **Hotel Palomar.** This luxury hotel rolls out the welcome mat for dogs, starting with a greeting from the Director of Pet Relations, a Beagle named Higgins Bottomley *(see photo on next page).* choice (Actually the fun starts before you even arrive; when the hotel knows a pet is arriving, Higgins will send a welcome email to your dog!) Four-legged guests find treats waiting for them at the guest room honor bar and food and water bowls at the ready; more treats, bottled water and plastic pick-up bags are available at the front desk. A grassy area for Rovers to romp includes waste bags and a disposal to keep the turf tidy. Grooming, pet-sitting, dog-walking and veterinary services are just a phone call to the concierge away. *Info: 5300 E. Mockingbird Ln.; (214) 520-7969; www.hotelpalomar-dallas.com.*

Hyatt Regency Dallas. Pet-friendly rooms cost an additional $35 per night for dogs weighing 50 pounds and under. Guests may have up to two dogs per room with a combined weight that does not exceed 75 pounds. With the pet fee, you'll receive use of a branded Hyatt pet bed, dog bowls with a small mat, a dog ID Tag with the hotel's address, a dog walking map, dog door hanger and doggie treats. *Info: 300 Reunion Blvd.; (214) 651-1234; www.dallasregency.hyatt.com.*

W Dallas Victory Hotel. A four-star friend to those with fur, this property's Pets Are Welcome (P.A.W.) program starts your Spot's stay with a pet toy, treat, a W Hotels pet tag and clean-up bags at check-in. Inside your room, Rover can take a cat nap on a custom W pet bed, dine and drink at a food and water bowl placed on a floor mat, and end the day with a special treat at turndown. A pet in-room door sign will notify cleaning staff of your pup's presence. The hotel's Whatever/Whenever service will also fetch pet products in need, including leashes, wee pads, waste removal bags and pet first aid kits. To comply with the program, dogs must weigh 40 pounds or less, and pet parents must not only pay a room rate $35 over the regular room charge, but also a $100 non-refundable cleaning fee. *Info: 2440 Victory Park Ln.; (214) 397-4100; www.wdallasvictory.com.*

Warwick Melrose. For a $50 non-refundable pet fee which is implemented every three days, one canine companion weighing 60 pounds or less can stay with a guardian in one of this hotel's 184 guest rooms. Guests must also sign a pet registration waiver prior to checking in to the upscale Uptown retreat, which has graced Dallas' cityscape since 1924. (A copy of the agreement can be viewed online.) *Info: 3015 Oak Lawn Ave.; (214) 521-5151; www.warwickmelrosedallas.com.*

Pawty Time

dogtipper
choice

March: Krewe of Barkus Mardi Gras Dog Parade and Festival. McKinney's historic downtown goes to the dogs when the Art Institute of McKinney and McKinney Main Street sponsor the annual Krewe of Barkus Mardi Gras Dog Parade and Festival. The event kicks off with a parade followed by a dog costume contest. *Info: Mitchell Park, McKinney; (972) 369-7911.*

June: Dallas Pet Expo. Free admission brings dog lovers to enjoy this all-day event with vendors, adoptables, training demonstrations, dock diving, and more. *Info: www.dallaspetexpo.com.*

November: Richardson Citywide Pet Day. This annual event in the suburb of Richardson welcomes dogs and dog lovers to Owens Farm for a day including a pooch parade, demonstrations, family fun, and plenty of adoptable dogs. *Info: www.cor.net.*

Six Flags Over Texas
Although this 200-acre theme park does not permit dogs (except service animals), it does offer air-conditioned kennels. Dogs and cats may be boarded for a fee at the Six Flags kennel, located at the parking lot gas station. The kennels are attended but dogs cannot be left at the facility after the park closes. *Info: 2201 Road to Six Flags; (817) 640-8900; www.sixflags.com/overTexas.*

December: Holiday Pet Expo. Ring in the holidays with Rover at this expansive expo featuring vendors, dog demonstrations, and plenty of cute adoptables if you'd like to add to your furry family. *Info: www.DallasPetExpo.com.*

Sniff Out More Information
Dallas Convention and Visitors Bureau; (214) 571-1000 or (800) 232-5527; www.visitdallas.com.

DENTON
Half an hour north of Dallas, Denton still holds to its own atmosphere, from its historic downtown to the parks for those looking to get away from the Metroplex hustle and bustle for a while.

Run, Spot, Run!
Ray Roberts State Park. This park, always popular as a weekend getaway from DFW, invites you and your dog to enjoy several distinct units. The Ray Roberts Greenbelt, a favorite with equestrians, is open to dogs on leash and offers 12 miles for equestrian and 10 miles for hike and bike use, starting at the Ray Roberts dam and ending at Lake Lewisville. The park itself has two units: the Isle du Bois Unit and the Johnson Branch Unit. Isle du Bois offers plenty of dog-friendly trails, swimming, picnicking and camping, while Johnson Branch has a primitive hiking trail, swimming, picnicking and camping. *Info: Isle du Bois Unit, 100 PW 4137, Pilot Point, (940) 686-2148; Johnson Branch Unit, 100 PW 4153, Valley View; (940) 637-2294; www.tpwd.state.tx.us. Fee.*

Wiggly Field Dog Park. This 2.75-acre park within Lark Forest Park caters to both small and large dogs with distinct sections for each. The dog park is open sunrise to sunset daily, except part of the day on Wednesday for maintenance. The park includes benches and fountains and, just outside the fenced area, a trail and a pond for some dog paddling. *Info: 1400 Ryan Rd.; (940) 349-8731; www.wigglyfielddogpark.com. Free.*

Fetch This!
PetSmart Denton. This PetSmart features a full-service Banfield hospital in case you have any veterinary needs on your trip. *Info: 1441 S. Loop 288; (940) 591-9895; www.petsmart.com.*

Stay, Lie Down

Denton is home to several dog-friendly budget hotel chains including **America's Best Value Inn**, **Comfort Inn**, **Days Inn**, **Homewood Suites**, **Howard Johnson**, **La Quinta**, **Quality Inn**, **Motel 6**, **Super 8** and more.

Pawty Time

May: Dog Days of Denton. For two decades, this annual event has put canines on center stage. Look for events that include paw readings, dogs on parade, agility and disc demos, freestyle dog dancing, arts and crafts, trick contests, and more. *Info: www.dogdaysdenton.com.*

Sniff Out More Information

Denton Convention and Visitors Bureau; (940) 382-7895 or (888) 381-1818; www.discoverdenton.com.

FORT WORTH

If there's one big city in Texas that has "the look" that many out of state visitors expect to see, it's probably Fort Worth. This city that calls itself "the place where the West begins" is home to the Fort Worth Stockyards, a National Historic District that's still home to cowboys on horseback, as well as dog-friendly historic hotels, western shopping, and an all-around good time.

Run, Spot, Run!

Bark Park. Located in the suburb of Bedford, this new dog park in Meadow Park features grassy areas for off-leash fun for both large and small dogs. The park includes a water fountain for people and pets. *Info: 3200 Meadowpark, Bedford; www.bedfordtx.gov. Free.*

Fort Woof. Located within Gateway Park, this popular off-leash park is one that we just love for its well-maintained appearance, large, grassy areas, and friendly atmosphere. The park is open 5:00 a.m. to 11:30 p.m. daily and is lighted. The park is very well groomed and includes a large parking lot, plenty of room for both large and small dogs to run, and quite a bit of agility equipment, especially in the small dog section. *Info: Gateway Park Dr. at Beach St.; fortwoof.org. Free.*

Fort Worth Stockyards. You and your dog have to mosey over to Fort Worth's Stockyards Historic District, an area that's surprisingly dog-friendly. Twice a day, at 11:30 a.m. and 4 p.m., you can experience the Fort Worth Herd, the world's only daily cattle drive. Cowboys drive the cattle along the streets of the Stockyards, a must-see event if you feel your dog won't be frightened by the sight of Longhorn cattle coming down the street. Any time you

visit, expect to see plenty of people in Western gear. You can also rent a GPS guided tour; the tours will take you by the Cattlemen's catwalk for a view of the cattle pens, the Cowtown Coliseum that's home to the world's first indoor rodeo, Mule Alley which was once called the world's finest stables, and Billy Bob's Texas, still holding the record as the world's biggest honky tonk. You'll find parking across from Cowtown Coliseum in Mule Alley, on the east end of Exchange Avenue at Stockyards Station, and one block north of Cowtown Coliseum at Billy Bob's Texas. *Info: www.stockyards station.com. Free.*

Villages of Bear Creek Park. Part of a 40-acre city park with picnic areas and walking trails, a three-acre dog park offers off-leash fun. A small dog section for pooches under 40 pounds and a large dog section are both behind double gates for safety. Open sunrise to sunset, the park is closed on Thursday for maintenance. *Info: 1951 Bear Creek Parkway, Euless; (817) 685-1650; www.eulesstx.gov. Free.*

Fetch This!

Jersey Lilly Photo Parlor. Want a photo of you and your dog as cowboys? Saloon girls? Gunfighters or gamblers? Here's your chance; this photo studio at the Texas Cowboy Hall of Fame welcomes people and pets. You'll have your choice of costumes and can pose on a historic stagecoach for an antique sepia-toned portrait. During peak travel times, a reservation for your portrait session is recommended at this studio located in the Stockyards. *Info: 128 East Exchange, Historic Barn A; (817) 626-7131; www.texascowboyhalloffame.org.*

Petco Westover Hills. You'll find several Petco stores in the suburbs that surround Fort Worth but this location is within the I-820 loop. *Info: 465 Sherry Ln.; (817) 377-1968; www.petco.com.*

PetSmart Fort Worth. You'll find numerous PetSmart stores in Fort Worth and the surrounding suburbs; this downtown store is the most central location. The store includes a Banfield pet hospital for your veterinary needs on the road. *Info: 415 Carroll St.; (817) 820-0630; www.petsmart.com.*

Treats and Eats

Black Rooster Bakery. Woof down a freshly-baked pastry or a straight-out-of-the-oven baguette as you sit with your barking buddy at one of the outdoor tables which hug the exterior of this cozy eatery. *Info: 2430 Forest Park Blvd.; (817) 924-1600; blackroosterbakery.com.*

Fort Worth Food Park. Fido-loving foodies who enjoy taking gastronomic journeys can park themselves at a picnic table and taste flavors from all four corners of the world at this venue. Peppered among the roster of regulars are rotating food trucks, which add spice to each visit. Open Thursday through Sunday. *Info: 2509 Weisenberger St.; (817) 878-2424; www.fwfoodpark.com.*

Lili's Bistro. Umbrellas shade the tables that line the entrance to this eatery, where patrons with pups can sit and watch the world go by as they sip one of the house wines. *Info: 1310 Magnolia Avenue; (817) 877-0700; lilisbistro.com.*

Love Shack. Chef Tim Love welcomes four-legged diners on the patio of this Stockyards area eatery that's right in the middle of the action. The night we visited, it was a bit loud for dogs but at quieter times you'll find popular options like Amore Caliente, a burger with poblano chile, guacamole, pepperjack cheese and lettuce, all on a flour tortilla. *Info: 110 E. Exchange Avenue; (817) 740-8812; www.loveburgershack.com.*

Riscky's Barbecue. Don't make the same mistake we did and, with dog leash in hand, head to Riscky's Steakhouse, also in the Stockyards. The Steakhouse isn't dog-friendly but the big, shaded patio at Riscky's Barbecue, just down the street in Stockyards Station, is. You'll find all the must-have barbecue fare including chopped beef sandwiches, beef brisket, and spare ribs. You'll even find a unique item: BBQ Bologna, thick slices of bologna rubbed with "Riscky's Dust" rub then smoked and served on a bun. *Info: 140 E. Exchange Ave.; (817) 626-7777; www.risckys.com.*

Spiral Diner and Bakery. A heaping helping of compassion is served with every order at this vegan venue, which sells tasty treats for two-legged customers. A wallet-friendly spot which also offers sustenance for the soul, a portion of the proceeds are donated to animal, human and environmental organizations. The eatery (which also has a Dallas location) includes an outdoor dining area for you and your dog. *Info: 1314 W. Magnolia Ave.; (817) 3-EATVEG; www.spiraldiner.com.*

Stay, Lie Down

You'll find all the major budget chains that are pet-friendly represented in Fort Worth but here's a look at several unique properties that welcome canines to Cowtown:

The Ashton Hotel. At the hub of all that's happening in Forth Worth, this historic downtown venue welcomes dogs under 50 pounds at no charge, but make sure that your tail-wagging chum is tidy during your stay, as there is a $150 charge if a mess is found after you check out. *Info: 610 Main St.; (817) 332-0100 or (866) 327-4866; www.theashtonhotel.com.*

Etta's Place. Named after Etta Place, the girlfriend of legendary outlaw Sundance Kid, the beauty of this boutique retreat will steal the heart of any pet parent traveling with a small dog under 20 pounds. The cozy 10-room inn charges a $25 pet fee per night, and canine companions must be crated when a guardian is not in the room. *Info: 200 W. Third St.; (817) 255-5760; www.ettas-place.com.*

Omni Fort Worth. Fort Worth will literally be at Fido's feet when you check into one of the 614 guest rooms or suites at this towering downtown hotel, which allows up to two dogs under 25 pounds for a $50 non-refundable cleaning fee per stay. *Info: 1300 Houston St.; (817) 535-6664; www.omnihotels.com.*

dogtipper choice

Stockyards Hotel. A Lone Star institution since 1907, you and your canine (or cat!) companion can follow in the footsteps of such  famous figures as Chuck Norris, Willie Nelson, Garth Brooks, Jim Belushi and Dan Ackroyd, and even notorious bank robbers Bonnie and Clyde by making this historic hotel home base during a visit to Fort Worth. For a $50 cleaning fee, there is no limit on the number or size of dogs per room. *Info: 109 East Exchange Ave.; (817) 625-6427; www.stockyardshotel.com.*

The Worthington Renaissance Fort Worth. Called "The Star of Texas," dog devotees will be in seventh heaven at this 504-room property, which has no pet fee and requires require a $200 refundable deposit only if you're paying in cash. *Info: 200 Main St.; (817) 870-1000; www.marriott.com.*

Pawty Time
October: Barktoberfest. This annual fundraiser for the Fort Woof dog park is held by the Fort Worth Dog Park Association. The event features plenty of costumed canines and an election for the mayor of Fort Woof. *Info: fortwoof.org.*

Sniff Out More Information
Fort Worth Convention and Visitors Bureau; (800) 433-5747; www.fortworth.com

GLEN ROSE
Nicknamed the Dinosaur Capital of Texas, Glen Rose makes a popular day trip from Dallas-Fort Worth. The city's Dinosaur Valley State Park is a one-of-a-kind attraction that welcomes you and your dog.

Run, Spot, Run!

Cleburne State Park. Located about 20 miles east of Glen Rose near the community of Cleburne, this state park is a favorite with mountain bikers but they'll also share their trails with you and your dog. The park's Cedar Lake is a great choice for dogs that are fearful of loud noises because this no-wake lake prohibits the use of jet skis and other personal watercraft so it's nice and quiet! Your dog will find plenty of spots along the lakeshore for a dip; you can extend your visit by camping here as well. *Info: 5800 Park Road 21, Cleburne; (817) 645-4215; www.tpwd.state.tx.us. Fee.*

dogtipper

choice

Dinosaur Valley State Park. It's not just everywhere you can compare your dog's paw to the footprint of a dinosaur...but here's your chance. This unique state park contains real dinosaur tracks right in the bed of the Paluxy River. You and Fido can wade in the river (some tracks are submerged, some are in the banks, depending on the water level) and touch the tracks made by Theropod and Sauropod dinosaurs. You'll also find plenty of swimming, hiking on trails, picnicking and camping, and you can't miss the two fiberglass dinosaur models in the park: a 70-foot Apatosaurus and a 45-foot Tyrannosaurus Rex. *Info: 4 miles west of Glen Rose; take US 67 to FM 205, continue for 4 miles to Park Road 59; (254) 897-4588; www.tpwd.state.tx.us. Fee.*

Dinosaur World. Friendly dogs on leashes are always welcome at this outdoor museum with over 150 life-sized dinosaur models. The park doesn't sell food but you're welcome to bring a lunch and use a picnic table (or have pizza delivered to you and your pooch at the park). Know that this is a popular attraction with schoolchildren, especially in the spring months of field trips and summer vacations, so time your visit carefully if your dog reacts to excited children. *Info: 1058 Park Road 59; (254) 898-1526; www.dinosaurworld.com. Fee.*

Meridian State Park. Located 27 miles south of Glen Rose near Meridian, you won't find dinosaur tracks at this park but you and your dog should be on the lookout for fossils in the limestone formations that surround Lake Meridian. The lake itself is encircled by a hiking trail; you and your dog will find plenty of water fun as well as camping and picnicking. *Info: 173 Park Road 7, Meridian; (254) 435-2536; www.tpwd.state.tx.us. Fee.*

Stay, Lie Down
Glen Rose is home to several dog-friendly budget chains including **America's Best Value Inn, Best Western, Holiday Inn, La Quinta** and others.

Sniff Out More Information
Glen Rose Convention and Visitors Bureau; (888) 346-6282; www.glenrosetexas.net.

LA GRANGE
Nearby destinations: Bastrop, Round Top, Smithville

If you've heard of the *Best Little Whorehouse in Texas* Broadway musical and movie, then you've heard of La Grange. The small, quiet town was in the spotlight with the unveiling of the Chicken Ranch. The infamous Ranch is long gone now, and today La Grange makes a good base to explore area lakes and parks.

Run, Spot, Run!

Monument Hill–Kreische Brewery State Historic Sites. This park is two in one, all perched on a 200-foot bluff high over the town of La Grange. Monument Hill Historical Park is the burial site for the Texans who died in the Dawson Massacre and the Mier Expedition, two historic Mexican conflicts that occurred in 1842, six years after the Texas Revolution. The Kreische Brewery State Historic Site recalls a far more cheerful time in Texas history. Heinreich Kreische, who immigrated here from Germany, purchased the hilltop and the adjoining land in 1849, including the burial ground of those Texas heroes, for his brewery site. Before closing the brewery in 1884, Kreische became the third-largest beer producer in the state. Your dog can't enter any of the buildings at the site but you'll find several trails to explore together including the Brewery Lane, Kreische Woods Nature Loop, Scenic and Historic Trail and more. Open daily 8 a.m. to 5 p.m. *Info: 414 State Loop 92; (979) 968-5658; www.tpwd.state.tx.us. Free.*

Oak Thicket Park. This 64-acre LCRA park welcomes pets in the camping and cabin sections (although only one pet per cabin). Located on the shores of Lake Fayette, the park is a popular fishing and swimming destination. *Info: 4819 W. State Highway 159, Fayetteville; (979) 249-3504; www.lcra.org. Fee.*

Park Prairie Park. Located on 2,000-acre Lake Fayette (a cooling lake for the Fayette Power Project), Park Prairie welcomes dogs for a day of fun or camping at unimproved campsites. *Info: 1250 Park Prairie Rd.; (979) 249–3504; www.lcra.org. Fee.*

White Rock Park. On the east bank of the Colorado River, just south of La Grange, this is one of the largest parks on the lower Colorado. Developed by the LCRA but operated by the City of La Grange, this day-use park welcomes your dog on leash for some river fun (there's even a canoe launch), hiking on trails, and picnicking. *Info: Mode Lane. From La Grange, take US 77 (Jefferson St.) south to Elbin Road, and continue about three-quarters of a mile to Mode Lane (CR 134). Take a right on Mode Lane and travel about a quarter mile to this park; (979) 968–5805; www.lcra.org. Free.*

Stay, Lie Down

Best Western Plus La Grange. Located out on the loop that surrounds La Grange, this property accepts dogs for a $15 per dog, per night fee. *Info: 600 E. TX 71 Bypass; (979) 968-6800; www.bestwestern.com.*

Wildlife Guesthouse. Pets (but not two-legged children) are welcome at this guesthouse located on a 60-acre exotic wildlife ranch between La Grange and Schulenburg. Your stay will include use of a golf cart to drive around the ranch to view deer, blackbuck antelope, wild turkeys, ducks, and geese. If you have a horse as well, you're invited to bring your own horse to ride. *Info: 7707 W. US 90, Schulenburg; (979) 224-6234; wguesthouse.com.*

Sniff Out More Information

La Grange Area Chamber of Commerce; (800) LAGRANGE or (979) 968–5756; www.lagrangetx.org.

LOCKHART

Nearby destinations: Austin, Luling

Known as the "Barbecue Capital of Texas," Lockhart, located just 23 miles south of Austin, is the stuff of Texas legend. Cattle drives. Comanche battles. Cotton. Oil. Through the years, this small town has seen them all.

Run, Spot, Run!

Lockhart State Park. We have to admit that we've lived all our lives in Texas and this little park is one that we only discovered a few years ago. Often called one of the hidden gems of the state park system, this 263-acre park welcomes you and your dog to enjoy Clear Fork Creek, hiking trails, and camping. The park's best known feature is its nine-hole golf course. Many of the facilities here were constructed by the Civilian Conservation Corps in the 1930s. *Info: 4179 State Park Rd.; (512) 398–3479; www.tpwd.state.tx.us. Fee.*

Treats and Eats

Lockhart is world-famous for its barbecue. **Smitty's Market** (*www.smittysmarket.com*), **Black's Barbecue** (*www.blacksbbq.com*) **Kreuz**—pronounced Krites—**Market** (*kreuzmarket.com*) and **Chisholm Trail** each draw a devoted following to enjoy tender brisket and spicy sausage. All the city's barbecue joints are great for take-out for a picnic for you and your dog but only Chisholm Trail features a convenient drive-through window for dog travelers.

Chisholm Trail BBQ Restaurant. Barbecue brisket is the headliner on this menu that also includes sausage, pork ribs, chicken, and beef fajitas, all served with your choice of sides. Barbecue makes a great picnic to take to Lockhart State Park! *Info: 1323 S. Colorado St. (US 183); (512) 398-6027; www.chisholmtrailbbq.com.*

Sniff Out More Information

Lockhart Chamber of Commerce; (512) 398–2818; www.lockhartchamber.com.

LULING

Nearby destinations: Lockhart, Seguin

Oil was discovered in Luling in 1922. Even today the "black gold" is still evident with pumpjacks around town and the surrounding area.

Run, Spot, Run!

Luling Zedler Mill Paddling Trail. Tell Fido it's time to trade in the dog paddle for the canoe paddle and a day of fun on the San Marcos River. This was the state's first paddling trail and starts six miles upstream from Luling; you'll come out at Zedler Mill inside within city limits. (There's a dam beyond the mill, so be careful not to go beyond the mill.) Check the web site for information on local canoe rentals, shuttles, and GPS coordinates along the river. *Info: Put in 5 miles west of Luling where US 90 crosses the San Marcos River; www.tpwd.state.tx.us. Free.*

Palmetto State Park. Located six miles southeast of Luling toward Gonzales, this park is like a secret tropical hideaway tucked among miles of ranch land. Thousands of years ago, the San Marcos River shifted course, leaving a huge deposit of silt that eventually became a marshy swamp estimated to be more than 18,000 years old. Today that swamp is filled with palmettos as well as moss-draped trees, 4-foot-tall irises, and many bird species. You and your dog can enjoy nature trails through the area or rent a paddleboat and enjoy an excursion on the San Marcos River together. The park has also has full hookups, tent sites, and plenty of picnic options. One precaution: those swamps mean mosquitoes so bring repellent and be sure your dog is current on heartworm preventative. *Info: 78 Park Road 11 South, Gonzales; (830) 672-3266; www.tpwd.state.tx.us. Fee.*

Sniff Out More Information
Luling Area Chamber of Commerce; (830) 875-3214; www.lulingcc.org.

MEXIA
One of the most mispronounced names in Texas (it's ma-HAY-ya), this community's slogan is "A great place, no matter how you pronounce it." You and your dog will find it an easy jumping off spot to several local state parks that welcome dogs with open paws.

Run, Spot, Run!
Fairfield Lake State Park. Thirty miles from Mexia in Fairfield, this 2,400-acre lake is known for its year-around warm waters (heated by the TXU Big Brown power plant) and for red drum fishing opportunities. Canines aren't permitted in the designated swimming area but you'll find plenty of other places in the park for a doggie dip. *Info: 123 State Park Rd. 64, Fairfield; (903) 389-4514; www.tpwd.state.tx.us. Fee.*

Fort Parker State Park. This state park holds special memories for Paris who took her first canine camping trip with her childhood dog Pepsi at this park when he was just a pup. Located seven miles out of Mexia, the park is best known for fishing on Fort Parker Lake and numerous hiking trails. You can extend your visit with a stay at one of the park's many campsites. *Info: 194 Park Road 28; (254) 562-5751; www.tpwd.state.tx.us. Fee.*

Sniff Out More Information
Mexia Chamber of Commerce; (254) 562-5569 or (888) 535-5476; mexiachamber.com.

PARIS

One of the most common questions Paris had growing up was "Were you born in Paris, Texas?" Well, the answer was no ... but in seeing the many great amenities the city and surrounding area offer dog lovers, we both agree that it sure would be a fun place to live.

Run, Spot, Run!

Bonham State Park. Forty miles west of Paris, this state park is built around Bonham State Park Lake, where you and your dog can enjoy swimming and boating (with paddleboat rentals available). Campsites are also available. *Info: 1363 State Park 24, Bonham; (903) 583-5022; www.tpwd.state.tx.us. Fee.*

Cooper Lake State Park. About half an hour's drive from Paris, this state park has two separate units. On the north side of Cooper Lake, the smaller Doctors Creek Unit offers you and your dog several hiking trails, camping, and picnicking as well as a boat launch. On the southern shores, the expansive South Sulphur Unit offers camping, hiking trails (including a horse trail to steer clear of if your dog is reactive), and even canoe rentals. *Info: Doctors Creek Unit, 1664 FM 1529 South, Cooper, (903) 395-3100; South Sulphur Unit, 1690 FM 3505, Sulphur Springs, (903) 945-5256; www.tpwd.state.tx.us. Fee.*

Eiffel Tower. Standing 65 feet tall, the tower may not be as tall as its French cousin but it has one distinction that's truly Texan: it's crowned with a red cowboy hat. Who can resist snapping a photo of their dog with this Texas version of the Eiffel Tower? *Info: Corner of Jefferson Rd. and Collegiate Drive, next to Love Civic Center. Free.*

Trail de Paris Rail to Trail. This non-motorized pedestrian/bicycle trail welcomes leashed dogs to enjoy miles of trails that include refurbished railroad bridges, creeks, wildflower fields, and more. *Info: starts at 12th S.E. St.; (903) 785-7353; www.traildeparis.org. Free.*

Fetch This!

Petco Paris. Located just off TX 286, this full-service pet supply store features quality foods and travel supplies. *Info: 3900 Lamar Rd.; (903) 739-2738; www.petco.com.*

Stay, Lie Down

Paris is home to several budget chains that welcome woofers including **Best Western**, **Days Inn**, **La Quinta**, and **Ramada**.

Sniff Out More Information

Lamar County Chamber of Commerce; (903) 784-2501; www.paristexas.com.

ROUND TOP

Nearby destinations: La Grange

Mention "antiques" and "Texas" in the same sentence and most people will assume you're talking about Round Top. This tiny community—the smallest incorporated town in Texas—may be small in residents but it's Texas-sized in the world of antiques. Twice a year, this town swells with shoppers from around the country during "Antiques Week." Held in the spring and fall (with limited shows in June, too), Antiques Week takes place at huge outdoor sales as well as some in show barns. Many of the shows are dog-friendly for leashed dogs (and many vendors bring their dogs, too!)

Pawty Time

Marburger Farm Antique Show. Dogs are welcome at this expansive sale which has been showcased in *Country Living* magazine. This event's 27 acres of parking gives you an idea of how popular the show has become. *Info: 2248 S. TX 237 between Round Top and Warrenton; (800) 999–2148; www.roundtop-marburger.com.*

Sniff Out More Information

Round Top Area Chamber of Commerce; (979) 249–4042 or (888) 368–4783; www.roundtop.org.

SEGUIN

Nearby destinations: Luling, San Marcos

Seguin (pronounced "se-GEEN") has one of the most unusual nicknames of any Texas city; it's "The Mother of Concrete Cities." A Seguin chemist held several concrete production patents, so don't be surprised at the many historic buildings utilizing concrete around town.

While dogs aren't that interested in concrete, they will definitely love Seguin's natural attractions, prime among them beautiful Starcke Park. The park is home to numerous pecan trees, an important crop that is honored with the "World's Largest Pecan," a statue located on the courthouse lawn at Court Street. It's no longer the world's largest but it still makes a fun photo with Fido!

Run, Spot, Run!

Seguin Dog Park. Located in shady Starcke Park, just off the busy highway but miles away in terms of peace and quiet, this dog park offers both large and small dog sections. Look for agility equipment and double gating; save time to enjoy the park (below) with your leashed dog, too. *Info: TX 123 Business in Starke Park; seguindogpark.com. Free.*

Seguin's Lakes. Seguin is surrounded by four lakes on the Guadalupe River that are known for their fishing but also offer your dog a place for a dip. The lakes include Lake Dunlap (I-10 to TX 46 exit west of Seguin, then 8 miles on TX 46); Lake McQueeney (I–10 to FM 78 exit, then west for 3 miles to FM 725, then turn right and continue for 1 mile); Lake Placid (I–10 to FM 464 exit, stay on access road); and Meadow Lake (I–10 to TX 123 bypass, then south for 4 miles). *Free.*

Starcke Park. Our dogs loved walking around this shady park after their visit to the dog park. Tall pecan, oak, and cypress trees and the Guadalupe River make this a great spot for a picnic with Fido. *Info: South side of town, off TX 123; (830) 401–2480. Free.*

Stay, Lie Down

Seguin is home to several pet-friendly hotel chains including **America's Best Value Inn and Suites**, **Days Inn**, and **Super 8**.

Sniff Out More Information

Seguin Convention & Visitors Bureau; (800) 580-7322; www.visitseguin.com.

SMITHVILLE
Nearby destinations: Bastrop, La Grange

Southeast of Austin, the small town of Smithville is tucked between railroad tracks, the Colorado River, and the Lost Pines
region.

Run, Spot, Run!
Buescher State Park. OK, here's another one of those Texas place
names that's a dead giveaway as to who's a visitor and who's a
resident. Buescher is pronounced BISH-er and often talked about
in conjunction with nearby Bastrop State Park. The parks may be
close by but they feature totally different environments. Unlike
the pines of Bastrop, Buescher is shaded by tall oaks and is the
home of a 30-acre lake. You and your dog can enjoy hikes, camping
and picnicking. *Info: 100 Park Road 1E, three miles north of town;
(512) 237–2241; www.tpwd.state.tx.us. Fee.*

North Shore Park. Along with a day of fishing, boating, and
swimming on Lake Bastrop, dogs are welcome in the campground
of this LCRA park as well. *Info: FM 1441; (512) 498-1922;
www.lcra.org. Fee.*

Railroad Historical Park and Museum and Depot. This small park
contains two cabooses and a depot relocated here from West
Point, a small community east of town. You'll find a Chamber of
Commerce office in the park. And you and your dog can't miss the
giant gingerbread man (actually a Texas-sized cookie sheet) that
stands in the park; he is a reminder of the Guinness World Record
that the town set in 2006. The cookie sheet was used to bake a 20-
foot-tall gingerbread man that weighed over 1,308 pounds. If only
he had been a dog treat! *Info: 100 W. 1st St.; (512) 237–2313. Free.*

Smithville Bark Park. The
Bark Park, with separate
small (under 30 pounds)
and large dog areas, is located at the end of the Railroad Park (see above). The
double-gated park includes
some agility equipment;
restrooms are located

nearby. If your dog has a phobia of loud noises (like our Irie), be aware that this park is immediately adjacent to the train tracks. *Info: TX 95 at W. 1st St; (512) 237-3282; www.ci.smithville.tx.us. Free.*

South Shore Park. Also located on Lake Bastrop, this park welcomes Fido for a day of swimming or fishing; you can also camp. Unlike other LCRA parks such as Lake Buchanan's Black Rock Park, however, this park does not permit dogs in its cabins. *Info: 375 South Shore Rd.; (512) 498-1922; www.lcra.org. Fee.*

Vernon L. Richards Riverbend Park. This Lower Colorado River Authority park is operated by the City of Smithville. Located on the banks of the Colorado River, the 50-acre park includes hike/bike trails, picnic facilities, campsites, and a boat ramp. *Info: TX 71 where it crosses the Colorado River, just north of Smithville; (512) 237-3282; www.lcra.org. Free.*

Sniff Out More Information
Smithville Area Chamber of Commerce; (512) 237-2313; www.smithvilletx.org.

WACO
Often called the "Heart of Texas" for its central location, Waco is located at the confluence of the Brazos and Bosque Rivers. The city became a center for commerce when it erected a suspension bridge across the Brazos. Designed by the same engineers who constructed New York City's Brooklyn Bridge years later, today this bridge welcomes you, Fido and other pedestrians to stroll across the Brazos.

Run, Spot, Run!
Cameron Park Trail System. Waco's largest park is home to 15 miles of multi-use trails, part of the National Recreation Trail system. You and your dog can walk or run the trails which range from beginner to expert. *Info: 2601 Sturgis Rd.; (254) 750-5980; www.waco-texas.com. Free.*

Dog Collectibles Museum. Just north of Waco in the Antiquibles Antique Mall lies what's billed as the world's largest dog collectibles museum. (The sign says "America's largest" but indoors

the museum proudly proclaims "world's largest"...and it very well might be.) With over 7,000 items on display, this Texas-sized collection includes all things canine: dog salt and pepper shakers, dog inkwells, dog buttons, dog figurines, and more. The collection began with the private collection of Barbara and David Hays who collected dog items on their travels; it later expanded and included the collection of Julia Speegle Hall, the aunt of Hollywood director Ron Howard. The collection includes everything from toys from the Sixties to a rare 1700s gun stock with a carved dog head plus plenty of examples of dogs in advertising, dogs in popular culture and more. When you're finished with the museum, have a look around the antiques mall, too; we found that several booths sell dog collectibles. *Info: I-35, exit 345; www.antiquibles.com. Free.*

Fort Fisher Park. This 30-acre park is a quiet contrast to nearby I-35. Located along the shady banks of the Brazos River, this park was once the site of Fort Fisher, an outpost of the Texas Rangers built in 1837. Today the park contains the City of Waco Tourist

Information Center, excellent for picking up travel information across the state, and the Texas Ranger Hall of Fame and Museum. Although your dog can't enter the museum, you'll find picnicking and walking paths to enjoy together. *Info: I–35, exit 335B; (254) 750-8631. Fee for camping.*

H.O.T. Dog Park. Open from dawn until dusk, the three-acre Heart of Texas (H.O.T) Dog Park offers big and small dog play areas. The park is owned by the veterinarian from the adjacent Texas Animal

Medical Center and they have a staff member on call at all times in case of emergency. *Info: 4900 Steinbeck Bend Rd. Free.*

Waco River Walk. Leashed dogs are welcome for a great riverside dog walk along the Brazos River. The walk includes the restored Suspension Bridge, today a pedestrian bridge, linking Indian Spring Park on the west bank and Martin Luther King Jr. Park on the east. On the west side, you'll find a walk to Fort Fisher Park in one direction and Herring Avenue Bridge in the other. In all, the Riverwalk spans seven miles. *Info: University Parks Dr. between Franklin and Washington Sts.; (254) 750-8080. Free.*

Fetch This!

Waco is home to a **PetSmart** with a Banfield veterinary clinic (4600 Franklin Ave.; 254-741-6847) and a **Petco** (2404 W. Loop 340; 254-662-4535).

Woof Gang Bakery and Grooming. You just never know where you going to run into fellow dog lovers. On a flight back to Texas from Orlando, we were looking through all the materials we'd picked up at the annual Global Pet Expo trade show. The next thing we knew, we were talking with the woman on the aisle seat; her daughter, a groomer, was opening a new Woof Gang Bakery in Waco. Opened in 2013, the location features all-natural foods and baked treats as well as pampering spa treatments for your pooch! *Info: 1210 Hewitt Drive, Suite 205; (254) 666-9663; www.facebook.com/ WoofGangBakeryGroomingWaco.*

Stay, Lie Down

Waco is home to many budget chains that accept pets including **Best Western**, **Clarion Inn**, **Days Inn**, **Extended Stay**, **Knights Inn**, **La Quinta**, **Motel 6**, **Super 8**, and others. Most are located along the I-35 corridor and near Baylor University.

The Cotton Palace. This Arts and Crafts–style 1910 home doesn't permit pets in the main house but The Carriage House welcomes pets for $20 per pet. Located near Baylor University, this property's innkeepers are all retired Baylor faculty members. *Info: 1910 Austin Avenue; (877) 632–2312 or (254) 753–7294; www.thecottonpalace.com.*

Hotel Indigo Waco-Baylor. Dogs of up to 80 pounds are welcome at this boutique hotel located across from the main entrance to Baylor University. Fees include a $10 per night fee, a $75 non-refundable cleaning fee, and a $150 pet deposit. Pets are permitted only in certain rooms. *Info: 211 Clay Avenue; (877) 846-3446; www.ihg.com.*

Sniff Out More Information
Waco Convention and Visitors Bureau; (800) WACO–FUN or (254) 750-8696; www.wacocvb.com.

WAXAHACHIE
Located just half an hour south of Dallas, Waxahachie (pronounced WALKS-a-hachie) was established on the Shawnee Trail where cattle were driven to markets in Kansas City. Cotton was king here for most of the town's history with Waxahachie at the center of a large agricultural base. The city was designated a National Main Street community in 2002 and a large portion of the historic downtown area has been restored to its former glory.

Run, Spot, Run!
Galaxy Drive-In. Pets are welcome at this nostalgic drive-in theater; if you decide to sit outside your car, be sure your dog's on a leash (and don't take him inside the snack bar...but you know that's best because he'd want to order everything anyway!) Vintage speakers hang from your car window or you can listen on FM. Seven nights a week, the drive-in shows two features per night for one price! *Info: located 13 miles east of Waxahachie at 5301 I-45 Frontage Road in Ennis; (972) 875-5505; www.galaxydriveintheatre.com. Fee.*

Wags-A-Hachie Dog Park. At press time, final plans were underway for the opening of Wags-A-Hachie Dog Park near the rodeo arena. *Info: Howard Road. Free.*

Waxahachie Creek Hike & Bike Trail. This six-mile-long trail follows Waxahachie Creek passing the Old City Cemetery. The concrete trail starts at Lions Park. *Info: 2303 Howard Road; www.traillink.com. Free.*

Stay, Lie Down

Waxahachie is home to several budget-friendly, dog-friendly hotel chains including **American's Best Value Inn**, **Comfort Suites**, **La Quinta**, **Super 8** and more.

Pawty Time

October: Texas Country Reporter Festival. Texas travelers will be familiar with Bob Phillips and the "Texas Country Reporter" TV series that's been a longtime staple. The television host and author puts on an annual party on the courthouse square featuring Texas music, food, and arts and crafts. Dogs on leash are welcome at this one-day event. *Info: (972) 937-2390; www.texascountryreporter.com.*

Sniff Out More Information

Waxahachie Convention and Visitors Bureau; (972) 937-0681; www.waxahachiecvb.com.

7. Panhandle Plains

Like the Big Bend area, much of the Panhandle Plains is composed of wide-open space, which our dogs love. Here, Amarillo and the nearby community of Canyon are the gateway to the nation's second largest canyon, Palo Duro Canyon State Park, a dog-friendly Texas-sized wonder that stretches 120 miles.

Amarillo has long been a stop for cross-country travelers thanks to the famous Route 66, which ran right through the heart of the city. South of Amarillo lies the cotton production capital of Lubbock now also known for its wine industry. Lubbock area grapes are shipped to wineries throughout Texas and their home product has won numerous international awards. Further south, the city of San Angelo grew from historic Fort Concho and Abilene, where history and culture join together. On the northern boundaries of this region lies Wichita Falls, just minutes from the Oklahoma border.

ABILENE
Founded by cattlemen as a railroad shipping point and named for Abilene, Kansas, this city has a long history as a cattle producing area. Later, it became a center for the oil and gas industry and today both form the backbone of the city's economy and it is the home of several universities. The historic downtown district, which includes several renovated turn-of-the-century buildings and one of the original Paramount Theaters, makes a fun morning dog walk.

Run, Spot, Run!
Abilene State Park. Located 15 miles south of Abilene, this state park offers you and Fido a full menu of outdoor activities including hiking trails, picnicking, fishing in Elm Creek and camping. You'll need to pitch a tent or travel in a trailer or RV to overnight here with your dog. Dogs are permitted throughout the park except in the buildings and swimming areas. As with most state parks, they must be on leash and should not be left unattended. *Info: RR 89 south to 150 Park Road 32, Tuscola; (325) 572-3204; www.tpwd.state.tx.us. Fee.*

Buffalo Gap Historic Village. The tiny town of Buffalo Gap, 13 miles south of Abilene, was originally a stop for cattle herds being driven to Dodge City, Kansas on the Great Western Cattle Trail. Your footprints and your dog's pawprints can follow in the hoofprints of those that came before you as you stroll on self-guided tours of the historic buildings. Your leashed dog is welcome outdoors throughout the village. *Info: 133 North William, Buffalo Gap; (325) 572-3365; www.tfhcc.com. Fee.*

Camp Barkeley Dog Park. Enjoy some leash-free fun at this expansive dog park with separate areas for large and small dogs. Along with a secure, double-gated entrance, you'll find drinking fountains, sitting areas and shade. Restrooms are provided for dog parents. The park is located east of downtown Abilene, near Grover Nelson Park. *Info: 2070 Zoo Lane; (325) 676-4068; www.facebook.com/campbarkeley. Free.*

Fort Phantom Hill. Established as an outpost of the U.S. Army in 1851 this 22-acre site north of Abilene is open during daylight hours for visitors to explore. Several of the original buildings remain with signage relating the fort's history. Leashed dogs are welcome to explore with you. There are no (human) restrooms or public water available in the fort so plan accordingly! *Info: 10767 RR 600 South; (325) 677-1309; www.fortphantom.org. Free.*

Fort Griffin State Historic Site. Forty miles northeast of Abilene, ruins of this fort which once guarded the frontier are now a state historical site. It is also the home to an official State of Texas Longhorn Herd which keeps alive the original Texas Longhorn bloodlines. You and your leashed dog can enjoy a walk around the fort as well as the adjacent nature trails. The site also has over 30 campsites, some with water and electricity. As at other state facilities, dogs are allowed in the RV and tent camping areas but not in the camp cabins or any

other park buildings. *Info: 1701 N. US 283, Albany; (325) 762-3592; www.visitfortgriffin.com. Fee.*

Fetch This!

PetSmart. If you need dog supplies in Abilene, this PetSmart has got you covered. The store has dog food, leashes, collars, beds and lots of other pet products. There is also a grooming salon and dog training center here. And, of course, your leashed dog is welcome to help you shop. *Info: 3501 Catclaw Dr.; (325) 692-9411; www.petsmart.com.*

Tractor Supply Company. Your pooch doesn't have to be a farm dog to appreciate the selection of pet products here including a large selection of dog food, treats and chews, toys, bedding and much more. Leashed dogs are welcome in the store, too. *Info: 4450 Southwest Dr.; (325) 691-8901; www.tractorsupply.com.*

Treats & Eats

Abi-Haus. This new restaurant is devoted to bringing a cool, hip atmosphere to downtown Abilene serving what the owners call "funky American" cuisine. Some menu choices include Beer Can Chicken and smoked lamb shank along with burgers, sandwiches and tacos. A full bar offers craft beers and specialty drinks. Dining is community style with long tables inside; an outdoor dining area seats 20. Dogs are welcome at the outdoor tables. *Info: 959 N. 2nd St.; (325) 672-7452; www.good-haus.com.*

Jason's Deli. Health conscious, eco-friendly and dog-friendly, this Jason's Abilene location serves organic, naturally sourced sandwiches, soups and salads. Leashed dogs are allowed to accompany diners in the outdoor dining areas of the restaurant. *Info: 3490 Catclaw Dr.; (325) 692-1975; www.jasonsdeli.com.*

Natural Food Center. This emporium has been the go-to place in Abilene for 25 years for healthy foods and organic produce. You and your dog can snag an outdoor table and peruse the lunch menu featuring fresh, organic menu choices as well as juices and desserts. Locals swear by their Soup of the Day and their sandwiches and wraps. *Info: 2534 S. 7th St.; (325) 673-2726; www.naturalfoodcenter.net.*

Stay, Lie Down

Abilene is home to several dog-friendly chain hotels including **America's Best Value Inn, Best Western, Comfort Suites, Days Inn, La Quinta, Motel 6, Quality Inn, Residence Inn, Sleep Inn, Super 8,** and more.

Abilene KOA. This shady campground is located right off I-20 on the north side of Abilene and is situated in what was originally a pecan tree grove. RVers are treated to large pull-through spaces, an outdoor pool, free Wi-Fi, cable TV and an on-site snack bar and convenience store. The park also has rustic cabins and tent camping sites with water and electricity. Dogs of any size are welcome without a surcharge, and the campground has a fenced dog park where Fido can roam leash-free. *Info: 4851 West Stamford St.; (325) 672-3681; www.texaskoa.com.*

Candlewood Suites Abilene. Located near Abilene Christian University, this extended stay property offers fully equipped kitchens with microwave, refrigerator, cooking range and pots, pans and utensils as well as cable TV, CD/DVD players, and Internet access. An on-site fitness center, pool, guest laundry facilities and an outdoor gazebo with barbecue grill are also provided. Dog lovers will appreciate the small, fenced dog-walking area. Dogs can stay with a non-refundable deposit of $25 per stay plus a daily pet fee of $15. *Info: 3050 Catclaw Dr.; (325) 437-4741; www.ihg.com.*

Sniff Out More Information

Abilene Convention and Visitors Bureau; (325) 676-2556 or (800) 727-7704; www.abilenevisitors.com.

AMARILLO

Nearby destinations: Canyon, Lubbock

Historic Route 66 runs right through the heart of this Panhandle city, and the buildings that once housed theaters, roadside cafes, and drugstores are now chock full of shops, diners, and buildings that hark back to the region's heyday. Amarillo is also the cultural and commercial capital of the Texas Panhandle. From a humble beginning as a staging area for the Fort Worth and Denver City Railroad in the 1880s, the city became a center for cattle ranching, wheat and cotton farming, and oil production. Amarillo is also the gateway to the nation's second largest canyon where you and your dog can get a taste of the Old West at Palo Duro Canyon State Park. Truly a Texas-sized wonder, this natural chasm stretches 120 miles.

Run, Spot, Run!

Amarillo Botanical Gardens. An outgrowth of Amarillo's first gardening club, the Botanical Gardens are an oasis of natural beauty in the city's Medical Center Park. Stroll with your (leashed) dog through four acres of gardens, including both native and exotic species with special exhibits devoted to butterfly, Japanese, fragrance and xeriscape plantings. *Info: 1400 Streit St.; (806) 352-6513; www.amarillobotanicalgardens.org. Fee.*

Buffalo Lake National Wildlife Refuge. Located about 30 miles southeast of Amarillo, this refuge consists of over 7,000 acres of native grassland and marsh areas which are home to a host of wildlife species including deer, prairie dogs, bobcats, coyotes, rabbits and over 300 species of birds. Driving tours of the refuge and hiking trails give visitors a chance to spot wildlife. Leashed dogs are allowed in the park but must not disturb wildlife. *Info: US 60 to Umbarger, then RR 168 to the entrance; (806) 499-3382; www.fws.gov. Fee.*

Ellwood Park. This fenced, small dog park is located near Ellwood Senior Park. *Info: 1100 S. Jackson St. at Washington; (806) 378-3036; www.amarilloparks.org. Free.*

Elkins Ranch. Just outside the entrance to Palo Duro Canyon State Park, this working cattle ranch offers several Jeep tours of the canyon as well as other events such as their Chuckwagon Breakfast and Chuckwagon Supper. The tours are a good way to take in the rugged beauty of the canyon and learn about its history. Tours last from one to three hours. Well-behaved dogs are allowed on some (but not all) of the Jeep tours. *Info: 25 miles south of Amarillo on TX 217; (806) 488-2100; www.theelkinsranch.com. Fee.*

John Stiff Memorial Dog Park. Spanning two acres, this park features some fun play equipment, benches, and drinking fountains (as well as biodegradable poop bags). *Info: Southwest 48th & Bell; (806) 378-3036; www.amarilloparks.org. Free.*

Lake Meredith National Recreation Area. This man-made reservoir on the Canadian River covers 10,000 acres and is a popular boating and fishing destination in the Amarillo area. There are also several camping and picnic areas around the lake and most of these allow leashed dogs. Some of the campsites are improved while others are primitive sites with no amenities. *Info: TX 136 to the town of Fritch; (806) 857-3151; www.nps.gov/lamr/. Free.*

Palo Duro Canyon State Park. We still talk about our visit to this amazing destination known as the "Grand Canyon of Texas." Palo

dogtipper

choice

Duro Canyon winds for 120 miles through the *Llano Estacado* ("staked plains") region of the Texas Panhandle south of Amarillo. Eroded for over a million years by a fork of the Red River, the canyon is the second largest in the U.S. and presents some of the most scenic vistas in the Southwest. The 20-mile-wide canyon is 800 feet deep at its deepest point. You and your dog will find plenty of fun among Palo Duro Canyon State Park's 25,000 acres of rugged landscape with opportunities for driving tours, hiking, camping, picnicking and nature study. Dogs are allowed in the outdoor areas of the park but cannot be in any of the park buildings. Although the park is well-known for its summer outdoor *TEXAS* musical drama, dogs are not permitted at the production. *Info: 11450 Park Rd. 5, Canyon; (806) 488-2227; www.tpwd.state.tx.us. Fee.*

Rock Island Rail Trail. Part of a national non-profit initiative, the Rails-to-Trails Conservancy, this four-mile hike and bike trail follows the path of a former railroad line from near downtown to the west side of Amarillo. Most of the route is asphalt surface and leads through urban areas (with cross traffic) and eventually through more natural areas with some shade and rest stops with picnic tables where you and Fido can take a break. *Info: trailhead at Seventh Ave. and Crockett St.; (806) 378-9397; www.traillink.com. Free.*

Southeast Dog Park. Especially popular for its small dog section (which includes benches as well as a dog drinking fountain), the large pups have a less-developed area to run and romp as well. *Info: S.E. 46th & Osage; (806) 378-3036; www.amarilloparks.org. Free.*

Thompson Dog Park. If your dog wants to take a dip on a hot Amarillo day, our dogs give this park a big paws up thanks to its pond (as well as agility equipment and benches). *Info: N.E. 24th and Fillmore; www.amarilloparks.org. Free.*

Fetch This!
Gander Mountain. If you need hiking supplies before you and Fido venture out to Palo Duro Canyon or just need general dog supplies, here's a pet-friendly place to shop. Dogs need to be leashed in the store. *Info: 10300 W. I-40; (806) 354-9095; www.gandermountain.com.*

PetSmart. If Rover needs some supplies, you'll probably find it in this expansive pet emporium. *Info: 2802 Soncy Rd.; (806) 351-1171; www.petsmart.com.*

Treats & Eats
The Bagel Place. This deli-style place doesn't just make bagels; they serve lots of other things as well: sandwiches, soups, salads and breakfast, too. Dogs are welcome on their outdoor patio area. *Info: 3301 S. Bell; (806) 353-5985; bagelplace.net.*

Burrito Stop. This coffee and Tex-Mex shop is located near downtown and is open for breakfast and lunch. Sit on the outdoor patio with Bowser while you enjoy a burrito. *Info: 114 Southeast 9th St.; (806) 418-2705; burritostop.com.*

Jason's Deli. Healthy choices coupled with good taste is the watchword at this national chain of sandwich shops known for fresh, natural ingredients. Leashed dogs are allowed on the outdoor patio. *Info: 7406 W. 34th Ave.; (806) 353-4440; www.jasonsdeli.com.*

Macaroni Joe's. This upscale Tuscan restaurant has an extensive wine list and their time-tested Italian menu has made it a favorite for lunch and dinner. Their steak, pastas and seafood entrees are their most popular choices. An outdoor patio is open for al fresco dining for you and your pooch. *Info: 1619 S. Kentucky; (806) 358-8990; macaronijoes.com.*

McAlister's Deli. This national chain is known for their jumbo sandwiches and their signature sweet tea (hey, this is Texas, after all). The Amarillo location on the western edge of town has an outdoor dining area where your dog is allowed to join you. *Info: 8605 West 34th Ave.; (806) 355-7500; mcalistersdeli.com.*

Ruby Tequila's Mexican Kitchen. Ruby Tequila's operates several Texas restaurants serving authentic south of the border dishes like mesquite-grilled steaks, ribs and fajitas and their "flaming skillet" dishes which are beef, fish or chicken, served in the pan with grilled vegetables. Pets are allowed in a grassy fenced area next to the restaurant's outdoor patio. *Info: 2001 S. Georgia St.; (806) 358-7829; rubytequilas.com.*

Stay, Lie Down

Amarillo is home to numerous dog-friendly chain hotels including **Baymont Inn, Best Western, Days Inn, Drury Inn, La Quinta, Microtel, Motel 6, Quality Inn, Residence Inn, Super 8**, and more.

Amarillo KOA. This KOA offers RV, cabin and tent camping on Amarillo's east side. Campers enjoy a heated swimming pool, new restrooms and showers, free cable TV and Wi-Fi access, a gift store and best of all, a fenced dog park for some leash-free romping (they must be leashed when in the other public areas, however). There are no extra fees for dogs here except for the cabins where a daily fee of $5 per pet is charged. *Info: 1100 Folsom Rd.; (806) 335-1762; www.amarillokoa.com.*

Ambassador Hotel Amarillo. Not all rooms here are pet friendly at this full-service hotel, so ask when you make your reservation. Your dog will be treated with a welcome pet goodie bag when you check in; there's a $50 non-refundable pet fee, per pet. *Info: 3100 I-40 W.; (800) 817-0521 or (806) 358-6161; www.ambassadoramarillo.com.*

Bar H Working Dude Ranch. Located 60 miles east of Amarillo (not that far by West Texas standards!), this family-owned ranch offers accommodations and ranch activities tailored to each individual guest. These include riding the trails on quarter horses, bird and wildlife watching, fishing and other recreational pursuits or you can also help the ranch hands mend fences, feed livestock or other chores. Guests stay in comfortable bunkhouses and are greeted each morning with a chuckwagon breakfast. The ranch also caters to day visitors with trail rides and dining. There is free Wi-Fi in the ranch dining room. Dogs are welcome on the ranch but visitors are asked to call ahead to determine the details. *Info: 12064 Bar H Ranch Rd.; (800) 627-9871; www.barhduderanch.com.*

Luxury Inn and Suites Amarillo. This smaller hotel has 50 guest rooms with TVs with premium channels, microwaves, refrigerators and hair dryers. The hotel, which has an indoor swimming pool with Jacuzzi and offers free Wi-Fi, serves a complimentary hot breakfast. Up to three dogs are allowed in your guest room with a daily pet fee of $5 per pet. *Info: 2915 I-40 E.; (806) 372-8101; www.luxuryinntexas.com.*

Overnite RV Park. Situated on the eastern side of Amarillo, this RV campground features large pull-through RV sites, a children's playground, heated pool, laundry room and a gift shop. All sites have access to free Wi-Fi and TV cable. Seven sites here are especially dog-friendly with fenced yards so dogs can roam leash free! Dogs must be leashed when in other areas of the camp. *Info: 900 S. Lakeside Dr. (off I-40 at exit 75); (806) 373-1431; www.overnitervpark.com.*

Red Roof Inn Amarillo. Located two miles from the center of Amarillo, Red Roof Inn offers free Wi-Fi, free Continental break

fast, a swimming pool and a coin laundry. Children 17 years and younger stay here free with adult. Rooms feature TVs with cable channels, hair dryers; some rooms also have microwaves and small refrigerators. Red Roof

Inn allows one dog per room at no additional fee. *Info: 1620 I-40 E.; (806) 374-2020; www.redroof.com.*

Sniff Out More Information
Amarillo Convention & Visitor Council; (800) 692-1338; www.visitamarillotx.com.

BIG SPRING
Big Spring is located where two landforms, the Edwards Plateau and the Caprock, converge. The area, once a stop on the Overland Trail in the 1800s, has been prized for centuries for its dependable water source. Today, those springs are part of Comanche Trail Park.

Run, Spot, Run!
Big Spring State Park. This smaller state park is unusual in several ways: it is a day-use only state park, it lies within the city limits of Big Spring, and it does not charge an entrance fee. Thanks to its convenient location, the park is popular for jogging, hiking and cycling—and dog walking. The loop road winds around the perimeter of the park's 382 acres and offers scenic views from atop high bluffs as well as several picnic area. *Info: No. 1 Scenic Dr.; (432) 263-4931; www.tpwd.state.tx.us. Free.*

Hangar 25 Air Museum. Housed in a WWII-era hanger at the former Webb Air Force Base, this museum features exhibits recalling the history of the base and the its bombardier training school. One interesting exhibit is the "Snoopy Sidewalk" honoring the well-known cartoon dog, the "World War One Flying Ace," made famous by the Peanuts comic strip. In the 1960s, students in the flying school chose Snoopy as their mascot and received permission from creator Charles M. Schultz to call their class the "Snoopy Flight." Shortly thereafter, one of the students drew Snoopy's likeness mounted on his Sopwith Camel doghouse in a wet concrete walk which was being poured near the flight line. Today, the famous Beagle's image and the names of the flight class are preserved for visitors to see. The Snoopy memorial and other outdoor areas of the museum are dog-friendly, although dogs are not allowed in the buildings. *Info: 1911 Apron Dr.; (432) 264-1999; www.hangar25airmuseum.com. Free, donations accepted.*

Lake Colorado City State Park. Located about 40 miles east of Big Spring, this state park, with its five miles of shoreline on Lake Colorado City, is popular for fishing, swimming and boating. Several hiking trails transverse the park's 500 acres and numerous campsites with water (some with electricity) are available for overnight stays. The park is closed on Tuesdays and Wednesdays. Dogs are allowed in the park's outdoor areas but not in any park buildings. *Info: 4582 FM 2836, Colorado City; (325) 728-3931; www.tpwd.state.tx.us. Fee.*

Treats & Eats
Sonic Drive In. There are two Sonic restaurants in Big Spring where Fido can sit with you while you eat in your vehicle. *Info: 601 East RR 700, (432) 263-2700; 1200 South Gregg St., (432) 263-6790; www.sonicdrivein.com.*

Stay, Lie Down
Big Spring is home to several dog-friendly chains including **La Quinta, Motel 6, Quality Inn,** and more.

Holiday Inn Express Big Spring. Located on Big Spring's north side, just off I-20, this limited service Holiday Inn welcomes dogs 30 pounds or less for a non-refundable fee of $30. The hotel includes a well-equipped fitness center, outdoor pool, guest laundry and a kids-eat-free policy; complimentary breakfast is served daily. *Info: 1109 N. Aylesford; (432) 263-5400; www.ihg.com.*

Texas RV Park of Big Spring. This full-service park is located just south of Big Spring and offers RV, cabin and tent camping. Amenities include cable TV, Wi-Fi, restrooms and showers, laundry facility, and picnic tables. Up to two dogs are allowed at the RV and tent camping areas, but not in the cabins or other buildings. The park also has some hiking trails to enjoy; dogs must be leashed. *Info: 4100 US 87; (432) 267-7900; www.txrvpark.com.*

Sniff Out More Information
Big Spring Convention and Visitors Bureau; (432) 263-8235 or (866) 430-7100; www.visitbigspring.com.

LUBBOCK
Nearby destinations: Amarillo

When Francisco Coronado and his explorers arrived in this region four centuries ago, they found the grass high and the terrain devoid of landmarks. The Spaniards drove stakes into the soil to mark their path across the region they dubbed *Llano Estacado* or "staked plains." Modern-day Lubbock is the center of a vast cotton-farming region and the Lubbock area is increasingly known as the heart of Texas's full-bodied wine business.

Run, Spot, Run!

American Wind Power Center and Windmill Museum. Surrounded by miles of plains, Lubbock is a natural setting for one of the most unusual museum venues in the region: the American Wind Power Center and Windmill Museum. Located in Mackenzie Park, the 28-acre museum showcases rare windmills, with information on the importance of harnessing this natural source of power. You and your (leashed) dog can stroll among the 100 windmills exhibited here including a full-sized reproduction of the Flowerdew Hundred Postmill, the first windmill built in North America in 1621. *Info: 1701 Canyon Lake Dr.; (806) 747-8734; www.windmill.com. Fee.*

Buffalo Springs Lake Recreational Area. This 200-acre reservoir is located nine miles east of central Lubbock and is a major destination for boating, fishing, camping, picnicking and hiking. Developed campsites with electric and water as well as primitive camping spots invite you and Fido to spend a few days kicking back and enjoying the Panhandle atmosphere. Dogs are permitted in the campgrounds without any extra fees. Dogs must be leashed and have proof of current vaccinations. *Info: 9999 High Meadow Rd.; (806) 747-3353; www.buffalospringslake.net. Fee.*

Lubbock Memorial Arboretum. This 93-acre site in the center of the city is located within the K.N. Clapp City Park. With a mission to beautify Lubbock through education, the Arboretum was established in the 1960s to determine the best plantings for the south Texas plains area. Bowsers will enjoy a walk through this park while you watch for local birds and take in the natural beauty. *Info: 4111 University Ave.; (806) 797-4520; www.lubbockarboretum.org. Free.*

McAlister Park. Located on Lubbock's southwest outskirts, this new city park has been developed to appeal to active families with a BMX track, baseball and disc golf fields, a skate park and natural birding areas. Soon it will also be the location of Lubbock's first dedicated dog park. As for now, dogs are allowed to hike and explore on leash. *Info: Marsha Sharp Freeway and Milwaukee Ave.; (806) 775.2687; www.visitlubbock.org. Free.*

Tech Terrace Park. This park near the center of the city offers lots of wide-open spaces to walk and benches when you and your dog are ready for a rest. *Info: 23rd St. and Flint Ave.; (806) 775-2687; www.visitlubbock.org. Free.*

Llano Estacado Winery. The rich soil and temperate weather of the high plains region has drawn numerous award-winning wineries and international acclaim to Lubbock. Probably the most celebrated winery in the state is Llano Estacado. Their award-winning red and white wines are produced from their own vineyard and from other vineyards in the area. The winery is open for tastings and tours; leashed dogs are allowed in the outside areas but not inside the buildings. *Info: 3426 E. FM 1585; (806) 745-2258; www.llanowine.com. Free.*

Stars and Stripes Drive-In Theatre. If you're looking for a unique activity to enjoy with your dog, this 1950s-style drive in theatre is just the place. Two movies are offered nightly on different screens. Just drive up and watch from your vehicle or next to it on your own folding chairs. Dogs are allowed to be inside the car or, if you are viewing from chairs, beside you on a leash. Although there is an 50s Cafe with outdoor seating, dogs are not allowed there. *Info: 5101 Clovis Hwy.; (806) 749-7469; driveinusa.com. Fee.*

Fetch This!

Gander Mountain. Specializing in outdoor outfitting, this store also has a large array of pet products with an emphasis on hunting dog accessories. If Rover needs a new doggie backpack, Gander is your place; your dog can even pick out his own accessories in the store as long as he's on leash. *Info: 4006 West Loop 289; (806) 785-1591; www.gandermountain.com.*

PetSmart. Two PetSmart locations in Lubbock each offer a wealth of pet products, premium foods, and travel accessories for pooches. *Info: 6801 Slide Rd., (806) 798-0717; 6046 Marsha Sharp Fwy., (806) 799-4637; www.petsmart.com.*

Treats & Eats

Firehouse Subs. Founded by firemen, this national chain of sandwich shops supports firefighters through various fund-raising initiatives. Their menu includes all kinds of subs, salads, soups and beverages. Rover is invited to join you on the outdoor dining area at this location near the Texas Tech campus. *Info: 411 University Ave.; (806) 747-9600; www.firehousesubs.com.*

Fuzzy's Taco Shop. You'll find more than tacos at this central Lubbock eatery; the Tex-Mex menu features burritos, nachos, quesadillas along with burgers, beer and margaritas. Open for breakfast, lunch and dinner; an outdoor dining area welcomes leashed dogs. *Info: 2102 Broadway St.; (806) 740-8226; www.fuzzystacoshop.com.*

Jason's Deli. Located in the Kings Park area of south Lubbock, Jason's offers healthy choice sandwiches, soups, and salads made from organic, natural ingredients without artificial additives. Jason's has an outdoor patio where leashed dogs are welcome. *Info: 4001 South Loop 289; (806) 799-8660; www.jasonsdeli.com.*

Stay, Lie Down

Lubbock is home to numerous budget chains with dog-friendly properties including **America's Best Value Inn, Baymont Inn and Suites, Best Western, Extended Stay America, Holiday Inn, La Quinta, Motel 6, Red Roof Inn, Sleep Inn, Studio 6**, and more.

Woodrow House Bed and Breakfast. This property is located near Texas Tech University and has 10 guest rooms, each with a private bath. Each room is decorated with a separate theme and offers free Wi-Fi and TVs. The inn has a swimming pool and hot tub and a full breakfast is served each morning in the common room. Some of the rooms here welcome dogs for a pet fee of $30. *Info: 2629 19th St.; (800) 687-5236 or (806) 793-3330; www.woodrowhouse.com.*

Sniff Out More Information
Visit Lubbock; (806) 747-5232 or (800) 692-4035; www.visitlubbock.org.

SAN ANGELO
The city of San Angelo was built around Fort Concho, a frontier fort established in 1867. Today, the city is a ranching center and home of the largest wool and mohair market in the country. Located on the Concho River, a treasure of the region are the pink Concho River pearls. Angelo State University, part of the Texas Tech University System, was founded in San Angelo in 1928.

Run, Spot, Run!
Fort Concho National Historic Landmark. This former military post is one of the best-preserved forts in the state containing 23 native-limestone buildings that once were part of the fort. At one time, the fort housed as many as 500 infantry and cavalry troops and covered over 1600 acres. Today the reconstructed fort in present-day downtown San Angelo covers about 40 acres. Leashed dogs are allowed in the outdoor areas of the fort and also in the Barracks 1 visitor center. *Info: 630 South Oakes St.; (325) 481-2646; www.fortconcho.com. Fee.*

River Walk. You and your fur-iend can follow the course of the Concho River through downtown San Angelo, past parks and gardens, picnic areas and more to Fort Concho National Historic Landmark. *Info: Several trailheads in downtown San Angelo; (325) 657-4279. www.sanangelotexas.us. Free.*

San Angelo State Park. Pitch a "pup" tent or camp in an RV at this park located a few miles west of San Angelo on the shores of OC Fisher Lake. This state park offers lots of outdoor recreation including fishing, camping, picnicking, birding and 50 miles of hiking trails to satisfy the most devoted dog walkers. *Info: 3900-2 Mercedes Rd.; (325) 949-4757; www.tpwd.state.tx.us. Fee.*

Pearls for Your Pooch?

San Angelo owes its existence to the **Concho River** that drew explorers and colonists here. The Concho, a major tributary of Texas' Colorado River, means "shell" in Spanish, so named for the large population of **freshwater mussels** found there. These mussels sometimes produce **pink, lavender or purple pearls** that are especially valued as they are produced only in the Concho River basin. These freshwater treasures were known to Spanish explorers in the 1600s, and one legend says that Concho pearls were incorporated into the Spanish crown jewels. Today, licensed pearl collectors scour the river, its tributary creeks and downstream lakes for these naturally occurring beauties.

Fetch This!

Petco. A full array of dog supplies and products fill the shelves here and your dog can help you make your selections. *Info: 4157 Sunset Dr.; (325) 223-8236; www.petco.com.*

PetSmart. This PetSmart location in San Angelo presents a large selection of dog food, leashes and collars, and more. *Info: 4439 Sunset Dr.; (325) 949-6160; www.petsmart.com.*

Stay, Lie Down

San Angelo is home to several dog-friendly chain properties including **Best Western, Days Inn, Microtel, Ramada, Rodeway Inn, Staybridge Suites**, and more.

Pawty Time

April: Dog's Day at the Park. This annual event at San Angelo State Park is a veritable canine fun fest with Wiener Dog Races, costume contests, obstacle courses and the Stupid Pet Trick contest. Product vendors and concessions are also on hand. *Info: sanangelolive.com.*

June: Sunset Mall Pooch Pageant. Held at San Angelo's Sunset Mall, this one-day event has several prize competitions including an owner and dog look-alike contest, best dressed dog, and best personality and the best tail wag. The event benefits a local dog rescue organization. *Info: www.conchovalleypaws.org.*

Sniff Out More Information

San Angelo Convention & Visitors Bureau; (325) 655-4136 or (800) 375-1206; www.visitsanangelo.org.

WICHITA FALLS

Just a few miles from the Oklahoma border lies the city of Wichita Falls, located on the Wichita River. Named for the Wichita Indians, this community was first an agricultural hub but boomed at the turn of the century with the discovery of oil. Although the modern oil industry of West Texas is a far cry from its boomtown days, reminders of the petroleum business are found throughout the city. Steel oil derricks point to the sky at Lake Arrowhead State Park as a reminder of those boomtown days.

Run, Spot, Run!

Lake Arrowhead State Park. Five miles of hiking/equestrian trails beckon Bowsers in this park on the shores of 14,000-acre Lake Arrowhead. You and your furry family member can enjoy fishing, boating, swimming, picnicking and camping at over 70 campsites (some primitive tent sites, some improved). Note that this park has a resident black-tailed prairie dog colony where dogs will *not* be welcome. *Info: 229 Park Road 63; (940) 528-2211; www.tpwd.state.tx.us. Fee.*

Off-Leash Dog Facility at Lake Wichita Park. Opened in 2011, this dog park has separate areas for large and smaller dogs, secure chain-link fencing and double entry gates. Dog water fountains are a new addition to the park. This facility is located within Lake Wichita Park on the banks of Lake Wichita. In addition to the off-leash park, Lake Wichita Park has a 2-1/2 mile walking trail along the lake and picnic areas, perfect for a (leashed) dog walk. *Info: 5205 Fairway Blvd.; (940) 761-7490; www.wichitafallstx.gov. Free.*

River Bend Nature Center. This centrally-located attraction is home to many animal and bird species in native forest and wetland areas. There are 15 miles of walking trails through bottom land and cultivated planting sections. A large indoor atrium hosts a butterfly garden and native flora. Leashed dogs are allowed in the outdoor areas of the nature center, but not in any buildings including the conservatory. *Info: 2200 3rd St.; (940) 767-0843; riverbendnature-center.wordpress.com. Fee.*

Wichita River Trail. Part of the national Rails to Trails initiative, this paved trail follows a former railroad line along the Big Wichita River from Lucy Park to Wichita Lake Park. This route is part of the citywide Circle Trail System covering some 18 miles in all. Pooches and people can begin and end their walks at a number of trailheads. The trail passes through several other wooded park areas and the River Bend Nature Works with a tall ornamental waterfall. *Info: Lucy Park trailhead at 100 Sunset Drive; (940) 761-7490; www.wichitafallstx.gov. Free.*

Fetch This!

Petco. If it's dog-related, you'll find it at this extensive pet product store. It's located on the city's southwest side, just down the street from Sikes Senter Mall. Dogs are welcome to shop with you. *Info: 4319 A. Kemp Blvd.; (940) 692-6244; www.petco.com.*

Tractor Supply Company. This store has a large inventory of farm and ranch needs as well as a good selection of dog products and food. Leashed dogs are allowed in the store. *Info: 2618 Southwest Parkway; (940) 696-8850; www.tractorsupply.com.*

Stay, Lie Down

Wichita Falls is home to numerous dog-friendly hotel chains including **America's Best Value Inn, Baymont Inn & Suites, Holiday Inn, La Quinta, Motel 6, Quality Inn, Ramada Limited**, and more.

Candlewood Suites Wichita Falls. Suites here feature free Wi-Fi, full kitchens with all necessary appliances and utensils, sofa beds in living rooms, cable TVs, stereos and DVD players. The hotel has an outdoor picnic area with barbecue grills, a complimentary laundry, free breakfast and a snack shop. Two dogs of up to 80 pounds are allowed with a non-refundable fee of $50 for up to six nights; $100 for 7 or more nights. *Info: 1320 Central Fwy.; (940) 322-4400; www.ihg.com.*

Coyote Ranch Resort. This guest ranch and event center just east of Wichita Falls offers cabin and RV camping and a nice array of amenities although only the RV areas are dog-friendly. You'll find 123 RV sites, most of them pull-throughs. The sites are equipped with water, electricity, and sewer connections, restrooms, laundry rooms and a fenced dog run. Other amenities include swimming pools, a stocked fishing pond, picnic tables, barbecue pits, catering service from the resort kitchen and lots of outdoor recreation. Dogs are welcome for no additional fees. *Info: 14145 US 287 North; (877) 767-6771; coyoteranchresort.com.*

The New Grand Hotel Of Wichita Falls. This large downtown hotel is built around a nice indoor atrium with a heated pool, sauna and hot tub, putting green, a shuffleboard court and a fitness center. A complimentary Continental breakfast is served daily and an elevator serves the upper floors. All rooms have high-speed Internet access and cable TV and suites have refrigerators and microwave ovens. Dogs of any size are allowed for a non-refundable fee of $150 per stay. *Info: 401 Broad St.; (940) 766-6000; www.grandhotelwichitafalls.com.*

Sniff Out More Information
Wichita Falls Convention & Visitors Bureau; (800) 799-6732; wichitafalls.org.

8. Gulf Coast

Beaches and bowsers go hand in paw, and Texas offers nearly 300 miles of coastline for the two of you to explore. From the Louisiana border to the Mexico border, the Gulf coast is lined with vacation options that range from big city bustle to nearly deserted stretches of Padre Island National Seashore accessible only by four-wheeler.

The northern stretches of the Gulf are the busiest. Communities like Beaumont and Baytown recall Texas's oil heritage. Galveston offers resort getaways with a true island atmosphere but a short drive inland, Houston is filled with world-class parks, shopping, and big city fun.

Midway down the Texas coast lies Corpus Christi and the Coastal Bend, populated by the communities of Port Aransas, Rockport and more. Continuing south, you'll find the southernmost reaches of Texas: Port Isabel, Brownsville, and South Padre Island, the vacation destination that's separated from the rest of Padre Island by a man-made channel.

ANAHUAC
Located where the Trinity River meets Galveston Bay, Anahuac began as a fortress that once held William B. Travis before he was rescued by the Texian troops during the Texas Revolution. That fort is today a dog-friendly park, one of two outdoor destinations in this small town that welcome you and your dog to explore the coastal marshes and bird habitat for which Anahuac is known.

A word of warning: Anahuac, the home of the annual Texas Gatorfest, is called the "Alligator Capital of Texas." Please keep your dog on a short leash at all times, don't let him near the water alone (gators can surge quickly out of the water), and don't let him bark at alligators.

Run, Spot, Run!
Anahuac National Wildlife Refuge. This 34,000-acre refuge is

home to over 250 species of birds either on a full-time or migrating basis. You're welcome to bring your dog on leash but be aware that the bayous and coastal marshes of this park on Galveston Bay are also home to alligators. The refuge includes walking and driving trails, fishing piers, and wildlife observation areas. *Info: 4017 FM 563; (409) 267-3337; fws.gov/refuge/Anahuac. Fee.*

Fort Anahuac Park. This historic park was once home to a fort used by Mexican troops to hold William B. Travis and other Texas insurgents. The Texians, in the first armed confrontation between the revolutionaries and the Mexican army, freed Travis. Although the fort's remains are gone, today the county park is a favorite for picnicking, camping (no hookups), or just dog walks. *Info: 1704 S. Main St. at Trinity Bay; (409) 267-2409. Free.*

Sniff Out More Information
Anahuac Area Chamber of Commerce; (409) 267-4190; www.anahuacchamber.com.

BAYTOWN
Nearby destinations: Houston

With a slogan as the place "where oil and water really do mix," you just might guess that Baytown was built on the oil industry. And you'd be right. The city continues to be very active in the petrochemical industry but it features several attractions for dog lovers as well. Located on the Great Texas Coastal Birding Trail, this city offers some quiet getaways, parks, and even a winery that welcomes Fido.

Run, Spot, Run!
Baytown Bark Park. Located in the city's W.L. Jenkins Park, the bark park is filled with five acres of off-leash fun. Large dogs have four acres to romp while small dogs have a dedicated one-acre

area. Warm weather visitors will appreciate the shade covers and drinking fountains for both two- and four-legged guests, especially after Fido takes a turn at the park's agility equipment. *Info: 4334 Crosby Cedar Bayou Rd.; www.baytown.org. Free.*

Yepez Vineyard. Home to two vineyards growing Blanc Du Bois and Black Spanish grapes, this family-owned operation welcomes you to bring a picnic and chairs—and your dog—and enjoy their outdoor facilities. The winery's tasting room is open Friday through Sunday. *Info: 12739 FM 2354; (281) 573-4139 or (281) 804-3410; yepezvineyard.com. Free.*

Fetch This!
Petco Baytown. If Fido runs out of food on the trip, you'll find quality foods as well as treats and toys at this store just off TX 146. *Info: 4665 Garth Rd.; (281) 427-4374; www.petco.com.*

Treats & Eats
Sonic Drive-In. Definitely high on the list of Irie and Tiki's favorite eateries, Sonic is found at two locations in Baytown. *Info: 3916 Garth Rd.; (281) 428-2531 and 7360 Garth Rd.; (281) 421-4763; www.sonicdrivein.com.*

Stay, Lie Down
Baytown is home to several pet-friendly budget chains including **Baymont Inn, Candlewood Suites, Comfort Suites, Econo Lodge Inn & Suites, La Quinta, Motel 6,** and **Super 8.**

Galveston Bay KOA. If you've got an RV or trailer (or have rented one for your vacation), this waterside campsite welcomes two dogs per campsite and has a dog walk area as well as a fishing pier right on Galveston Bay. *Info: 2000 Tri-Cities Beach Rd.; (281) 420-3200; www.galvestonbaykoa.com.*

La Quinta Inn & Suites Houston Baytown East. We love La Quinta's dog-friendly policy (two dogs per room without a fee). This hotel, located near the San Jacinto Mall, is located near numerous fast food restaurants. *Info: 5215 I-10 E.; (281) 421-5566; www.lq.com.*

Sniff Out More Information
Baytown Chamber of Commerce; (281) 420-5311; www.baytown.org.

BEAUMONT

Located nearly 90 miles east of Houston, Beaumont earned its place in the Texas history books with the 1901 discovery of oil at Spindletop, a salt dome. Beaumont quickly became a boomtown. Today Beaumont is a port city and is also a gateway to Big Thicket National Preserve.

Run, Spot, Run!

Gulf Terrace Hike & Bike Trail. Leashed dogs are welcome on this 3.5-mile trail near the Cris Quinn Soccer Complex. A 10-foot-wide cement trail is shared by the one-way traffic including cyclists, runners, and walkers. *Info: 9310 Phelan Blvd. Free.*

dogtipper
choice

Fire Museum of Texas. Don't forget to pack the camera for a visit to this museum, home of what was once the world's largest fire hydrant! The 24-foot-tall, 4500-pound, Dalmatian-spotted hydrant that sits in front of the Fire Museum was donated by Walt Disney Studios to celebrate the rerelease of *101 Dalmatians.* For special events, the fire hydrant sprays water but every day it's available for some fun photos with your dog. Unless packed with school groups, dogs are generally permitted inside the museum as well where you'll find a doghouse in the shape of a fire hydrant, displays on the history of fire dogs, and much more. *Info: 400 Walnut St.; (409) 880-3927; www.firemuseumoftexas.org. Free.*

Ira Reed Dog Park. This dog park, located just off I-10, is open from dawn to dusk. Dogs under 30 pounds are allowed only on the south side of the park; dogs over 30 pounds are allowed only on the north side of the park. *Info: 2348 Louisiana St., www.beaumontrecreation.com. Free.*

Fetch This!

Petco Beaumont. Premium foods and travel needs as well as professional grooming are available at this store. *Info: 4175 Dowlen Rd., (409) 895-0440; www.petco.com.*

PetSmart Beaumont. Located just south of US 287/69/96, this PetSmart has anything you might have forgotten at home, from leashes to premium foods. *Info: 4045 Dowlen Rd.; (409) 924-0247; www.petsmart.com.*

Puppy Love. This premier boutique carries everything from designer duds for dogs to top of the line doggie treats. *Info: 3939 Dowlen; (409) 892-WOOF; www.puppylovedogstore.com.*

Stay, Lie Down

Beaumont is home to numerous dog-friendly chain hotels including **America's Best Value Inn, Candlewood Suites, Days Inn, Holiday Inn, Howard Johnson, Knights Inn, La Quinta, Red Roof Inn, Residence Inn, Rodeway Inn, Studio 6, Super 6**, and more.

MCM Elegante Hotel & Conference Center. Dogs of 50 pounds or less are welcome at this hotel that's often lauded as one of the town's best. Up to two dogs per room are accepted, and guests will need to show Fido's proof of immunizations at check-in. Pet rooms are found in the non-poolside portion of Cabana Building. The hotel does not charge a fee for pets but there is a $100 refundable deposit at this hotel that includes a fitness center, a day spa, three restaurants, a tropical outdoor pool, and free wireless Internet. *Info: 2355 I-10 S.; (409) 842-3600; mcmelegantebeaumont.com.*

Pawty Time

October: DOG-tober Fest. This free event puts the spotlight on Fido starting with the Strut your Mutt parade which kicks off a full slate of dog-centric activities including paw readings, Neiman Barkus shopping area, a look-alike contest, best tail wagging contest, most talented dog contest, and much more. *Info: www.beaumontmainstreet.com*

Sniff Out More Information

Beaumont Convention and Visitors Bureau; (409) 880-3749; www.beaumontcvb.com.

BROWNSVILLE
Nearby destinations: South Padre Island

The largest city in the Rio Grande Valley as well as the southern-most city in Texas, Brownsville began as Fort Texas, later renamed Fort Brown. The fort marked the US boundary and its establishment ignited the Mexican-American War.

Today Brownsville moves at a peaceful pace, a favorite getaway with birders who travel from around the world for the chance to spot the nearly 400 bird species that have been identified in this region.

Run, Spot, Run!
Catherine B. Stillman Dog Park. Located next to the animal shelter, this park has sections for large and small dogs as well as water fountains for Fidos. *Info: 416 FM 511; (956) 542-2064. Free.*

Historic Battlefield Trail. This 8.5-mile trail runs from downtown Brownsville to the Palo Alto Battlefield National Historical Park. The trail, which includes benches and water fountains, got its start when the city purchased a portion of an abandoned railroad corridor. *Info: trailheads at E. Harrison St. to Entrance of Palo Alto Battlefield on FM 1847; www.traillink.com. Free.*

Palo Alto Battlefield National Historical Park. The National Park Service operates this small, free park that is located at the site where the Battle of Palo Alto took place in 1846 during the Mexican-American War. *Info: 5 miles north of downtown Brownsville at intersection of FM 1847 (Paredes Line Rd.) and FM 511; (956) 541-2785; www.nps.gov. Free.*

Resaca De La Palma State Park. This 1,200-acre state park is part of the World Birding Center, a network of birding sites through the Rio Grande Valley and a favorite with birders. The ancient riverbed of the Rio Grand moved through the years and created prime territory for wildlife. Today the park has a picnic area and numerous trails that welcome you and your leashed dog. The park also has a tram that offers a 3.2-mile loop; it's up to the discretion of the driver and the other passengers if your dog is permitted on the tram. *Info: 1000 New Carmen Rd., four miles west of Brownsville* *on US 281; (956) 565-3919; www.tpwd.state.tx.us and www.worldbirdingcenter.com. Fee.*

Stay, Lie Down
Brownsville is home to several dog-friendly hotel chains including **Homewood, Motel 6, La Quinta, Red Roof Inn, Residence Inn, Super 8** and more.

Sniff Out More Information
Brownsville Chamber of Commerce; (956) 542-4341; www.brownsvillechamber.com.

CORPUS CHRISTI
Nearby destinations: Port Aransas, Rockport

The Coastal Bend has been a magnet for travelers since the days of buccaneers and Spanish conquistadors. Today's visitors are drawn by a relaxed atmosphere and coastal beauty, turning Corpus Christi, the capital of the Coastal Bend, into one of the state's top travel destinations.

The waters of Corpus Christi Bay are calm, protected from the Gulf of Mexico by the barrier islands of Padre and Mustang, which served as pirate hideouts even after the area was charted in 1519 by Spanish explorer Alonzo Alvarez de Pineda. He bestowed the bay with its name, which means "body of Christ."

Today Corpus Christi is a thriving city, consistently ranking as one of America's busiest ports. High-rise luxury hotels, specialty shops, and seafood restaurants overlook the bay. The heart of Corpus Christi is Shoreline Boulevard, with its proud palms and spectacular views of the water. Beyond Corpus Christi lies Padre Island (often referred to as "Upper Padre Island" to differentiate it from

South Padre Island near Brownsville.) Both Padre Island and nearby Mustang Island provide miles of beaches that welcome your dog!

Run, Spot, Run!

Barkaritaville Pet Resort Dog Park. Corpus Christi is home to a private dog park at Barkaritaville, a boarding, day care, grooming and training facility. The double-gated, 22,000-square-foot off-leash area includes agility equipment, a self-serve dog wash, and watering stations. The park is for members only but you can purchase a single visit pass for $15 ($10 per additional dog). *Info: 6617 Jefferson St.; (361) 814-2275; barkaritavillepetresort.com. Fee.*

Corpus Christi Bay Trail. This nine-mile trail winds along the waterfront by many top Corpus Christi attractions including the Art Museum of South Texas, Museum of Science and History, and Corpus Christi Marina. It also links six parks along Ocean Drive on Corpus Christi Bay. (Portions of the trail are actually a bike lane.) *Info: www.traillink.com. Free.*

Corpus Christi Beaches. Unlike Padre Island, the barrier island that lies beyond the city, Corpus Christi isn't located on the Gulf of Mexico but on Corpus Christi Bay. You and your dog will need to head out to Padre for huge beaches but, within Corpus Christi, you do have some easy, convenient options for a sandy romp:

- **Cole Park.** This 43-acre park on Corpus Christi Bay is a popular place for city events and music in an outdoor amphitheater. There is also a lighted fishing pier, a playground and lots of shady picnic spots where you and your pooch can enjoy the scenic views of the Bay. *Info: Ocean Dr.; (800) 766-2322. Free.*
- **North Beach.** Located across the Harbor Bridge, this expansive beach includes both a busy section of sunbathers and swimmers, complete with picnic tables and showers, as well as a quiet section on the north end, perfect for solitary dog walks. *Info: Off TX-35/US-181 at Corpus Christi Beach exit (near Texas State Aquarium). Follow the exit towards Burleson St., turn right on Burleson St. and continue on Breakers Ave.; (361) 826-3469. Free.*
- **McGee Beach.** This downtown beach is a favorite with families with small children so, if your dog is reactive, choose your times accordingly. The beach has umbrellas for rent during the

summer months; year-around you'll find a large fishing pier and concession stand. From the beach, you can enjoy a walk on the Seawall. *Info: Shoreline Blvd. and Schatzell St.; (361) 826-3469. Free.*

Harbor Ferry. The 90-foot Harbor Ferry transports visitors – and their crated dogs — from the Peoples Street T-Head to the Texas State Aquarium/North Beach area. The pedestrian ferry costs $3 round trip and runs daily during the summer as well as spring break, weekends only in spring and fall months. *Info: Peoples St. T-Head; (361) 883-2287; ccrta.org. Fee.*

Hans and Pat Suter Wildlife Refuge. This coastal marshland on Oso Creek offers a one-mile trail as well as an 800-foot-long boardwalk. A favorite with birders for a chance to view brown pelicans as well as ducks and shorebirds, the refuge is also a great spot for dog walks. You'll also find picnic tables scattered throughout the facility. *Info: Ennis Joslin Rd. at Nile. Free.*

Lake Corpus Christi State Park. Located west of Corpus Christi near the little town of Mathis, this 14,000-acre park has lots of water recreation including swimming, boating, fishing as well as hiking, birding and camping (with both improved and primitive camp-sites). Dogs are allowed in the park campsites and on the trails, provided they are leashed and under control. They are not allowed in any park buildings and cannot be left unattended. Keep an eye out for javelina. *Info: 23194 Park Rd. 25, Mathis; (361) 547-2635; www.tpwd.state.tx.us. Fee.*

Padre Island. The 110-mile-long Padre Island, a barrier island that protects the south Texas coast from hurricanes, is reached by crossing the Intracoastal Waterway via the JFK Causeway Bridge. Don't confuse Padre Island with South Padre Island. Padre Island is the northern stretch of island paralleling the area from Corpus Christi to Port

dog**tipper**

choice

Mansfield; from that point south to the tip of Texas, the land mass is named South Padre Island. The surf is usually gentle and shallow enough to walk for hundreds of yards before reaching chest-deep water. Occasionally undertow is a problem, but on most summer days the waves are gentle and rolling, and the water is warm. Padre Island is home to several parks:

- **Padre Balli Park.** Padre Balli Park is named for the priest who managed a ranch on the island in the early nineteenth century. Operated by the county, this park includes both RV and primitive camping that offers plenty of beach fun for you and your leashed dog. *Info: 15820 Park Rd. 22 (South Padre Island Dr.); (361) 949-8121; nuecesbeachparks.com. Fee.*
- **Padre Island National Seashore.** Further south, the Padre Island National Seashore also welcomes dogs on leash. Although the

dogs are not permitted at the improved facilities at Malaquite Beach Visitor Center, you'll find miles of beach just beyond Malaquite where Fido can splash in the waves. Our dogs loved this beach! Vehicles are allowed on Padre beaches but after first few miles, only four-wheel drive vehicles should continue. Be sure to keep your dog close to you on the beach because, with the sound of the waves, it is difficult to hear cars on the soft sand. Five campgrounds are available (no reservations are accepted) for both tent campers and RVers although sites do not have hookups. *Info: 20420 Park Rd. 22; (361) 949-8068; www.nps.gov/pais. Fee.*

South Texas Botanical Gardens and Nature Center. This 180-acre park, located on the Great Texas Coastal Birding Trail, features native South Texas plants and winding trails through subtropical foliage. The gardens welcome "controllable and friendly pets on leashes only." *Info: 8545 S. Staples Dr.; (361) 852–2100; www.stxbot.org. Fee.*

Fetch This!

Petco Calallen. Located northeast of the city, this Petco offers food, treats, travel needs, and grooming. *Info: 4101 US 77; (361) 241-2072; www.petco.com.*

Petco Corpus Christi. If your visit to the beach has left Fido needing a freshwater bath, this Petco has a self-service dog wash! *Info: 6418 S. Staples St.; (361) 986-9222; www.petco.com.*

PetSmart Corpus Christi. Located just off South Padre Island Drive, this expansive store also includes veterinary services at Banfield Pet Hospital seven days a week. *Info: 5214 Blanch Moore; (361) 993-8882; www.petsmart.com.*

Treats & Eats

Landry's Seafood House. This restaurant, housed in a restored two-story barge, has long been one of our Corpus Christi favorites. The outdoor patio dining welcomes your four-legged travel companion (of any size). Although you'll find steaks and pasta dishes on the menu, Gulf seafood is the specialty of the house, all enjoyed with great views of the surrounding bay. *Info: 600 N. Shoreline Dr. on the Peoples St. T-Head; (361) 882–6666; www.landrysseafood.com.*

Stay, Lie Down

Corpus Christi is home to numerous dog-friendly, budget-friendly hotel chains including several **Comfort Suites**, **Econo Lodge**, **Homewood Suites**, **Knights Inn**, **La Quinta**, **Plaza Inn**, **Quality Inn**, **Red Roof Inn**, **Super 8**, and more.

Best Western Marina Grand Hotel. We loved the convenience of this hotel that's centrally located just across Shoreline Boulevard from the seawall and the Lawrence Street T-Head and one block east of the Water Street Market area with its bars, restaurants and the Texas Surf Museum. This high-rise hotel is dog-friendly. Dogs smaller than 80 pounds are welcome, two per room, and the hotel also offers special dog packages. Packages include the $20 per day dog fee and goodies for your four-legged travel companion. The 11-

dogtipper

choice

story hotel offers complimentary breakfast, covered parking, and laundry facilities. *Info: 300 N. Shoreline Blvd.; (361) 883-5111; www.marinagrandhotel.net.*

Holiday Inn Emerald Beach. The only hotel in downtown Corpus Christi on the beach (albeit a small one), this property is very popular with families and welcomes any dog, any size. There's a $30 dog fee per stay, and the hotel welcomes multiple dogs per room. The 368-room hotel is adjacent to Magee Beach. *Info: 1102 South Shoreline Blvd.; (361) 883–5731; www.ichotelsgroup.com.*

Omni Corpus Christi Hotel. Easy to spot on the Corpus Christi skyline, this elegant 475-room hotel overlooks the bay and welcomes dogs 25 pounds and under with a one-time fee of $50. Many of Corpus Christi's main attractions lie within walking distance. *Info: 900 N. Shoreline Blvd.; (800) THE–OMNI or (361) 887–1600; www.omnihotels.com.*

Puerto Del Sol RV Park. If you're coming in by RV, this bayside park is a convenient choice. Located on the water's edge near the

---

Beach Safety

Water, water everywhere, and not a drop to drink! Well, unfortunately most dogs will think there's plenty of water to drink and will try to lap up some of the salty sea on a beach visit. **Be sure to watch your dog and stop him from drinking saltwater;** too much and he'll have a nasty case of diarrhea and a tummy ache. Always carry fresh water and offer it often.

The beach itself makes the perfect place for a nice, long dog walk but you'll need to keep an eye out for a few troublemakers including the Portuguese Man-Of-War jellyfish. The tentacles of these iridescent purple creatures produce a nasty sting. A far less dangerous, but very annoying, aspect of the Gulf beaches are **tar balls**. These black clumps, formed by natural seepage and offshore oil spills, wash up on the beach and stick to shoes and paws alike. Many hotels have a tar removal station to help you remove the sticky substance but, for dogs, the safest way to remove the tar is with baby oil.

Harbor Bridge, this park offers waterfront and off-water sites as well as fishing piers and fish cleaning stations. Dogs on leash are welcome guests as well. *Info: 5100 Timon Blvd.; (888) 353-5373 or (361) 882-5373; www.puertodelsolrvpark.com.*

Sniff Out More Information
Corpus Christi Convention & Visitors Bureau; (800) 678-6232; visitcorpuschristitx.org.

GALVESTON
Once the busiest city in Texas and a major center of commerce, in 1900 the town then called "Wall Street of the Southwest" was struck by the most devastating hurricane in US history. Today the city, which is located 50 miles from Houston on Galveston Island, recalls its roots with a 36-block historic district. The city and island are popular tourist destinations and dogs are welcome on the beaches and in many local establishments.

Run, Spot, Run!
BayWatch Dolphin Tours. Your dog can ride for free on this cruise that visits dolphins in their native habitat. The 45-minute tours are held on a boat with a covered interior; the boat has no propeller to keep the dolphins safe. Tours are conducted daily, departing from Pier 21. *Info: 2101 Harborside Dr.; 832-859-4557; www.galvestonbaywatch.com. Fee.*

Bolivar Ferry. This free ferry travels from the east end of Galveston to the Bolivar Peninsula. Your dog will have to remain in your vehicle but keep an eye out for porpoise as well as gulls. Ferries leave about every 20 minutes; the ride lasts 18 minutes. You can drive your car onto one or step onboard the 185-foot-long ferry as a passenger. *Info: To reach the ferry, follow Broadway/Avenue J (TX 87) east through town until it merges with Seawall Boulevard, then turn left on 2nd Street which becomes Ferry Road; you'll see signs directing you toward the landing; (409) 795-2230; txdot.gov. Free.*

East Beach. Often called the "party beach" (a hint at the activity level you'll find here), this beach gets its reputation because alcohol is legal on this beach. If your dog doesn't mind crowds, this beach on the eastern tip of the island welcomes him. During the summer months, you'll find chairs for rent here as well as umbrellas. *Info: 1923 Boddeker Rd.; (409) 797-5111; www.galveston.com/beachparks. Fee.*

Fort Travis Seashore Park. Located on the Bolivar Peninsula (see the Bolivar ferry, above), this site has long served as a fortification, first by the Spanish and later by the Confederates and US military in a fort built at the site. Although dismantled in 1949, today some reminders of the early fort remain along with picnic grounds, a seawall, and the Fort Travis Interpretive Trail that invites you and your dog to explore. The park also includes campsites. *Info: 900 TX 87; (409) 684-1333 or (409) 934-8100 for reservations; www.galvestonparks-seniors.org. Fee.*

dogtipper **Galveston Island State Park.** Located on the west end of the island,

choice

this nearly 2,000-acre park spans the entire width of the island, including both beach and salt marsh frontage. Texas Parks and Wildlife Department runs Galveston Island State Park, located at 14901 FM 3005. This is a great place to see wildlife, including birds and ducks, raccoons, marsh rabbits, and even the occasional armadillo. Admission is $5 per person. *Info: 14901 FM 3005; (409) 737-1222; www.tpwd.state.tx.us. Fee.*

Galveston Beach Pocket Parks. Whether your pooch is pocket-sized or not, he'll enjoy a visit to one of the island's "pocket parks," small beachside parks that promise Spot plenty of fun in the sun. The pocket parks are located on the island's West End. Sea Gull Shores Beach Pocket Park 1 is located on Galveston Island's west end at FM 3005 at 7 1/2 Mile Road. Sand Castle Beach Pocket Park 2 is located at 11745 FM 3005 at 9 Mile Road. Sea Shell Beach Pocket Park 3 is located on Galveston Island's west end at 13315 FM 3005 at 11 Mile Road. With 10 miles of beaches, this pocket park is the largest. Each of the pocket parks is open only from March through September. *Info: www.galveston.com. Fee.*

Island Carriages. Hop a carriage for a horse-drawn tour of the Strand district with this dog-friendly company. They'll pick you up at your hotel or at a restaurant in the historic district for a tour that averages about $1 per minute for the entire carriage (which holds about four adults). *Info: (409) 765-6951. Fee.*

Stewart Beach. Considered the best family beach on the island (so expect numerous children, just in case they make your dog nervous), this beach welcomes dogs on leash. You'll find chair and umbrella rentals and expect special events ranging from sand  castle building contests to volleyball tournaments during peak months. *Info: 201 Seawall Blvd.; (409) 797-5182; www.galveston.com/stewartbeach. Fee.*

Fetch This!

Galveston has three fun shopping districts that, if nothing else, make for some fun window-shopping for you and your dog. **Seawall Boulevard**, which runs alongside the wall built to protect the island from storms, is lined with stores selling all kinds of beach gear and souvenirs. **Postoffice Street** is lined with antiques shops and art galleries as well as restaurants and bars. **The Strand** is perhaps the most famous of the shopping districts, spanning a five-block area from 20th to 25th Street along Avenue B/Strand Street. Here the Victorian buildings are filled with everything from souvenirs to artwork.

Buster's Old Time Photos Galveston. Buster's welcomes your own four-legged Buster to join in the photo fun at this studio known for its historic style photos. Props and costumes are available for everything from a Wild West to a pirate photo. *Info: 2217 Strand St.; (409) 497-2521; bustersoldtimephotos.com.*

Treats & Eats

Float Pool & Patio Bar. Part of the wildly popular Yaga's franchise, this island-style bar welcomes your dog for afternoon, evening, or late night fun with live music. *Info: 2828 Seawall Blvd.; (409) 765-7946; www.yagaspresents.com/float.*

The Mosquito Cafe. Often lauded as one of the best restaurants in the region, this eatery, tucked in the East End Historical District, features a menu that ranges from ahi tuna sandwiches to shrimp cake slides. Arrive early to make sure you and Fido get a seat on the patio! *Info: 628 14th St.; (409) 763-1010; www.mosquitocafe.com.*

Yaga's Cafe and Bar. You and your dog can dine out on the patio on Caribbean dishes like jerk chicken or the Rasta Pasta salad but you'll also find plenty of pizzas and burgers on this menu. *Info: 2314 Strand St.; (409) 762-6676; www.yagaspresents.com/yagascafe.*

Stay, Lie Down

As one of Texas's most popular family vacation destinations, it's no surprise that the island is home to many budget chain properties including **Candlewood Suites**, **La Quinta**, **Motel 6**, **Travelodge**, and more.

Avenue O Bed and Breakfast. Located in the historic Silk Stocking  District of Galveston, pets are welcome at this B&B although not at breakfast (you can leave your dog crated in your guest room). The 1923 Mediter-ranean-style former home has a lush tropical back yard that's often used for weddings but provides a shady place for a dog walk. *Info: 2323 Ave. O; 409-457-4255; www.avenueo.com.*

Beach home rentals. Galveston has numerous condo and beach house properties for rent; the minimum stay on these varies by season with a minimum one-week rentals at some properties during the summer months. Pet policies can vary as well; check the Galveston.com site for a list of beach rental companies for more on this option. You'll find a full range of prices and properties that range from one-bedroom condos to expansive homes. *Info: www.galveston.com/vacationrentals.*

Dellanera RV Park. Operated by the Galveston Park Board of Trustees, this RV park welcomes you and your dog with 1,000 feet of beach frontage including 63 full RV hook-ups and day parking. Tent camping is not permitted on the beach. *Info: 10901 San Luis Pass Rd. (FM 3005 at 7 Mile Rd.); (409) 797-5102; www.galveston.com/dellanera.*

Pawty Time

March through October. Movie and Music Nights on The Strand. Grab Fido's leash as well as your chair, blanket or pillow and head to downtown Galveston for this free movie or music event. Movie Night on The Strand takes place at 7 p.m. every first Saturday of the month at Saengerfest Park, located at the corner of 23rd and Strand Streets. On the 2nd and 4th Saturdays, you can catch free live concerts from 6-9 p.m. in Saengerfest Park. *Info: www.galveston.com.*

April: A Bark in the Park. Held in Kempner Park, this annual event begins with the Blessing of the Dogs before moving into the competitions (which welcome all dogs, regardless of breed or breed mix). Along with classification competitions (including a special competition for mixed breeds), there's a trick contest, costume contest, and more. The event, which benefits the Galveston Island Humane Society, also includes seminars, vendors, and local adoptables. *Info: www.galvestonislanddogshow.com.*

Sniff Out More Information

Galveston.com & Company Tourism & Marketing; (888)939-8680; www.galveston.com.

HOUSTON

Nearby destinations: Richmond-Rosenberg, Spring

Mention Houston as a vacation destination and the superlatives start to fly. Fourth largest city in the country. World's eighth busiest airport. World's largest medical center. World's largest rodeo.

178 TEXAS WITH DOGS!

But Houston is also a leader when it comes to the dog world. One of the country's largest dog events is held here every July. Numerous parks throughout the city—including a large collection of dog parks—tempt with four-legged fun. And Houston now offers restaurants the option of purchasing a permit to herald their patios as dog-friendly, a trend that many have fetched and run with, offering a large number of patio bars and restaurants for Rover to enjoy.

Pets in carriers are permitted on Houston's METRO including trains and buses. *Info: (713) 635-4000; www.ridemetro.org.*

Run, Spot, Run!

Alexander Deussen Dog Park. Located on Lake Houston, this doggedly devoted area within Alexander Deussen Park offers tiny tail-waggers and big barking buddies their own places to play, with double gated entries leading to separate areas which feature gravel trails, water fountains, benches and doggie bags. *Info: 12303 Sonnier St.; (281) 454-4108. Free.*

Bay Area Bark Park. From 7 a.m. until dusk Rovers over the age of four months can romp in this 5.3-acre Pasadena playground for pooches which provides plenty of shady spots for rests in both its large and small dog sections; water fountains for both people and pets; a dog shower; a path for a stroll and waste bag stations. *Info: 7500 East Bay Area Blvd., Pasadena; (281) 326-6539. Free.*

Baytown Bark Park. Found next to Jenkins Park, large dogs have four acres complete with dog agility equipment, while little dogs have their own one-acre area. Both areas offer a walking trail, water fountains, benches and shade covers. *Info: 4334 Crosby Cedar Bayou, Baytown; (281) 420-6597. Free.*

Bear Branch Dog Park. Offering more than two acres of tree-lined fun, this park in The Woodlands has separate areas for dogs 25 lbs. and over and for more light-weight tail-waggers. Doggie bags and waste receptacles are available, as are water fountains and benches. *Info: 5200 Research Forest Dr., The Woodlands. Free.*

Buffalo Bayou Park. With downtown Houston as a backdrop, this extensive park is a major destination for joggers, cyclists, and other outdoor enthusiasts. The park is one in a series of parks and greenbelts that follow the slow-moving Buffalo Bayou. The area of the park where dog lovers have traditionally gathered is being developed into a formal, fenced dog park with benches, water fountains and other amenities. Other areas of the park are for leashed dogs only. *Info: 2700 Allen Pkwy. at Studewood; (832) 395-7000. Free.*

Burroughs Dog Park. Located in Tomball, a far north suburb of Houston, this big shady dog park covers six acres and has separate areas for large and small dogs. Other amenities here include walking trails through the pines, benches, pet drinking fountains, dog-washing stations and (human) restrooms. The park is open from 7 a.m. to dark daily. *Info: 9738 Hufsmith Rd., Tomball; (281) 353-4196; www.hcp4.net. Free.*

Cattail Dog Park. As is the case with all dog parks in The Woodlands, pooches over the age of four months can enjoy this one-acre puppy playground, which offers separate areas for both small and large dogs and a water source. *Info: 9323 Cochran's Crossing Dr., The Woodlands. Free.*

Congressman Bill Archer Bark Park. Along with Millie Bush, this park is one of the most lauded in the Houston area. From 7 a.m. until dusk dogs can show off their skills on a dog agility course, splash in a dog bone-shaped pond, enjoy a canine constitutional with their human companion on a 0.81-mile granite trail for large dogs or a 0.29 mile granite loop for small dogs, get a drink at a water fountain and cool down with a dog shower. Bag dispensers and trash receptacles are readily available, and benches and covered areas are conveniently located both near the ponds and along the trails. *Info: 3201 TX 6 N.; (281) 496-2177. Free.*

Danny Jackson Family Dog Park. Since 2005, Rovers have romped in this 2.76-acre dog park, which offers granite trails, dog lakes and a water fountain in separate areas for large and small dogs, as well as a dog wash area. Convenient for both early birds and night

owls, hours are from 5 a.m. - 10 p.m. *Info: 4700 Westpark; (281) 496-2177. Free.*

Discovery Green Park. Located downtown just north of Houston's central business district, this park has an array of features including performance space for music and other public events, playgrounds, gardens, hiking and jogging trails, art exhibit space, even an ice rink on Kinder Lake. There are two off-leash areas for dogs: the Kinder Large Dog Run for dogs 15 inches or taller and the Joe Foster Small Dog Run for small pooches. The dog parks have gravel paths, water fountains and benches. Dogs need to have current licenses. *Info: 1500 McKinney; (713) 400-7336; www.discoverygreen.com. Free.*

Gene Green Beltway 8 Park Dog Park. Featuring Harris County's first Dog Spray Park (open from the first Saturday in April until the final Saturday in October), this park has separate big and small dog areas located conveniently close to the park's main entrance. *Info: 6500 E. Sam Houston Pkwy. N.; (281) 452-1182. Free.*

Houston Arboretum & Nature Center. In Memorial Park, just outside Loop 610 on Houston's west side, this 155-acre nature center strives to educate about the natural world with five miles of hiking trails through wooded, wetland and meadow environments. The nature center building houses hands-on exhibit halls and a gift shop. Leashed dogs are allowed throughout the outdoor areas and even inside the building lobby. They need to be under control and are not allowed in the ponds. *Info: 4501 Woodway Dr.; (713) 681-8433; www.houstonarboretum.org. Free.*

Katy Dog Park. West of Houston in the community of Katy, this 14-acre park has provided lots of four-legged fun. A favorite site for such Fido-centric festivities as the city's annual HOWL-o-WEEN event and PAWS in the Park Easter Egg Hunt, in 2013 this 14-acre off-leash dog park underwent renovations to its now concrete-lined dog pond and lighting for the convenience of early morning strollers along its oval walking trail. The area also features fountains for both pets and their human parents, and custom dog showers. The off-leash park is open daily from dawn to dusk and makes a great place to let your dog run on acres of shaded grass, splash in the wading pools, or walk with you on the oval walking path. You'll also find doggie showers here for a quick cleanup before heading back in the car. *Info: 5414 Franz, Katy; (281) 391-4840; cityofkaty.com. Free.*

Market Square Dog Park. Decorated with sculptures of man's best friend, since 2011, pups have played in the venue's separate, enclosed areas for large and small dogs, trotted along the well-lit crescent-shaped dog run and quenched their thirst at a dog fountain. *Info: 301 Milam; (713) 223-2003. Free.*

Maxey Bark and Run Park. Offering almost 13 acres of fenced-in fun for Fido, the park features both a big and dog and small dog area, drinking fountains, a dog shower; a waste disposal station and several benches sprinkled throughout so pet parents can watch their pup at play. *Info: 601 Maxey Rd. Free.*

Memorial Park. Known as the largest urban park in the state, Memorial Park covers some 1,400 acres on Houston's west side. A wide array of activities are supported here including the 18-hole Memorial Park Golf Course, tennis courts, softball fields, a fitness center, pool and six miles of hiking and jogging trails. Leashed dogs are allowed throughout the park; off-leash areas are located at the adjacent **Houston Arboretum & Nature Center.** *Info: 6501 Memorial Dr.; (832) 395-7000; www.houstontx.gov. Free.*

Millie Bush Bark Park. Named in honor of one of the former President's First Fidos, this dog park's 100 parking places offers proof of how popular this spot for Spots is truly is. Fifteen acres separated into sections reserved for small and large Rovers offer several water features, including a dog shower and three dog ponds, and two gravel walking trails. Open daily to the public from 7 a.m. until dusk. *Info: 16101 Westheimer Pkwy.; (281) 496-2177. Free.*

dogtipper choice

Paws in the Park Dog Park. Spanning nearly two acres consisting of a small dog and a large dog section, this dog park is located in Pasadena, 15 miles southeast of downtown Houston. The facility includes some agility equipment and doggie pools, and, especially important during the hot Texas summer, shaded pavilions and benches. *Info: 5170 Burke Rd., Pasadena; (713) 475-7048; www.ci.pasadena.tx.us. Free.*

Pawm Springs Bark Park. Located in Sugar Land Memorial Park, this dog park is a six-acre tropical puppy paradise complete with palm trees (both real and a tree-shaped sprinkler that will spritz Spots on hot summer days); a dog pond in the fenced-in big dog area, a shade pavilion and lounge chairs. Open sunrise to sunset from Tuesday through Sunday. *Info: 15300 University Blvd., Sugar Land; (281) 275-2825. Free.*

Sam Houston Park. First opened in 1899 as Houston's first public park, this 20-acre downtown park is now a historical park under the supervision of the Houston Heritage Society. It features a number of historic houses that were moved here and beautifully restored. Leashed dogs are allowed in the park's outdoor areas but not in the houses. *Info: 1000 Bagby St.; (832) 395-7000; www.houstontx.gov. Free.*

San Felipe de Austin State Historic Site. When you're ready for a break from the busy Houston atmosphere, you and your dog can head out to this small park, operated by the Texas Historical Commission, and the neighboring Stephen F. Austin State Park in the small community of San Felipe. This site is home to the original San Felipe town site and includes a statue of Stephen F. Austin, the father of Texas, as well as a log cabin replica of his headquarters and a small museum. *Info: 15945 FM 1458, San Felipe; (979) 885-2181; visitsanfelipedeaustin.com. Free.*

Stephen F. Austin State Park. Located just down the road from San Felipe de Austin State Historic Site in the community of San Felipe, this state park makes an easy getaway from the Bayou City. Located on the Brazos River, the park offers you and Fido a place to picnic and camp or enjoy a hike on nature trails. *Info: Park Rd. 38 (From I-10 West, head north on FM 1458; then take a left on Park Rd. 38); (979) 885-3613; tpwd.state.tx.us. Fee.*

Terramont Dog Park. Located in The Woodlands, this is an exclusive playground for our tail-wagging chums who are 25 pounds and under. *Info: 8500 Terramont Dr., The Woodlands; (281) 210-3800. Free.*

Terry Hershey Park Hike & Bike Trail. Winding along the banks of Buffalo Bayou, this 10-mile trail follows a greenbelt in west Houston. Along the way are exercise stations, picnic tables and a playground. The trail varies from asphalt to grass to gravel, in different spots. Dogs are allowed on the trail, but they must be leashed and under control. *Info: 15200 Memorial Dr.; (281) 496-2177; www.traillink.com. Free.*

Fetch This!
Bass Pro Shop. This sportsman's wonderland has two locations in the Houston area and is a great place to get outfitted for a camping trip. They also sell a variety of dog-related merchandise including treats, outdoor apparel, medications, doggy backpacks and much more. Bass Pro Shops are pet friendly; leashed dogs are welcome in the stores. *Info: 1000 Basspro Dr., (713) 770-5100; 5000 Katy Mills Circle, (281) 644-2200; www.basspro.com.*

Funny Fur. If your dog is begging for some trendy threads, you'll both find what you want in this ritzy River Oaks boutique. Designer fashions and accessories, themed costumes, doggie furniture, grooming supplies and holistic and organic treats fill the shelves. Your dog is welcome to help you pick out just what she wants. *Info: 3268 Westheimer Rd.; (713) 239-0133; www.funnyfur.com.*

Orvis Company Store. Purveyors of upscale outdoor clothing, accessories and gear, this Orvis retail store has plenty of pet products as well. And, your leashed dog can come inside and pick out his own merchandise here. *Info: 5727 Westheimer Rd.; (713) 783-2111; www.orvis.com/houston.*

The Pet Stop. This pet boutique in west Houston has a full selection of pet products including premium food and treats, grooming supplies, pet clothing, toys, beds and lots more. If you need something not on their shelves, they will special order it for you. *Info: 6401 Woodway Dr.; (713) 266-5869; petstoponline.com.*

Petco. This centrally located Petco store has tons of dog food and supplies plus training classes and dog grooming. This store also hosts vaccination clinics and adoption events. Open daily. *Info: 2110 S. Shepherd; (713) 521-1005; www.petco.com.*

PetSmart Houston (Heights). In the central Heights area, this PetSmart offers plenty of choices in dog products as well as offering dog training classes, grooming and a Banfield Pet Hospital on-site. *Info: 1907 Taylor St.; (713) 863-0533; www.petsmart.com.*

dogtipper choice

Rocky & Maggie's Petshop. Doggedly devoted both to each other and their four-legged family members, in 2011 Bill Klein and Jen Arnold from the TLC series "The Little Couple" embarked on a business venture inspired by and named after their Chihuahua/Terrier mix. Along with toys, apparel, bedding, grooming products and food, Rocky and Maggie's carries a wide range of items for the traveling dog, including bike baskets, car seats, carriers and strollers. *Info: 2535 Times Blvd.; (713) 492-0656; www.rockyandmaggies.com.*

Treats & Eats

Barnaby's Cafe. Named after a beloved four-pawed pal from the proprietor's past, cheerful, child-like drawings of Barnaby the Sheepdog decorate the interior of this popular restaurant chain, while out on the patio patrons can enjoy a mouth-watering meal with their own canine companion. Menu items include Danish Baby Back Ribs, Grilled Salmon Filet, Flatiron Steak and Hawaiian Pork Chops. *Info: 5750 Woodway Dr. (in Woodway), (713) 266-0046; 1701 S. Shepherd (in River Oaks), (713) 520-5131; 414 West Gray (in Midtown), (713) 522-8898; 604 Fairview, (713) 522-0106; 801 Congress (Downtown), (713) 226-8787; www.barnabyscafe.com.*

BlackFinn American Grille. Join the pack of foodies and Fidos dining on the patio at this Midtown eatery that features traditional restaurant fare as well as items to satisfy those with a curiosity for more adventurous culinary creations. *Info: 1910 Bagby St.; (713) 651-9550; houston.blackfinnamericangrille.com.*

The Boneyard Dog Park & Drinkery. If you are over the age of 21, you can drink a toast to your tail-wagging chum at The Boneyard Drinkery's 7,000-square-foot dog park, a fenced-in, double-gated area that offers community dog bowls and bagging stations. No children allowed at any time. Although they don't sell food at the Drinkery, you'll often find food trucks just outside. *Info: 8150 Washington; (832) 494-1600; www.boneyardhouston.com.*

dogtipper
choice

Café Mezza & Grille. Featuring potted palms and soft lighting in the evening, this Mediterranean/American restaurant has created the perfect recipe for a relaxing meal out on the patio with a four-legged friend. We enjoyed dinner here with two dogs at our table but there were several other dogs on the patio as well relaxing as their parents enjoyed a great meal. *Info: 6100 Westheimer; (713) 334-2000; www.cafemezza.net.*

Gratifi Kitchen + Bar. Proud to proclaim itself the first restaurant in the city to obtain a "Paws on Patio" permit, pup-loving patrons who mull over the menu at this eatery will find Doggie Dinners listed. Fido can feast on Taste of the Wild High Prairie Dog Food, served with a side order of a bacon dog treat made in house. *Info: 302 Fairview at Taft; (832) 203-5950; gratifikitchenandbar.com.*

King's Head Pub. Toes tap and tails wag in time to the beat of live music performed on the patio at this English-style pub, which is a popular spot for sports fans. King's Head features nearly 30 beers on tap. *Info: 1809 Eldridge Pkwy.; (832) 379-1000; www.kingsheadpubhouston.com.*

Natachee's Supper 'n Punch. Enjoy some of the best comfort food in the city and relax with Rover in Natachee's back yard at an umbrella-shaded picnic table. Favorite treats here include a Yan-kee Chili Mac and the Skillet Licker Burger. *Info: 3622 Main St.; (713) 524-7203; www.natachees.com.*

Niko Niko's Market Square. Take a gastronomic journey to Greece as you sit on the patio with your pooch and enjoy a gyro sandwich or kebob. The Milam Street location is at Market Square Park, where patrons and their pups can stroll in the dog runs after a meal. *Info: 301 Milam (at Congress); (713) 224-GYRO (4976); www.nikonikos.com*

Petite Sweets. Your tail-wagging chum can chill out on the patio with a chicken pupsicle while you beat Houston's heat with a frozen custard sundae or gelato. *Info: 2700 W. Alabama; (713) 520-7007; www.petitesweetshouston.com.*

Tila's Restaurante and Bar. If you have a hunger for an authentic Mexican meal you can enjoy dishes created from family recipes as you sit on the patio with your four-legged family member. *Info: 1111 S. Shepherd; (713) 522-7654; www.tilas.com.*

Stay, Lie Down

Houston and its satellite cities are home to many dog-friendly chain properties including **Candlewood Suites**, **La Quinta**, **Motel 6**, **Red Roof Inn**, and more.

dogtipper choice

Hotel Derek. Thanks to the Derek Loves Dogs amenity package complete with a dog bowl, treats and a stylish Hotel Derek bandana, this four-star venue will feel like a home away from home for traveling tail-waggers. A portion of the $100 pet fee will be donated to the Houston SPCA, making checking into the boutique retreat with a canine companion a fun way to help animals in need of a forever home. The hotel has no limit on the number of dogs or the size (or breed) of dogs that you share your room with, a policy we love! *Info: 2525 West Loop S.; (713) 961-3000; www.hotelderek.com.*

Hotel Granduca. Combining the ambiance of Old World Italy with old-fashioned Texas hospitality, your barking buddy will receive treats and bowls for their stay at this palazzo-inspired paradise, which is conveniently located near Memorial Park. For a $125 non-refundable pet deposit, pet parents can check in with up to two four-legged friends, provided that each weigh less than 60 pounds. A hotel with heart, a portion of the pet deposit will be donated to Friends for Life, a nearby no-kill shelter. *Info: 1080 Uptown Park Blvd.; (713) 418-1000; www.granducahouston.com.*

Hotel Icon, Autograph Collection. Once the Union National Bank Building, time spent at with your dog at this architectural A-lister will leave you with a wealth of memories, starting with the treats and toys your pet receives upon check in. Located near a dog walk at Market Square, guests with dogs must pay $20 per night, for up to two small pets who weigh a maximum of 35 pounds. Pets must be kenneled if the guardian is away. *Info: 220 Main; (713) 224-4266; www.hotelicon.com.*

Hotel Indigo Houston at the Galleria. After paying a $75 non-refundable pet fee, guests can relax with Rover in one of the hotel's 131 rooms. For the traveler who wants to mull over merchandise, the hotel is conveniently located near the Galleria Mall. *Info: 5160 Hidalgo St.; (713) 621-8988; www.uptownhoustonhotel.com.*

Hotel ZaZa. Both Fidos and felines can enjoy a taste of the good life at this unique retreat, which offers a "Pampered Pet Menu" complete with meals catered to the health-conscious canine (roasted chicken and rice); sports-loving Spots (a hot dog served with a side of french fries) and the dog with a hankering for down home cooking (tenderloin with carrots and potatoes).

dogtipper choice

The hotel charges a $75 one-time fee and there's no limit on the size or breed of dog visitors! *Info: 5701 Main St.; (713) 526-1991; www.hotelzaza.com.*

The Lancaster. For a $250 deposit at check in ($100 of which is non-refundable) Rover can be your roomie at this Lone Star landmark, which has just undergone a $10 million renovation. *Info: 701 Texas St.; (713) 228-9500; thelancaster.com.*

The St. Regis Houston. This hotel rolls out the welcome mat for dogs with bowls and bed for Fidos who weigh 80 pounds or less. (Dogs over the desired weight may be approved in advance at the hotel's discretion.) Pet parents can check in with one or two canine companions after signing a waiver. *Info: 1919 Briar Oaks Ln.; (713) 840-7600; www.stregishoustonhotel.com.*

Pawty Time

February: Picassos By Paws. Artistic tail-waggers can unleash their inner Leonardog da Vinci or Henri Mutt-isse as they help to draw attention to an organization that helps to paint a brighter tomorrow for our four-legged friends at this annual paw-ty. Benefiting SNAP (Spay-Neuter Assistance Program), for a donation dogs dip their digits in safe, water-based paints to create masterpieces for their pet parents, then enjoy a splash at the wading pool station and dog treats at the Happy Tails Cocktail Hour. *Info: www.bayoucityoutdoors.com or www.archwaygallery.com.*

March, November: Chilly's Pet Pals Game. Sports fans and their Fidos can watch the Houston Aeros AHL team take to the ice for a game that offers an assist to companion animals in need of forever homes. *Info: www.aeros.com.*

April: Houston Pet Expo. Amazing Pet Expo's annual ode to all our furry, finned and feathered friends includes appearances by celebrity animal advocates, Animals Got Talent and pet costume contests for your canine companion to enter, agility demonstrations, pet/parent musical chairs, adoptions and more than 100 pet-related vendors. *Info: www.houstonpetexpo.com.*

 July: The Reliant Park World Series of Dog Shows. Five days devoted solely to Fidos includes not only pedigreed pups vying for a prize, but also agility course demonstrations, flyball teams, dog health and training clinics, and AKC My Dog Can Do That! events for non-registered Rovers. *Info: reliantdogshows.com.*

September: Dog Day at Minute Maid Park. Baseball buffs and their barking buddies can cheer for the Houston Astros as they step up to the plate to help a paws cause, with a portion of ticket sales benefiting the Houston Humane Society. Along with watching the game, sports-loving Spots can take part in a costume contest and promenade with their pet parent in a pooch parade around the warning track. *Info: houston.astros.mlb.com.*

October: Katy Dog Park Howl-o-ween: Bring your dog in costume to the off-leash dog park for a day of play for a paws cause. Starting with a one-mile constitutional for canines and their human companions, the morning of dogged devotion continues with advice from pet nutrition experts, groomers and trainers, and adorable adoptables from Houston-area animal rescue organizations. *Info: www.cap4pets.org.*

Sniff Out More Information
Houston Convention and Visitors Bureau; (800) 4-HOUSTON; www.visithoustontexas.com.

PORT ARANSAS
Nearby destinations: Corpus Christi, Rockport

dogtipper
choice

A favorite beach getaway with many Texans, Port Aransas (often just called "Port A") is a laid-back destination that welcomes dogs. Although it's best to avoid this town during spring break season when it swells with revelers, the rest of the year the town is relaxed and quiet, perfect for long beach dog walks.

Run, Spot, Run!
I. B. Magee Beach Park. Located at the Horace Caldwell Pier, this pet-friendly park offers a relaxing place to walk, watch the boat traffic from an observation deck, fish, do some birding, or even camp in one of the 75 RV and tent sites. *Info: 321 North on the Beach; (361) 749-6117; www.nuecesbeachparks.com. Free.*

Mustang Island State Park. Just down the island from Port Aransas lies this state park with freshwater showers, picnic tables, and tent and RV camping. The park offers vehicular beach access but we headed to the pro-

dogtipper
choice

tected portion of the beach with our Irie and Tiki, an area with a paved parking lot separated from the beach so no cars were permitted on the beach and adjacent sand. Here free picnic shelters offer your dogs shade and you a place to keep your items off the sand. Dogs are permitted throughout the park on a leash no longer than six feet long (and this includes in the water as well). *Info: Park Rd. 53, southwest of Port Aransas; www.tpwd.state.tx.us. Fee.*

Port Aransas Beach. Many dog-friendly properties in Port Aransas are within walking distance of the beach (and golf cart rentals are very popular) but you can also drive to the beach and park in the designated parking areas. A parking pass, sold at convenience stores throughout town as well as at the Port Aransas Visitors Center at 403 W. Cotter across from the ferry landing, costs $12 and is valid all year; there's no fee for just driving along the beach.

Roberts Point Park. Located at the turn for the ferry landing, this small park offers manicured grounds great for dog walking as well as an observation deck for watching both boat traffic and dolphins in the channel. This park is a good option when you and Fido are ready to take a break from the beach. *Info: JC Barr Blvd.; (361) 749-4158. Free.*

San Jose Island. You and your dog can hop the Jetty Boat from Fisherman's Wharf to this uninhabited island (also called St. Jo) where pirate Jean Lafitte is said to have camped. Although your dog can run off-leash here, be aware that there are rattlesnakes on the island and no public facilities. It is a quiet getaway for fishing, beachcombing, swimming, or shelling. *Info: 900 Tarpon St.; (361) 749-5448; www.jettyboat.net. Fee.*

Fetch This!

Port Aransas is not a shopping mecca by any stretch so don't look for cute canine boutiques here. You will find Texas-sized gift shops filled with all things beachy but the best part are the store facades: giant sharks, lighthouses, seahorses, and more lure shoppers (and offer some great photo ops for you and your dog!) Most gift shops are located on Alister and on Avenue G.

Family Center IGA. The island's largest grocery store is the IGA with mass-market pet foods, cleaning products, picnic supplies, sunscreen, and more. *Info: 418 S. Alister; (361) 749-6233; www.familycenteriga.com.*

Treats & Eats

The Back Porch Bar. This laid-back bar located right on the marina is a favorite watering hole with Port A regulars. Dogs on leashes are welcome (you'll find biscuits at the bar). Music in the evenings might limit this stop to dogs that don't mind noise and crowds. For food, you'll find barbecue on Friday nights. Open afternoons and evenings. *Info: 132 W. Cotter St.; (361) 749-2800; www.pabackporchbar.com.*

Fins Grill and Icehouse. Located right on the waterfront, you and Fido can watch the boats come and go from the patio restaurant as you wait for your order of fresh burgers or seafood (which we selected). If you'd prefer to take out, just call ahead. Open for lunch and dinner. *Info: 420 W. Cotter St.; (361) 749-ToGo; www.finsgrillandicehouse.com.*

dog**tipper**

choice

Port A Pizzeria. After a long drive to the coast, we enjoyed pizza delivery from this local restaurant. Delivery was fast and free; they also offer carry-out if you and your dog would like to grab a pizza on the way out to Mustang Island State Park, Padre Island, or points beyond. Open for lunch and dinner. *Info: 407 E. Ave. G; (361) 749-5226; www.portapizzeria.com.*

San Juan Restaurant. If you're looking for a bargain take-out, we definitely recommend San Juan. We ordered two complete take-out dinners for just $12 and were pleased with the large, tasty servings of enchiladas, rice and beans. Morning fare includes breakfast tacos, pancakes and more, especially popular with anglers before they head over to the marina for a day of fishing. Open for breakfast, lunch, and dinner. *Info: 410 South Cut-Off Rd.; (361) 749-6521; sanjuanrestaurant.net.*

Stay, Lie Down

A Laughing Horse Lodge. Perhaps the most dog-friendly lodging on the Texas coast, we loved the convenience of this property just two blocks from the beach. We stayed in a two-bedroom, free-

standing cottage; some rooms share a duplex but all include at least basic kitchen facilities (ours included a full kitchen as well as a dining area). Although it's no-frills (no maid service and you'll need to take out your own trash and do the dishes), the property offers many extras for its four-legged guests. Dog extras include a self-service dog bath (great on return from the beach!), complimentary dog tags with the hotel address and phone number, a list of veterinarians and dog-friendly patios, dog bowls, and poop bags. The grounds also include a large lot for dogs; two of the cottages (#11 and 12) face the lot. Pet fees are $25 for one dog, $35 for two dogs, or $50 for three or more dogs, covering the length of your stay. Our dogs absolutely loved this property! *Info: 503 E. Ave. G; (361) 749-5513; www.alaughinghorselodge.com.*

Double Barr Cottages. In easy walking distance of the beach, this complex of 14 cottages includes several that are specifically designated as pet friendly. Cottages include a full kitchen and use of a shared barbecue area. Up to two pets can be accommodated per cottage with a fee of $15 per pet per night. *Info: 415 Ave. G; (361) 749-5582; www.portagetaway.com.*

Pawty Time

April: Texas Sand Fest. The largest Master Sand Sculpting Competition in the country, Sand Fest draws 100,000 visitors for three days of sand castle competition, lessons on how to make a successful sand sculpture, and general party fun on the beach. Bowsers on leash are welcome. *Info: www.texassandfest.com. Admission. For More Information: visit Port Aransas Convention and Visitors Bureau, www.portaransas.org; (800) 45-COAST.*

Sniff Out More Information
Port Aransas Chamber of Commerce and Tourist Board; (800) 45-COAST; www.portaransas.org.

Ferries & Four-Legged Visitors
The main way to reach Port Aransas is aboard the **free ferry** that runs from Aransas Pass to Port Aransas. Operated by the Texas Department of Transportation, these open-air ferries provide a short ride. Although on our most recent trip we had no wait any of the four times we took the ferry, during peak summer months there can be a wait so tune into AM 530 for an update. Our dogs did well during the crossing although the ferry is somewhat loud. You'll need to turn your car off so windows will be down during hot weather; be sure your dogs are restrained in the car. (You're allowed to get out of your car during the crossing but your dogs must remain in the vehicle.) Occasionally the ferry will need to blow its horn at passing boat traffic and the noise is exceptionally loud so plan accordingly so your dog doesn't try to escape out the car window. If you can't handle the idea of the ferry, you can also drive to Port Aransas by means of Corpus Christi and South Padre Island Drive to the causeway to Padre Island, turning and traveling TX 361 down the length of Mustang Island into Port Aransas.

ROCKPORT-FULTON
Nearby destinations: Port Aransas

The adjoining fishing villages of Rockport and Fulton lie along scenic Aransas Bay and are havens for snowbirds of all varieties, from 5-foot-tall whooping cranes to those in 30-foot-long Winnebagos.

Rockport is nationally recognized in the birding world because it boasts over 500 species on record. From late August through September, thousands of tiny hummers from as far as Canada use Rockport and other nearby coastal communities as filling stations. They stop and refuel before the arduous, non-stop journey over the Gulf of Mexico on their way to warmer climes in Mexico and Central and South America.

During the fall migration, bird lovers come to see the humming-birds, an annual pilgrimage which has become a festival — the Hummer/Bird Celebration. The Coastal Bend Audubon Society together with the neighboring communities of Rockport and Fulton have come together to host the four-day event, always scheduled for early September.

Run, Spot, Run!

The Aquarium at Rockport Harbor. This non-profit aquarium ex-hibits the marine life of the area, from red drum found in the bays to sea urchins and sergeant majors seen around the jetties. Al-though nowhere the size of the Texas State Aquarium, this facility is free and a fun choice for families who are curious about the marine life below the surface of Rockport's waters. Friendly, leashed dogs are welcome here. *Info: 702 Navigation Circle; (361) 729-2328; www.rockportaquarium.com. Free.*

Aransas National Wildlife Refuge. This refuge is the prime winter-ing ground for the endangered whooping crane, plus hundreds of other bird species. The park is also home to a variety of waterfowl and shore birds and has hiking trails, camping, and picnic sites. Leashed dogs are allowed on certain trails where alligators are not present. *Info: From Rockport, 10 miles northeast on TX 35, then east on Park Rd. 13; (361) 286-3559; www.fws.gov/refuge/Aransas. Fee.*

Goose Island State Park. This 314-acre park is the home of "the Big Tree," the coastal live oak state champion. The park is also home to a variety of waterfowl and shorebirds. Leashed dogs are welcome as you pay your re-spects to the big tree. Open daily. *Info: TX 35 and Park Rd. 13, 21 miles northeast of Rockport; (361) 729–2858; www.tpwd.state.tx.us. Fee.*

Rockport Dog Park. We loved our visit to this dog park that opened in 2012 in Memorial Park, a great destination in itself for dogs and for leisurely walks on its nature and birding trails. The dog park is double gated and has separate small and large dog sections. Very shaded, the surrounding park offers benches and water fountains for dogs as well. *Info: In Memorial Park off Pearl St.; www.rockportdogpark.com. Free.*

dog**tipper**

choice

Rockport Beach. Dogs are NOT permitted on Rockport Beach, located right in town. However, your dog can play on leash at a small beach just at the entrance to Rockport Beach. *Info: 911 Navigation Circle; (361) 729-6661; www.rockportbeach-texas.com. Free.*

Treats & Eats
Moon Dog. This seaside eatery offers fresh seafood, burgers and other American dishes in a casual beach shack setting. Dogs are welcome on the outside decks as long as they are leashed and on their good behavior. Open for lunch and dinner. *Info: 100 Casterline Dr.; Fulton. (361) 729-6200.*

Stay, Lie Down
Rockport-Fulton has a selection of accommodations, ranging from fishing cottages to elegantly furnished condominiums. Because of the large number of Winter Texans who call Rockport home during the cooler months, many RV and trailer parks and condominiums lease by the day, week, or month. For a brochure listing all of Rockport-Fulton's varied lodgings, call the Chamber of Commerce office at (800) 242–0071.

Days Inn Rockport. This budget property is located just two blocks from the beach. It offers a free Continental breakfast and has an outdoor pool and hot tub. Rooms are equipped with microwave ovens and refrigerators and have free Wi-Fi. A maximum of three dogs are allowed here per room for a daily fee of $15 per dog. *Info: 1212 Laurel East, Rockport; (361) 729-6379; www.daysinn.com.*

Key Allegro Rentals. Key Allegro is a small island linked to Rockport by an arched bridge. The lovely drive here is your first hint at the elegant accommodations awaiting visitors in this area. Nicely appointed condominium units and upscale homes located on the water's edge afford beautiful views of Rockport's fishing vessels heading out for the day's catch. Rental homes and condominiums are available by the day or week. Note that some, but not all properties offered by Key Allegro Rentals are pet-friendly so it's best to ask when booking. *Info: 1798 Bayshore Dr., just over Key Allegro Bridge on Fulton Beach Rd.; (800) 348–1627 or (361) 729–3691; www.keyallegro.com.*

Laguna Reef Condominium Resort. This pet-friendly, waterfront hotel and condominium resort has an unbeatable view of the bay, especially for early risers who want to watch the gorgeous sunrise. Each fully furnished unit has a private balcony, kitchen, and dining/living room. After a day of sightseeing, take a walk along the complex's beach or down the long fishing pier. The units rent by the day, week, or month. A maximum of two dogs are allowed for a daily fee of $15 per pet. Dogs must be leashed when outside the units and you will need proof of vaccinations and a letter from your vet when you register. *Info: 1021 Water St., Rockport; (800) 248–1057 or (361) 729–1742; www.lagunareef.com.*

Sniff Out More Information
Rockport-Fulton Area Chamber of Commerce; (361) 729-6445; www.rockport-fulton.org.

RICHMOND-ROSENBERG
Nearby destinations: Houston

Just under 40 miles southwest of Houston, the neighboring Fort Bend County towns of Richmond and Rosenberg are alive with Texas history. In 1822, the area became home to the first settlement by members of Stephen F. Austin's colony, the Old 300. Fifteen years later Richmond became a city, its name borrowed from that of Richmond, England. Within the next few years,

Richmond, Texas, began to establish itself as a ranching and cattle center. Rosenberg emerged in 1880, after the Gulf, Colorado & Santa Fe Railway came to the area.

Run, Spot, Run!

Brazos Bend State Park. Outdoor enthusiasts consider this one of Texas's best state-run parks. The 5,000-acre park's Brazos River location makes it a popular place to fish and spot alligators and freshwater snakes. While hiking or biking along the 20 miles of trails  here, you're likely to spot coyotes, bobcats, deer, foxes, and more than 275 bird species. Visit the Nature Center to sign up for a free guided hike on the weekend or to learn about the local wildlife in the Habitats and Niches display. It is also possible to camp here. Camping fees range from $12 to $25 per night. Dogs are welcome at the campsites and on the trails, provided they are on a leash no longer than six feet. Dogs are not allowed in park buildings and they should not be allowed to drink water from the ponds in the park. Since alligators are present, pet parents should be watchful as they hike. *Info: 21901 FM 762, Needville (23 miles south of Rosenberg); (979) 553-5102; tpwd.state.tx.us. Fee.*

The Swimming Hole Private Dog Park. Located by J-Canine Pet Resort, this private park features two fenced acres with a three-quarter acre pond for plenty of dog paddling. Non-member passes are available for $25 per visit for two dogs living at the same address. You'll need to provide proof of vaccination. Although the park can be reserved for private groups, it's open weekdays 7 a.m. – 5:30 p.m., Saturday 8:30 a.m. – 12:30 p.m., and Sunday noon – 5:30 p.m. You'll check in at the J-Canine Pet Resort. *Info: 1525 Anton Stade Rd.; (281) 633-2675; www.swimminghole.net. Fee.*

Stay, Lie Down

Knights Inn Rosenberg. This hotel near downtown Rosenberg offers an outdoor pool, complimentary breakfast and free Wi-Fi in all guest rooms. There is an outdoor area with barbecue grills and a game room that kids will appreciate. Rooms also have small refrigerators and microwaves. Dogs are allowed here for a non-refundable charge of $20 per pet. *Info: 26010 Southwest Freeway, Rosenberg; (281) 342-6671; www.knightsinn.com.*

La Quinta Inn & Suites. This property offers a lot of value for a modest price including free wireless Internet, a fitness center, a pool, a business center, and complimentary breakfast. The 3-story property has 56 rooms and 16 suites with refrigerators, microwave ovens, and premium cable TV channels. Dogs are welcome here without an additional pet fee. All sizes are accepted. *Info: 28332 Southwest Fwy. 59, Rosenberg; (832) 595-6111; lq.com.*

Sniff Out More Information

Central Fort Bend Chamber Alliance; (281) 342-5464; www.cfbca.org.

SOUTH PADRE ISLAND
Nearby destinations: Brownsville

All too often, this southern island is mistaken for her sister, Padre Island. Originally, the two were one single island. In 1964 South Padre Island became a separate entity with the completion of the Port Mansfield Gulf Channel. Today South Padre is the capital of tourism in this tropical tip of Texas.

South Padre stretches for 34 miles, hugging the Texas coastline as a protective barrier against Gulf storms. At its widest point, the island is only a half-mile across, providing every one of the 5,000 hotel rooms with an unbeatable view. For some visitors, the chance to enjoy miles of pristine beach is reason enough to journey to South

Padre. Miles of toasted sand invite travelers and their dogs to enjoy wave hopping in the surf.

Run, Spot, Run!

Andy Bowie Park. This county park is located on the northern end of South Padre and offers plenty of beachy fun for humans and their dogs. Leashed dogs are welcome here without extra fees. *Info: Park Rd. 100; (956) 761-3704; www.co.cameron.tx.us. Fee.*

Isla Blanca Park. Along with day use, this county park with its white sand beaches is also one of Texas's largest RV parks offering Gulf view sites as well as lower-priced sites with partial or full hookups (and even tent sites). The park includes frontage on the Laguna Madre with a boat ramp, bait shop, and activity center. Dogs are welcome here; they must be on leash and owners are responsible for quick clean ups if necessary. Dogs cannot enter the park buildings. *Info: 33174 State Park Rd. 100; (956) 761-5494; www.co.cameron.tx.us. Fee.*

Laguna Atascosa National Wildlife Refuge. This enormous federal refuge covers nearly 100,000 acres of native wetlands, bays, and South Texas brush country and is populated with many species of birds and animals including the endangered ocelot. In addition to providing habitat for wildlife, the refuge is open to the public for hiking, birding, and driving tours. Limited camping is available at the Adolph Thomae Jr. County Park located on the northern side of the refuge near the small town of Rio Hondo. The rest of the refuge is open from dawn to dusk. Leashed dogs are allowed in the refuge but you are strongly cautioned to keep close watch on your dog, as alligators are common in some parts of the refuge. *Info: TX 100 to FM 510 at Laguna Vista past the Cameron County airport road then watch for Laguna Atascosa sign; (956) 748-3607; www.fws.gov/refuge/Laguna_Atascosa. Fee.*

Laguna Madre Nature Trail. We love this quiet trail on the north side of town at the South Padre Island Convention Centre. This boardwalk crosses four acres of coastal wetlands and offers some great bird and nature watching opportunities. Your leashed dog can accompany you but watch for alligators and make sure he stays on the boardwalk. *Info: 7355 Padre Blvd.; (956) 761-6433; www.sopadre.com. Free.*

Fetch This!
Paragraphs On Padre Boulevard. This full-service bookstore in a Victorian-styled building on Padre Boulevard has a nice selection of good reads for all ages. The store hosts public events here as well such as author readings and signings. Shoppers are invited to hang out on comfortable seating to read, use the store's free Wi-Fi or play board games. Your dog is welcome to browse the store with you. *Info: 5505 Padre Blvd.; (956) 433-5057; paragraphsonspi. blogspot.com.*

Treats & Eats
Boomerang Billy's Beach Bar and Grill. This party-hearty spot is located right on the beach and it makes a fun spot for lunch. Their menu runs to Tex-Mex and burgers and service is friendly. It's pet friendly, too, with its outside veranda overlooking the action on the beach where dogs are welcome. *Info: 2612 Gulf Blvd.; (956) 761-2420; www.boomerangbillysbeachbar.com.*

Yummies Coffee Shack. This little spot has become the go-to place for breakfast in South Padre thanks to their premium coffee drinks and hand made dishes that delight visitors and locals alike. Yummies is also open for lunch. Be warned, seating is limited here. Leashed dogs are welcome on their outdoor patio area. *Info: 700 Padre Blvd.; (956) 761-2526.*

Stay, Lie Down
Being such a popular vacation destination, South Padre Island has several national chain hotels with permissive pet policies. These include: **Econo Lodge, La Quinta Inn & Suites, Motel 6,** and **Ramada Limited.**

The Tiki. Well, of course we noticed this condominium property for the name (after all, we are pet parents to Tiki!), but we soon found out that it also offers dog-friendly condominiums for those with dogs 20 pounds and under. Not all units accept dogs but those that do charge a flat fee of $35 per pet. Each condo features a fully furnished kitchen, satellite TV, Wi-Fi, and maid service. *Info: 6608 Padre Blvd.; (956) 761-2694; www.thetikispi.com.*

Wanna Wanna Inn. This small, funky hotel sits right on the beach and keeps the spring break spirit going all year with live music on weekends and an open air beach bar and grill. Rooms here are basic

> ## Spring Break
> South Padre Island is one of the state's, if not the nation's, biggest spring break destinations. Tens of thousands of merrymakers fill the beaches in March making it tough to get a hotel room...and even more difficult to enjoy a good dog walk. You have been warned! *Info: whosyourpadre.com.*

with air-conditioning, cable TV with some premium channels, refrigerator and microwave. Most rooms and public areas have free Wi-Fi, too. Dogs are welcome to stay for a daily fee of $10 per pet and leashed dogs are allowed at the outer tables in the restaurant. *Info: 5100 Gulf Blvd.; (956) 761-7677; www.wannawanna.com.*

South Padre Island is awash in **condominium rentals** and many of these properties are pet friendly. There are number of rental agencies in town which will help you find a pet friendly condo on the beach. Pet policies vary from unit to unit so be sure to discuss this before booking. As a rule, condo properties are quieter than the beachside hotels, especially during Spring Break time, so if your dog likes a calmer environment a condo rental might be the best option. Some agencies with pet-friendly properties include:

- **Seaside Services, LLC**. *Info: (956) 761-6104; www.southpadre-beach.com.*
- **South Padre Beach Houses and Condos, Inc.** *Info: (956) 761-6554; www.sopadrerentals.com.*
- **Affordable Beach House Vacation Rentals SPI Inc**. *Info: (956) 761-8750; www.padrebeachhouses.com.*
- **Padre Getaways.** *Info: (956) 761-8888; www.padregetaways.com.*

Sniff Out More Information
South Padre Island Convention and Visitors Bureau; (800) SOPADRE; www.sopadre.com.

SPRING
Nearby destinations: Houston

Just 25 miles north of Houston, Spring built up around the rail yards. Today the heart of that historic district is known as Old

Town Spring and is filled with shops and is often the site of festivals and special events. Spring is often mentioned with its neighboring community, The Woodlands, a planned community with upscale shopping and residential enclaves tucked back into the pines. Both Spring and The Woodlands have quick access to Lake Conroe.

Run, Spot, Run!

Bibi and Mini-Me Bush Dog Park at Pundt Park. Named for the Maltipoos whose parents happened to be former President George H.W. Bush and Barbara Bush, this dog park was dedicated in 2012 by the former First Lady. The four-acre park has one acre just for little pooches and also includes concrete-floored dog wash areas (near the entrance gates) for rinsing wet rovers, a crushed granite walking trail, mulch to prevent mud, and benches with plenty of shade. *Info: 4129 Spring Creek Dr.; (281) 353-4196. Free.*

Montgomery County Preserve. A favorite with nature lovers and dog walkers, this 71-acre preserve includes trails that wind along Spring Creek through the pine and hardwood forest. Nicknamed "The Little Thicket," the preserve is part of the Spring Creek Greenway connecting 12,000 acres of forest on both sides of Spring Creek. *Info: 1118 Pruitt Rd.; (281) 367-7283; springcreekgreenway.org. Free.*

dogtipper choice

Rummy's Beach Club. This unique facility in Spring offers therapeutic swims in a heated pool for dogs and their people! Inspired by Rummy, a blind Husky who was rescued from a homeless life on the streets of Houston, the club was founded to provide a fun, safe way for dogs with joint problems or injuries to exercise in a custom-designed pool. The pool even operates in the winter when a cover is in place to conserve the heated environment. Rummy's also offers beginning dock diving classes during warm weather months. *Info: 22111 Fields Ln.; (713) 446-3805; rummysbeachclub.com. Fee.*

Treats & Eats

Bruster's Real Ice Cream. When you're ready for a sweet treat—for you and for Fido—don't miss Bruster's. Malts, banana splits, waffle cones and flavors ranging from Coffee Cake Streusel to Cotton Candy Explosion await. And for your dog, Bruster's gives every dog visitor a free doggie sundae topped with a dog treat! *Info: 7939 Louetta Rd.; (832) 717-7775; www.brusters.com.*

Hyde's Cafe. This casual eatery doesn't just have a dog-friendly patio; it also boasts a big grassy area where four-legged diners can play. Burgers, chicken-fried steak, sweet potato fries, fried okra, and pecan pie tempt diners; you can also bring your dog to listen to live music on Sundays. *Info: 26608 Keith St.; (281) 350-8530.*

Pizza Tonight. If you and Fido are tired from your day of exploring, you can order pizza delivered from this local eatery. Pizzas are created using fresh ingredients on a thin New York-style crust. Along with pizza, Greek salad, pasta, hot wings, and subs round out the menu. *Info: 27190 Glen Loch Dr.; (281) 465-4774; www.pizza-tonight.com.*

Stay, Lie Down
Spring and the nearby The Woodlands are home to numerous dog-friendly chains including **Drury Inn and Suites, Extended Stay America, Motel 6**, and more.

Rayford Crossing RV Resort. This private RV park is designed to appeal to campers who want a full range of activities and amenities for their stay. You'll find hiking trails, fishing in a stocked pond, a heated swimming pool, sport courts, playgrounds and game room for the children, modern showers, a convenience store and a fitness center. Campsites have concrete pads, cable TV and free Wi-Fi. Non-aggressive dogs are welcome here but they must be on leash when outside except when in the resort's fenced dog park. *Info: 29321 South Plum Creek Dr.; (281) 298-8008; www.rayfordcrossing.com.*

Sniff Out More Information
Old Town Spring Visitors Bureau; (888) U-STOP-IN or (281) 288-2355; www.shopspringtexas.com/shops.html.

9. Big Bend Country

Big Bend Country is the Texas of the movies: vast canyons, border excitement, and miles of open space. Miles of rugged plains. Oil derricks on the horizon. Tumblin' tumbleweeds rolling across a quiet highway.

The portion of Texas known as Big Bend Country is known for its untamed beauty and rugged parks but you'll find several small communities including Marfa, Fort Davis, and Alpine plus Del Rio in the eastern reaches.

For all its open country, this area is also home to the largest city on the U.S.-Mexico border: El Paso, a destination filled with south-of-the-border charm. And the neighboring West Texas cities of Midland and Odessa maintain a friendly competition for vacationers, each offering its own assets and located in Texas oil country.

ALPINE
Nearby destinations: Fort Davis, Marathon, Marfa

The seat of the largest county in Texas (larger than the state of Connecticut), Alpine is perched at an elevation of 4,485 feet, lofty by Texas standards. The mountainous climate makes the town a popular vacation spot, and travelers can enjoy mountain climbing, horseback riding, rock hunting, and more.

Run, Spot, Run!
Elephant Mountain Wildlife Management Area. Located about 25 miles south of Alpine, the Elephant Mountain Wildlife Management Area consists of 23,147 acres of desert ecosystem which is open for hiking and camping. A driving tour through the area is open May 1 through August 31. Although the park has few established hiking trails, many hikers simply follow the interior roads within the park. Only primitive campsites are available, and campers and hikers must bring their own drinking water and must register at the check station when they arrive. Leashed dogs are

allowed to accompany hikers and campers but they cannot be left unattended. Rattlesnakes populate this area so watch your dogs carefully. *Info: office at 109 South Cockrell, Alpine; WMA is 26 miles south of Alpine on TX 118; (432) 837-3251; www.tpwd.state.tx.us. Free.*

Kokernot Municipal Park. Located on the north side of town, off TX 118, Alpine's largest city park has some nice walking trails, along with picnic tables and sports fields. Dogs are welcome on leash. A number of the trails are paved. *Info: 801 Fighting Buck Ave.; (432) 837-2732. Free.*

Stay, Lie Down

Antelope Lodge. This hotel with its distinctive red tile roofs was originally a motor court built in 1949. Today it's been restored with a few modern amenities like air conditioning, cable TVs, and limited business services. It has kept its "rustic casual" vibe going with stone porches with rocking chairs and outdoor picnic tables and barbecue pits. The Lodge office contains a gift shop and The Last Frontier Museum of Rocks and Gems. Multiple dogs of any size are welcome for a daily $15 per pet fee. *Info: 2310 W. US 90; (432) 837-2451; www.antelopelodge.com.*

Best Western Alpine Classic Inn. This Best Western property is located near Sul Ross University. It features complimentary breakfast, a pool and hot tub, guest laundry facilities, a business center and Internet access. Some of the public spaces are decorated with murals illustrating Alpine's history. This hotel allows multiple dogs of any size for a $25 fee. *Info: 2401 E. US 90; (432) 837-1530; www.bestwestern.com.*

The Holland Hotel. Dating back to 1928, the Holland Hotel has long been a landmark in this community. After a renovation, it has returned to its former glory and now welcomes guests—and their dogs—in 25 guest rooms and suites decorated in West Texas

and Mexico style. *Info: 209 W. Holland Ave.; (800) 535-8040 or (432) 837-2800; thehollandhoteltexas.com.*

Lost Alaskan RV Park. If you are hauling your home around, you'll find this RV park more than adequate. This park accepts any size dogs without a pet surcharge. Dogs must be kept inside the trailer or on leash. There is also a fenced "Paw Paw Park" where dogs can roam leash-free. *Info: 2401 N. TX 118; (800) 837-3604; www.lostalaskan.com.*

Oak Tree Inn Alpine. Part of the Oak Tree Inn boutique hotel chain, this property prides itself on providing a restful environment with rooms designed for maximum quiet including well-insulated walls, ultra-quiet air conditioning systems, even "sound-therapy clock radios" in every room. Amenities include free breakfast at Penny's Diner, free wireless Internet access, cable TV, and a fitness center. The Oak Tree Inn Alpine is very pet friendly: dogs of any size are accepted without a pet surcharge. *Info: 2407 East Holland Ave.; (432) 837-5711; www.oaktreeinn.com.*

Ramada of Alpine. This hotel features 61 guest rooms (including 8 suites) with numerous amenities including complimentary breakfast with an omelet station, cable TV, the Lizard Springs Pool, Bar and Restaurant. Ramada of Alpine allows dogs of any size with a charge of $25 per room. *Info: 2800 W. US 90; (432) 837-1100; www.ramada-alpinetexas.com.*

Value Lodge. This modest property features rooms with small refrigerators and microwave ovens, wireless Internet and cable TV. Some rooms are pet-friendly, allowing dogs of any size for a daily $12 fee per pet. *Info: 2000 E. US 90; (432) 837-1200; www.valuelodgealpine.com.*

BIG BEND

Picture a map of Texas and where the river (and thus the international boundary) makes a big bend, well, you guessed it. This remote region is home of two enormous parks where you can get away from the crowds. With truly Texas-size proportions, Big Bend National Park spans over 800,000 acres—plenty of space for travelers looking for lots of elbow room. And, just to the west, Big Bend Ranch State Park boasts 311,000 acres of Chihuahuan Desert scenery including two mountain ranges. Several Texas towns make good jumping off places to explore the two natural areas including the nearby Lajitas and Terlingua and the more distant Alpine, Fort Davis, Marathon, and Marfa.

Run, Spot, Run!

Big Bend National Park. We love Texas's national parks but, like most of the national park system, this park has strict rules regarding pooches and the park. Because of the delicate ecosystem in this desert, Big Bend National Park has even more restrictions that you see at many of the other parks throughout the country. Although you can bring Fido with you when you explore the park, the National Park Service has these fairly stringent pet rules to keep in mind:

- Pets are not allowed on any trails. We had heard that there was a single trail that permitted pets; we have talked with park rangers, and they explained that dogs are prohibited from using *any* trail. Dogs are only permitted on the roads and in campsites that you can reach by car.
- Pets must be always be leashed or in a crate. Leashes should be 6 feet or less in length.
- Pets can go anywhere your vehicle can go including campsites.
- Pets cannot be left unattended in vehicles if it creates a dangerous situation for them or for other park visitors. This can be especially true during hot weather. Planning to hike the trail or take a guided walking tour? If so, someone must be left to attend your pet while you are gone. The nearest boarding facility (and veterinary office) is in Alpine.
- Pet owners must tidy up after their pets.
- Pets cannot enter park buildings.

With those restrictions in mind, visiting Big Bend can still be an adventure you can share with your dog. Enjoy a scenic drive through the huge park for an overall look at the scenery; the best vistas are found on the Ross Maxwell Scenic Drive and the road to the Chisos Mountain Basin. (Don't try these two while towing a trailer, though.) You'll also see plenty of dirt roads crisscrossing the park, but these are only recommended for those with high-clearance vehicles. *Info: travel from Marathon (70 miles) on US 385 to the north entrance of the park or on TX 118 from Alpine (108 miles) to the west entrance. The west entrance can be reached by taking RR 170 from Presidio to Study Butte then TX 118 to the west entrance; (432) 477-2251; www.nps.gov. Fee.*

Big Bend Ranch State Park. Like neighboring Big Bend National Park, Big Bend Ranch State Park is bounded to the west by the Rio Grande. Within its 311,000 acres (the largest of the Texas state parks), it presents rugged mountains, some of which are extinct volcanoes, canyons, and more than 500 sites which are noted for their archaeological significance including Native American pictographs dating from the Late Prehistoric and Protohistoric eras. The high desert environment of Texas's largest state park is rich with plant and animal life with ample opportunities for hiking, camping, birding, and observing the natural wonders of the park. While dogs are not exactly encouraged here, they are allowed to enter the park with restrictions. Like other state parks, they're prohibited from entering buildings but they also cannot go on hiking trails, with the exception of the Closed Canyon Trail and the Hoodoos Trail and are prohibited from approaching any wildlife. They are limited to venturing more than 1/4 mile from a campsite or a park road. Both the Closed Canyon Trail and the Hoodoos Trail are fairly short hikes (1.4 mile and 1 mile respectively) but they both offer spectacular desert scenery. Closed Canyon Trail is accessed through a "slot," a narrow passageway which opens up to a view of the surrounding desert. The Hoodoos Trail is named for striking natural rock formations that line portions of the trail. *Info:*

There are two entrances to the park. The western entrance is through the Fort Leaton State Historic Site on RR 170, a few miles east of Presidio. The eastern entrance is at the

Barton Warnock Visitor Center located a mile east of the town of Lajitas on RR 170; (432) 358-4444; www.tpwd.state.tx.us. Fee.

Stay, Lie Down

There are limited camping opportunities in the park and in nearby Terlingua. For additional dog-friendly accommodations, see the towns of Lajitas, Alpine, Marfa, Marathon, and Fort Davis, each covered in this section.

Big Bend Holiday Hotel, Terlingua. You'll need prior approval to bring a dog to this Terlingua hotel and only some rooms are dog-friendly. The hotel charges a $25-$35 pet fee but donates 10 percent of those fees to the local animal adoption center. *Info: Terlingua; (432) 201-1177; www.bigbendholidayhotel.com.*

Camping in Big Bend National Park. You and your dog will find several frontcountry developed campgrounds; two of them offer a limited number of reservations from mid-November through mid-April only. Pets are also allowed in backcountry campsites accessible by vehicle and must always be leashed. Primitive roadside camping requires a backcountry permit obtained in person at the visitors center. *Info: for camping reservations, visit recreation.gov; (877) 444-6777.*

Camping in Big Bend State Park. In Big Bend State Park, campers have several options. Developed campsites are found at Rio Grande Village (100 sites), Chisos Basin (63 sites), and Cottonwood (31 sites). Each of these sites has water and restrooms. No hookups are available. Each campsite is limited to eight campers and two vehicles. Leashed dogs are only permitted within a quarter mile of the campsites. There is no advance reservation system on these sites so it's first-come, first-served. *Info: (432) 358-4444; www.tpwd.state.tx.us.*

Chisos Mining Co. Motel, Terlingua. This 41-unit motel sits outside the park in the ghost town of Terlingua. There's a $20 per pet fee for your stay in any room, and pets cannot be left unattended in the room unless kenneled. Accommodations range from economy motel rooms to cabins with kitchen facilities. *Info: 23280 FM 170, Terlingua; (432) 371-2254; www.cmcm.cc.*

Chisos Mountains Lodge, Big Bend National Park. The only lodging in Big Bend National Park has three cabins available for pet travelers: Roosevelt Stone Cottages 101-103. These charming, free-standing stone cottages start at $150 per night and have stone floors, refrigerator and microwave, coffee pot and ceiling fan. Summer travelers: please note that there is no air-conditioning in these rooms! You may want to lie on that stone floor with your dog to stay cool during the heat of the summer so please plan your trip accordingly. There's a $10 per pet, per night fee as well. Dogs cannot be left unattended in the cabin. *Info: Big Bend National Park; (855) 584-5295; www.chisosmountainslodge.com.*

Lajitas Golf Resort and Spa. It might seem a little strange to find a five-star, world-class resort out in the middle of West Texas but here it is. Here travelers find an 18-hole PGA championship golf course, the Agave Spa, equestrian center, and hunting lodge—not to mention a private airport in case you and Fifi jet in aboard your own ride. The resort also has two restaurants and the Thirsty Goat Saloon. A full menu of outdoor activities are offered including hiking, birding and horseback riding. Rooms at the resort offer luxurious amenities and services and welcome up to two dogs of any size per guest room for a surcharge fee of $50 per pet per stay. If your dog is frightened of gunshots (like our Irie), please note that one of the big activities at this resort is skeet shooting. *Info: 100 Main St.; (432) 424-5000; www.lajitasgolfresort.com.*

Maverick Ranch RV Park. Part of Lajitas Golf Resort and Spa, the RV park offers full hook-ups, Wi-Fi, cable TV and nice shower and laundry facilities. Guests at the RV park can use many of the upscale features at the main resort including the spa, convenience store, fitness center and restaurants. The RV park has its own pool and picnic area and access to the resort's hiking trails and primitive campsites. Dogs are allowed but must be leashed when in the public areas and are not allowed in the pool area or in the buildings. *Info: 100 Main St.; (432) 424-5180; www.lajitasgolfresort.com.*

Prepare for the Desert

Remember, parts of this region are right on the desert floor. Here temperatures can be griddle-like in the summer months, but in the mountains you'll find more temperate conditions. The hottest months are May and June, with cooling rains usually starting in July and continuing through October. Winter temperatures are usually comfortable but light snow can occur.

The best packing tips for this park are to come prepared (you're not going to run out to the Wal-Mart and grab and extra layer if it does turn chilly). Be sure to bring a hat. (Short- or sparsely-haired dogs may need sun protection, too but be sure to use only sunscreen which is approved for canine use. Zinc-based lotions are toxic to dogs.).

Bring at least a gallon of water per person and per dog for every day you'll be in the parks, comfortable walking shoes, and any must-have items. Insect repellent is a must during summer months. And watch out for snakes; the emergency vet is a long drive away!

DEL RIO

Del Rio stands apart from other border cities because of its abundance of water. The town is literally an oasis in the semiarid climate at the edge of the Chihuahuan Desert. Tall palm trees, lush lawns, and a golf course dotted with water hazards are all part of Del Rio. The San Felipe Springs pump ninety million gallons of water daily. The crystal-clear water has drawn inhabitants to this region for 10,000 years. Del Rio lies 15 miles from the Amistad Dam and Lake Amistad, the result of a cooperative effort between Mexico and the United States.

Run, Spot, Run!

Amistad National Recreation Area. Fifteen miles north of Del Rio, this 57,292-acre park along the Rio Grande is also bordered by Lake Amistad which straddles the border with Mexico. The park is notable for its excellent pre-historic Native American rock pictographs. Activities here include birding, camping, hiking, and fishing. Dogs are welcome in outdoor areas of the park, but not in any park buildings. *Info: Off US 90; (830) 775-7491; www.nps.gov. Free; fee for use of lake.*

Kickapoo Cavern State Park. Located northeast of Del Rio, this park is home to numerous caves including Stuart Bat Cave, a protected (closed) habitat. The caves are home to populations of Mexican free-tailed bats during warm weather months seen exiting at sunset. Year around, you and your dog can camp, hike, picnic, or enjoy the peace and quiet of this serene park. *Info: RR 674 22 miles north of Brackettville; (830) 563-2342; www.tpwd.state.tx.us. Fee.*

Seminole Canyon State Historical Park. Seminole Canyon was first occupied by early humans about 8,500 years ago. Little is known of that culture, but archaeologists believe these people were hunter-gatherers, living on plants and small animals. The early residents left paintings on the caves and canyon walls that represent animals, humans, and supernatural shamans, but their meaning is still unknown. In the park campground, both tent and trailer sites are available, along with electrical and water hookups. You and Fido are invited to explore 10 miles of hiking trails, but dogs cannot go on the guided tours to the pictograph areas. During the warmer months, be sure to make this an early morning trip because the canyon can be very hot during the afternoon. *Info: West about 45 miles from Del Rio on US 90, 9 miles past the town of Comstock; (432) 292–4464; www.tpwd.state.tx.us. Open daily. Fee.*

Val Verde Winery. Italian immigrant Frank Qualia established this winery in 1883, drawn to the area by its flowing springs and fertile land. The oldest winery in Texas, this enterprise is now operated by third-generation vintner Thomas Qualia. Val Verde produces many wines, including award-winning Don Luis Tawny Port. Tours and tastings are available on a drop-in basis. You and your dog are welcome to stroll along the winery's public outdoor areas. *Info: 100 Qualia Drive; (830) 775–9714; www.valverdewinery.com. Open daily except Sunday. Free for grounds.*

Whitehead Memorial Museum. You and your dog are welcome to explore this museum—both indoor and outside areas—best known for its replica of the Jersey Lilly, Judge Roy Bean's saloon and courtroom. (The original Jersey Lilly remains in Langtry, about 60 miles west of Del Rio.) Judge Bean and his son Sam are buried behind the replica of the saloon, their graves marked with simple headstones. The museum boasts more than twenty exhibit sites, including an 1870s store, a windmill, a log cabin, a caboose, and the Cadena Nativity, a cultural folk art exhibit. *Info: 1308 South Main St.; (830) 774–7568; www.whiteheadmuseum.org. Fee.*

Treats & Eats

Manuel's Steakhouse. Located in the middle of downtown Del Rio, Manuel's Steakhouse is an upscale eatery serving steaks and seafood as well as authentic Mexican and Tex-Mex dishes. Save Spot a bite of your steak when the two of you enjoy Manuel's outdoor patio dining area. *Info: 1312 Veterans Blvd.; (830) 488-6044; www.manuelssteakhouse.com.*

R & R's BBQ. Tin building? Check. Gravel parking lot? Check. Lots of locals here at lunch? Check. Must be an authentic Texas barbecue hotspot! R & R's is located a few miles west of Del Rio, right on the shoreline of Lake Amistad and serves up barbecued brisket, ribs, chicken and sausage and all the trimmings that you can enjoy alongside your four-legged buddy in the outdoor dining area. *Info: Hwy. 90 W. (3-1/2 miles past US 277 intersection); (830) 778-2800; www.rrsbbqdelrio.com.*

Stay, Lie Down

Best Western, La Quinta, Motel 6, Ramada, and other pet-friendly chains are represented in Del Rio.

Broke Mill RV Park. Located a few miles north of Del Rio on US 90, this RV park offers large, full-service hookups and pads and welcomes non-aggressive dogs. The park has a designated dog walking green space where dogs can run unleashed but the area is unfenced. *Info: 6069 W. US 90; (830) 422-2961; www.brokemillrvpark.com.*

Ay, Chihuahua!

The **Chihuahuan Desert** that makes up much of this region is named for the nearby Mexican state of Chihuahua. The second largest desert in North America also shares a name with the smallest canine: the Chihauhua, also named for the Mexican state.

Sniff Out More Information

Del Rio Chamber of Commerce; (800) 889-8149 or (830) 775-3551; www.drchamber.com.

EL PASO

Looking for the excitement of a south of the border getaway without crossing the border? Check out El Paso, the largest city on the U.S.-Mexico border. A bilingual community with 76 percent of the population of Hispanic descent, the city also has both Southwestern and Native American influences. We always enjoy our visits to this city where Paris lived as a child; along with its big-city buzz, it's just a short drive to the surrounding Franklin Mountains, the southernmost tip of the Rocky Mountains. This region is part of the Chihuhuan Desert, although with altitudes that vary from 3,762 feet in the city to 7,200 feet in the mountains, climate can vary.

Run, Spot, Run!

Arroyo Park. This city park has some nice hiking trails. Dogs must be leashed to accompany hikers here. *Info: Robinson Ave. and Rim Rd. Open 6 a.m.- 10 p.m. Free.*

Ascarate Lake City Park. You and Rover will find lots of room to roam and explore in this park on the banks of the 48-acre Ascarate Lake. Tree-lined trails invite you to enjoy a shady dog walk. *Info: 6900 Delta Dr.; (915) 772-5605; www.epcounty.com/ascarate/. Free.*

Chamizal National Memorial. Located near the Bridge of the Americas, this memorial commemorates the resolution of a border dispute in 1963 caused by the shifting of the Rio Grande. The

Memorial grounds include the historic border markers between the two nations, hiking trails and picnic facilities. Throughout the year, cultural and musical events are held here as well. Leashed dogs can accompany walkers on the trails and throughout outdoor areas of the park. *Info: 800 S. San Marcial St.; (915) 532-7273; www.nps.gov. Free.*

Eastwood Dog Park. This fenced, dedicated dog park is located within Album Park. It has a gravel surface and a dog obstacle course as well. *Info: 3110 Parkwood Drive. Free.*

Franklin Mountains State Park. At over 24,000 acres, Franklin Mountains State Park is the largest urban wilderness park in the country and is one of our favorite stops in the region. The park's

dogtipper choice

borders begin in El Paso and continue through the Chihuahuan Desert to the Texas-New Mexico border. Park activities include primitive tent camping, a limited number of RV campsites, miles of hiking trails to explore the Franklin Mountain range, and a gondola which transports visitors to the top of the 5,632-foot-high Ranger Peak. Dogs on leashes are permitted on the trails and in the primitive camping areas. If your dog is small enough to hold, he'll be allowed to accompany you on the Ranger Peak gondola. *Info: 1331 McKelligon Canyon Rd.; (800) 792-1112 or (915) 566-6441; www.tpwd.state.tx.us. Fee.*

Hueco Tanks State Park. Historically a sacred place for Native Americans in the area, Hueco Tanks are a series of natural stone cisterns which capture and store rain water, a valuable resource in the arid climate of West Texas. You'll find plenty of opportunities to walk and hike with your dog in this 860-acre park that also offers the chance for some rock climbing. Extend your stay by camping in the dog-friendly campgrounds here. *Info: 6900 Hueco Tanks Rd. No. 1 (32 miles northeast of El Paso); (915) 857-1135; · www.tpwd.state.tx.us. Fee.*

Railroad and Transportation Museum. The route of America's second transcontinental railroad led through El Paso and this museum commemorates the historic event through extensive exhibits. The star of the museum is a restored 1857 steam locomotive engine. If you're prepared to perform a quick cleanup in case of a doggy accident, you're welcome to bring your dog inside the museum! *Info: 400 W. San Antonio Ave.; (915) 422-3420; www.elpasorails.org. Free.*

Tierra Este Dog Park. This fenced dog park, protected by a secure doubled-gated entrance, is mostly grass with a large area for Fido to run. The park does not have water, so bring plenty for your and your dog when you visit. *Info: 12701 Pebble Hills. Free.*

Westside Community Dog Park. This nicely maintained, fenced park has separate sections for large and small dogs. It also has a drinking water station. *Info: 7400 High Ridge Drive; (915) 587-1623. Free.*

Zin Valle Vineyards. This winery is located 15 miles north of El Paso in a Rio Grande valley named the Mesilla Valley Appellation near the small town of Canutillo. Family-owned Zin Valle produces a number of fine vintages including Zinfandel, Gewurztraminer, Malvasia, Pinot Noir, Sangiovese, French Burgundies and Chianti's. Dog people will especially appreciate the winery's "Man's Best Friend" Merlot, a medium-bodied red which features dogs on the label. Part of the proceeds from this wine is donated to the El Paso Humane Society. Your dog can join you in exploring the winery's outdoor areas. *Info: 7315 Canutillo La Union Rd., Canutillo; (915) 877-4544; zinvalle.com. Free for grounds.*

Treats & Eats

Café Central. This historic restaurant began across the border in Juarez and moved to downtown El Paso in the 1930s. Winner of numerous awards for its menu and wine selection, Café Central is an elegant restaurant with a soft spot for canines. Dogs are allowed in the outdoor dining areas; the eatery is open for lunch and dinner and has a nice bar area. *Info: 109 N. Oregon St.; (915) 545-2233; www.cafecentral.com.*

Charcoaler Drive In. This El Paso institution is definitely old school with a vibe recalling the 1950s and 1960s. It's a car dining experience where you order your burger and shake through a parking lot speaker, then pick up your order at the window. Although the drive-in doesn't have either inside or outside dining areas, your pooch can sit with you in your car and perhaps "help" you finish your french fries. *Info: 5837 N. Mesa St.; (915) 581-0660.*

Fetch This!

Las Palmas Marketplace. This large outdoor mall on the southeast side of El Paso is popular for shopping and dining. The Marketplace allows leashed dogs to walk around the public areas of the mall; some shops here also welcome dogs. *Info: 1317 George Dieter Drive; (915) 633-8841; www.dunhillpartners.com.*

PetSmart El Paso. Along with a Banfield Veterinary Hospital, grooming salon and a training school, this central PetSmart store stocks a huge array of pet products. *Info: 10501 Gateway West; (915) 594-1696; www.petsmart.com.*

Stay, Lie Down

El Paso is home to numerous dog-friendly chains including **America's Best Value Inn, Comfort Inn, Extended Stay America, Homewood Suites, La Quinta, Microtel, Quality Inn, Red Roof Inn,** and more.

Chase Suite Hotel by Woodfin. This all-suite property allows any sized dog to stay for a fee of $10 per pet. A grassy area is suitable for dog walking. Human amenities include an evening reception with appetiz-  ers on Mondays through Thursdays, full complimentary break-fasts, free Internet access, two outdoor pools, a hot tub, outdoor barbecue area, a sport court and complimentary use of a nearby health club. *Info: 6791 Montana Ave.; (915) 772-8000 or (800) 237-8811; www.chasesuitehotels.com.*

Holiday Inn Sunland Park El Paso. Located on the city's west side, this Holiday Inn welcomes dogs and charges a non-refundable fee of $50 for the stay. All rooms here have outdoor entrances, allow-ing easy access for dog walking. *Info: 900 Sunland Park Drive; (915) 833-2900 or (800) 315-2621; www.holidayinn.com.*

Wingate By Wyndham El Paso. This comfortable hotel offers a free Continental breakfast and newspaper, free Wi-Fi, a fitness center and pool and a pet-friendly attitude. Medium-sized dogs (up to 50 pounds) are allowed to stay here. Wingate charges a refundable pet deposit of $75 as well as a $10 fee per pet for each night's stay. *Info: 6351 Gateway Blvd. W.; (915) 772-4088; www.wingatehotels.com.*

Sniff Out More Information
El Paso Convention & Visitors Bureau; (800) 351-6024 or (915) 534-0600; visitelpaso.com.

FORT DAVIS
Nearby destinations: Alpine, Marfa

One of the gateways to the Big Bend region, this community began as a U.S. Army post in the mid-1800s at the intersection of two important mail routes. Located in the Davis Mountains, Fort Davis has an elevation of 5,050 feet, providing a cool respite from the heat of the surrounding Chihuahuan Desert. Fort Davis, the "High-est Town in Texas," is one of our favorite dog destinations in West Texas.

Run, Spot, Run!
Chihuahuan Desert Nature Center. Located five miles south of Fort Davis, this extensive nature area was established in 1974 to preserve and study the fragile desert ecology. You and Fido can explore several miles of hiking trails, a desert botanical garden, a greenhouse with various native cacti and succulent species and other exhibits among the Center's 500 acres of high desert land-scape. *Info: 43869 TX 118; (432) 364-2499; cdri.org. Fee.*

Davis Mountains State Park. As you might guess from the name, this park is located in the heart of the Davis Mountains, the most extensive mountain range that's fully contained within the state boundaries. Your dog will give this park a big paws up thanks to its mile high location, making it a cool getaway in a hot region during much of the long Texas summer. Miles of hiking trails invite you and your four-legged travel companion to explore and to enjoy the scenic vistas of this park. At night, sit out together and take in the blanket of stars. *Info: TX 118; (800) 792-1112 or (432) 375-2370; www.tpwd.state.tx.us. Fee.*

Fort Davis National Historic Site. Located at the site of the fort built in 1854 to protect the 600-mile-long San Antonio-El Paso Road, Fort Davis National Historic Site is considered one of the best examples of a frontier military post. Connected by hiking trails from neighboring Davis Mountains State Park (above), this fort was once a  bustling military establishment with over 100 buildings including barracks and officers' quarters. Today a number of the buildings have been restored to their original condition; while your dog cannot enter the buildings, you can explore the park with your leashed dog. Note: if your dog spooks at loud sounds, please note that the park plays an audio Retreat Parade with the sounds of hoofbeats and bugle calls at 11 a.m., 2 p.m. and 4 p.m. so plan accordingly. Our Irie hates loud, unexpected sounds so we avoided this period. *Info: 101 Lieutenant Henry Flipper Drive; (432) 426-3224; www.nps.gov. Fee.*

Stay, Lie Down

Fort Davis Motor Inn and Campground. Located on the north side of Fort Davis, this motor court offers complimentary breakfast and free Wi-Fi, large screen TVs with premium channels and mini refrigerators in the rooms. The adjacent RV park has full hookups and weekly rates. Dogs are welcome with no size restrictions. If you and your dog stay in the Inn, expect to pay a $10 per night pet fee for each dog. There is plenty of room for dog walking on the grounds. *Info: 2201 TX 17 N.; (800) 803-2847 or (432) 426-2112; www.fortdavisinn.com.*

Hotel Limpia. Built in 1912 and styled in art deco, this historic hotel on the town square is constructed of locally mined pink limestone and boasts the only bar in Jeff Davis County. The hotel is home to the Blue Mountain Bistro restaurant, the bar, some kitchenettes, some microwaves, and some in-room hot tubs, and cable TV. Dogs are welcome with a $30 per day fee for each pet. *Info: 101 Memorial Square; 800-662-5517; www.hotellimpia.com.*

dogtipper

choice

Overland Trail Campground. We love this convenient and dog-friendly private campground that, since the 1940s, has offered all kinds of camping adventures: RV camping, tent camping and cabins (including some parked Airstream trailers). Located about one mile south of Fort Davis National Historic Site, this camp-

---

Guadalupe Mountains National Park

Even by West Texas standards, Guadalupe Mountains National Park is a remote wilderness area. It is located some 230 miles north of the Big Bend park area on U.S. 62/180, 110 miles east of El Paso and touches the border with New Mexico.

The park is probably best known as the site of **El Capitan**, the iconic peak that rises in stark splendor above the Chihuahuan desert landscape. Some 80 miles of hiking trails transverse the park, though only one, the Pinery Trail, permits leashed dogs. This 3/4-mile trail begins at the Pine Springs Visitor Center so it is a convenient hike for dog lovers. In general, dogs are welcome in campground areas and parking lots, but they must be leashed. They cannot enter any park buildings.

Several areas of the park are ideal for picnicking with your pooch including an area near the Visitor Center and at the Frijole Ranch which has water and tables under shade trees.

Keep in mind that this is a very remote location with no services like gasoline or food, so plan your trip carefully. Potential dangers to dogs include rattlesnakes, spiny desert vegetation and, in the summer, hot temperatures. *Info: US 62/180, near the town of Salt Flat; (915) 828-3251; www.nps.gov.*

ground welcomes leashed dogs of all sizes in the RV area, the cabins and Airstreams (but not in the tent campsites). Overland Trail also offers full RV hookups with pull-throughs, shaded picnic areas, restrooms and showers and a camp kitchen facility. The cabins are equipped with air conditioning, TVs with cable service, kitchens with microwaves and refrigerators and Wi-Fi. There is a $6 per day pet fee for cabin use. If you are staying in your own RV, no pet fee is charged. *Info: 520 State St. N.; (432) 426-2250; www.texascamping.com.*

Sniff Out More Information
Fort Davis Chamber of Commerce; (800) 524-3015 or (432) 426-3015; www.fortdavis.com.

FORT STOCKTON
This West Texas community lies in the heart of the Chihuahuan Desert and is a popular stop on the road to or from El Paso. Fort Stockton holds the designation as a Main Street City and has refurbished many storefronts to their original historic appearance. Buildings such as the 1884 jail and the Grey Mule Saloon recall the days when this was a frontier army post.

Run, Spot, Run!
Annie Riggs Memorial Museum. Built in 1899 as the Adobe Hotel, today this museum is filled with local history exhibits and memorabilia from Fort Stockton's early days. Although your hound may be a history buff, he can't enter the building but the two of you can enjoy the museum's outdoor garden area which includes some shady areas and benches. *Info: 301 S. Main St.; (432) 336-2167; www.annieriggsmuseum.com. Fee for touring museum; garden is free.*

Historic Fort Stockton. Fort Stockton was established in 1858 to protect the frontier area from Comanche attacks. Today, the original and reconstructed buildings include the officers' quarters, a guardhouse, and a jail. Leashed dogs are allowed in the fort's extensive outdoor areas. *Info: 300 E. Third St. (entrance is on Fifth St.); (432) 336-2167; www.historicfortstockton.com. Fee.*

Paisano Pete. A truly Texas-sized statue, this 22-foot-tall fiberglass bird is probably the largest statue in the world commemorating the Roadrunner, a native species of West Texas. You can make a quick stop here to pose your own Wile E. Coyote in front of the statue for a unique photo op. *Info: Dickenson and Main Sts. Free.*

Stay, Lie Down
With its location along I-10, it's not surprising that Fort Stockton is home to many dog-friendly chain hotels including **Days Inn**, **La Quinta**, **Motel 6**, **Quality Inn**, **Sleep Inn**, and more.

Candlewood Suites Fort Stockton. This Fort Stockton all-suites hotel makes a great pet-friendly first impression: a bowl of dog treats on the counter! The hotel has an outdoor pool and patio area with a barbecue grill. Suites have free Wi-Fi, full modern kitchens and, maybe the best amenity in a pet-friendly property: efficient soundproofing in each suite. A complimentary breakfast begins the day here and if you and your pooch want to watch a movie the hotel offers a library of DVDs and free microwave popcorn. Up to two dogs each weighing 80 pounds or less are welcome. There's a $35 fee for stays under six nights; for longer stays, you'll be charged $5 per night. One caveat: all pet rooms are on the third floor. *Info: 2469 W. I-10; (432) 336-8070; www.ihg.com.*

Fort Stockton RV Park. This large, well-maintained park is located on the eastern outskirts of Fort Stockton and has 118 RV sites with full hookups (but no cable TV) as well as grassy areas for tent camping. The park has a large outdoor pool, guest laundry and showers, Wi-Fi and hiking trails which are ok for dog walking. It is also the home of Roadrunner Cafe which is open for breakfast and dinner. Pets stay here without additional fees. *Info: I-10 and Warnock Rd.; (432) 395-2494; www.ftstocktonrvpark.com.*

Hilltop RV. If you and your pooch travel in your own RV or trailer, this park has a lot to recommend it. Facilities here are new and well maintained and they have a fenced "Puppy Patch" dog park for off-leash fun and exercise. Other amenities include large pull-through sites with picnic tables, free Wi-Fi, a pool with covered patio, shower suites, a TV lounge and DVD library, and a community firepit area. *Info: 4076 I-10 W.; (432) 336-6090; www.ftstocktontexasrvpark.com.*

Sniff Out More Information
Chamber of Commerce Visitor Center; (800) 336-2166; www.fortstockton.org.

MARATHON
Nearby destinations: Alpine, Marfa

With a motto of "Marathon, Texas: Where There's Nothing 'To Do'" you probably have a clue to the best activity for you and your dog to enjoy: relax and slow down. The small (really small) town has one of the darkest skies in the lower 48 states, the perfect place to enjoy some star gazing. (Watch for Sirius, the dog star!)

Stay, Lie Down
Gage Hotel. Built in 1927, the Gage Hotel remains one of the best-known accommodations in West Texas. The original historic hotel

dogtipper choice

still offers rooms (with either private or down the hall bathrooms) and in Los Portales, adobe brick rooms, as well as in nearby historic homes. Your dogs are welcome to join you for a $20 per night per pet fee. Best of all, the hotel's Gage Gardens—a favorite wedding venue—also includes an off-leash area! *Info: 102 NW 1st St. (U.S. 90 W.); (800) 884-GAGE; www.gage hotel.com.*

Sniff Out More Information
Marathon Chamber of Commerce; visitmarathontexas.com

MARFA
Nearby destinations: Alpine, Fort Davis, Marathon

Located on a high desert plateau, this west Texas community was named for a character in *The Brothers Karamazov* and originally thrived as a railroad stop. Today, the community is often visited by those traveling to Big Bend and by vacationers seeking to spot the mysterious Marfa Lights, a phenomenon that has been seen since pioneer days but never completely explained. Marfa has also prospered in recent years as an artists' colony valued for its temperate climate and clear desert light. There is also a Hollywood connection; several movies have been filmed here. Who knows? That character walking down the street in cowboy hat and boots could be a genuine cowboy from a working ranch or a famous actor who just wandered off the set.

Run, Spot, Run!

Marfa Lights Viewing Area. Are these mysterious lights a natural phenomenon, an optical illusion or evidence of UFO activity? The debate has raged ever since a local rancher first reported the hovering lights in 1883. Research suggests that the lights were also observed much earlier by Native Americans. Whatever the cause, the Marfa Lights mystery remains a central attraction and has become an icon of Marfa's funky ambience. Each Labor Day weekend the town hosts the Marfa Lights Festival to celebrate the mystery. A visitors center located nine miles east of Marfa displays information on the mysterious lights and provides a good lookout spot. Visitors gather here at sundown to watch for the lights that can appear early or late in every season and any kind of weather. They don't always appear, so it may take more than one visit to spot them. If your dog is the patient type who is not likely to bother the other guests, he can wait with you and help you spot the lights. *Info: 9 miles east of Marfa on US 67/90; (432) 729-4942 or (800) 650-9696; www.marfacc.com. Free.*

Treats & Eats

Squeeze Marfa. Since 2004, this trendy place has been serving fresh-squeezed fruit drinks and gourmet coffee in its eclectic shop in downtown Marfa. Over the years, they have added more goodies like sandwiches, salads, soups, smoothies and shakes. Squeeze Marfa is also the sole U.S. distributor for Vollenweider Swiss chocolate. Fortunately for dog lovers, Squeeze Marfa is dog-friendly and welcomes canines with a bowl of water in its cozy outdoor dining area. Open for breakfast and lunch. *Info: 215 N. Highland Ave.; (432) 729-4500; www.squeezemarfa.com.*

Stay, Lie Down

Chinati Hot Springs. While not in the town of Marfa, this dog-friendly place is a "mere" two-hour drive west. (Hey, that's just around the block in West Texas!) The natural mineral hot springs here have been visited by people seeking therapeutic benefits since prehistoric times. You and your dog can choose from among seven rustic guest cabins done up in rock or adobe with air-conditioning and heat in each room; some rooms also have refrigerators. Activity here centers around the outdoor hot and cool soaking pools and the communal kitchen. There are also several campsites that are accessible by vehicle which can be rented. Day visitors to the site are accommodated according to availability so call before visiting. Leashed dogs are welcome everywhere except in the pool area and the community buildings. Chinati Hot Springs charges a $15 pet fee. *Info: 1 Hot Springs Rd., Presidio; (432) 229-4165; www.chinatihotsprings.net.*

El Cosmico. Set on 18 acres of land on the south side of Marfa, El Cosmico offers several kinds of "concept lodging" to allow visitors to experience West Texas in non-traditional ways. Alternatives here include restored  vintage trailers, teepees, safari tents and scout tents as well as sites where you can erect your own tent. Amenities (and prices) vary with the type of accommodation but rest assured that plenty of creature comforts are provided. The El Cosmico compound also includes communal areas such as a kitchen/dining area, community lounge with Wi-Fi, and a "hammock grove." Dogs are welcome to stay in any of the accommodations for a one-time charge of $10. *Info: 802 S. Highland Ave.; (877) 822-1950 or (432) 729-1950; elcosmico.com.*

Hotel Paisano. This historic boutique hotel has been restored to its former glory with some modern touches such as Wi-Fi and upscale bathrooms with rainforest showers. Some of the rooms feature private patios with *chiminea* fireplaces. There is also a restaurant and bar on-site. Small dogs are allowed throughout the property except inside the restaurant but your dog is welcome to join you on the restaurant patio. The hotel charges a pet fee of $20 per night.

Pet weight restrictions are flexible, so call ahead of your visit. *Info: 207 Highland St.; (432) 729-3669; www.hotelpaisano.com.*

Tumble Inn RV Park. This RV park is located just 1/4 mile east of Marfa and takes pride in its scenic views of the surrounding high desert. It features 14 variously-sized RV sites with Wi-Fi, electric and water hookups and modern bathrooms and showers. Check-in here is self-serve: just look for the antique Mobile Scout trailer. Dogs are welcome to stay without extra fees but they must be leashed when outdoors. A gravel road adjacent to the park is a popular dog walking spot. *Info: 93320 US 90; (432) 242-1962; tumbleinmarfa.com.*

Sniff Out More Information
Marfa Chamber of Commerce; (432) 729-4942 or (800) 650-9696; www.marfacc.com.

MIDLAND-ODESSA
These sister cities share a rich history in a Texas-sized industry: petroleum drilling and development. This area is the hub of the Permian Basin's oil and gas reserves and many businesses in the city are related to the industry. Midland is also famous as the birthplace of former President George W. Bush and First Lady Laura Bush.

Run, Spot, Run!
Hogan's Run Dog Park. This large fenced dog park is located on Midland's north side, near Hogan Park and next to the Sibley Nature Center. Although the address is on Wadley Avenue, the entrance to the park is around on Sibley Circle. The park is open during daylight hours (but closed for maintenance Monday mornings) and has lots of pet amenities including water fountains, seating, shady areas and agility equipment. It has a separate area for smaller dogs and a restroom for humans. *Info: 1201 E. Wadley Ave., Midland; (432) 685-7424; www.midlandtexas.gov. Free.*

Odessa Meteor Crater. A unique stop near Odessa, the 40-acre crater site has been designated by the National Park Service as a National Natural Landmark. Formed over 62,000 years ago, this crater (the nation's second largest) can be viewed by visitors at the Odessa Meteor Crater Museum. Located west of town, the visitor center and museum tells a fascinating story of the crater's origin. Travelers can take a marked trail through the crater. You and your dog are welcome to stroll the site together but dogs cannot enter the buildings. *Info: 3100 Meteor Crater Rd. (8 miles west of Odessa via I-20 at exit 108), Odessa; (432) 381-0946; www.netwest.com/ virtdomains/meteorcrater/index.htm. Free.*

Stonehenge Odessa. It's probably the last thing you expect to see in West Texas: an almost full-sized replica of Stonehenge. Built in 2004, the limestone construction has the same footprint of England's ancient original and it is 70 percent as high. Situated on the campus of The University of Texas of the Permian Basin it makes a good place to walk Fido and pose him for some dramatic photos. *Info: 4901 E. University, Odessa; (432) 552-2806. Free.*

The Permian Basin Petroleum Museum. This museum tells a detailed story of Midland's biggest industry, petroleum energy. One of its most popular exhibits is the Chaparral Gallery where a number of Chaparral race cars are displayed. The museum also has an extensive archives section and a library dedicated to the petroleum industry. Dog are permitted to walk on the grounds of the museum, provided they are leashed and under control. *Info: 1500 I-20 W., Midland; (432) 683-4403; petroleummuseum.org. Fee.*

Fetch This!
Stock up on anything your dog needs at these extensive, full service pet stores:

PetSmart Midland. *Info: 4206 W. Loop 250; (432) 520-3134; www.petsmart.com.*

PetSmart Odessa. *Info: 2022 E. 42nd; (432) 362-1614; www.petsmart.com.*

Treats & Eats
The Blue Door. This full-service bar opened in 2012 on Midland's north side and offers a huge beer selection along with wine and mixed drinks. It is a hip, trendy oasis which welcomes pooches on its outdoor patio. The drinks here are not the cheapest in town but the pet-tolerant atmosphere and big-city vibe makes it worth visiting. *Info: 4610 N. Garfield, Midland; (432) 218-8793.*

Fuddruckers. If you are a hamburger connoisseur, Fuddruckers has you covered, offering a wide variety of choices including traditional burgers as well as an expanded menu of more exotic varieties like buffalo, elk, wild boar and ostrich. The Midland and Odessa locations each have an outdoor dining area which welcomes leashed dogs. *Info: 4511 N. Midkiff Rd., Midland, (432) 689-0448; 4101 East 42nd St., Odessa; 432-362-4330; www.fuddruckers.com.*

Jason's Deli. Jason's offers a wide selection of health-conscious choices utilizing USDA certified organic ingredients. Sandwiches, soups and salads are featured along with a separate kids' menu. Leashed Lassies are welcome at their outdoor dining area. *Info: 4610 N. Garfield Rd., Midland; (432) 682-2200; www.jasonsdeli.com.*

Stars Drive-In. At the four Stars Drive-In locations in Odessa, diners order right from their car and the meals are delivered by car hops. This Texas chain also offers slushes, frozen drinks and other delights. Dogs are welcome to join you for some car dining. *Info: 1015 East 8th St., (432) 337-5141; 3836 Andrews Hwy., (432) 362-8591; 1402 West County Rd., (432) 333-4741; 9012 W. University, (432) 381-0612.*

Strawberry Café. Featuring organic food choices, the Strawberry Café is located within the Natural Foods Market that sells produce and natural health products. The café offers a health-conscious menu which changes daily but which always includes a vegetarian menu in addition to their regular offerings. Meals are prepared from ingredients which are produced without genetically modification or chemical fertilizers and pesticides. The café has an outdoor dining area which allows dogs. Dogs need to be leashed and under control. *Info: 2311 W. Wadley Ave., Midland; (432) 699-4048; www.naturalfoodsmkt.com.*

Stay, Lie Down

Midland and Odessa each boast numerous dog-friendly chains including **Best Western, La Quinta, Residence Inn, Studio 6, Travelodge,** and more.

Midessa Oil Patch RV Park. This full-service park is located halfway between Midland and Odessa. Pets are welcome to stay here with no additional fees. A highlight is the "Puppy Playground" a grassy, fenced dog park where pooches can roam leash free. The park also has a nice heated outdoor pool, children's' playground, picnic tables and Wi-Fi. Other amenities include a convenience store, laundry, showers and restrooms. In addition to the RV sites, the park has a tent camping area. *Info: 4220 S. CR 1290 (exit 126 from I-20), Midland; (432) 563-2368; midessaoilpatchrvpark.com.*

MCM Grande Hotel Fundome. This 245-room hotel has its own eatery, Polly's Restaurant, serving breakfast, lunch and dinner (breakfast is complimentary for guests) and Toby's Bar which serves complimentary drinks in the afternoons. Rooms feature premium bedding and high-speed Internet access. The "Fundome" is an indoor atrium with miniature golf, an indoor/outdoor pool, whirlpool and sauna, fitness center and a kids' playground. Up to two dogs are allowed for a refundable deposit of $50; they are allowed in outdoor areas and in the Fundome. *Info: 6201 East US 80, Odessa; (432) 362-2311; mcmgrandeodessa.com.*

Monahans Sandhills State Park.
Much of the West Texas desert areas are either rugged mountains or desert flats covered with native vegetation. Monahans Sandhills State Park is different, with nearly 4,000 acres of white sand dunes that are endlessly reconfigured by the West Texas winds. The most popular activity here is sand surfing: trekking to the top of a dune then riding down on a sliding device. The park has sand toboggans and simple disks for rent or you can bring your own. The Sandhills Interpretive Center furnishes information on the origin and history of the dunes and there are campsites available if you want to stay overnight. Leashed dogs are allowed all over the outdoor areas of the park including the campsites without additional fees. *Info: From I-20, take exit 86 to Park Rd. 41; (432) 943-2092; www.tpwd.state.tx.us. Fee.*

TownePlace Suites By Marriott Odessa. This all-suites property is located near the University of Texas Permian Basin and is set up for extended stays. Each suite here has a full-sized kitchen with refrigerator, microwave, cooking range and a dishwasher as well as separate sleeping and living areas. Suites are generously-sized with premium TV channels, complimentary Wi-Fi, and upgraded bedding and a choice of pillows. Complimentary breakfast and an evening reception with complimentary beer and wine are offered daily. Dogs up to 50 pounds are permitted for a non-refundable fee of $100 per dog. There is an outdoor picnic/barbecue area where dogs can be walked. *Info: 4412 Tanglewood Lane; (432) 362-1077; www.marriott.com.*

Sniff Out More Information
Midland Convention & Visitors Bureau; (800) 624-6435; www.visitmidlandtexas.com; Odessa Convention & Visitors Bureau; (800) 780-HOST (4678); www.odessacvb.com.

VAN HORN
Located about half way between Fort Stockton and El Paso on I-10, Van Horn is a small ranching town that began as a stop on the Overland Mail Route and later on the Texas and Pacific railroad line. It is the westernmost town in the Central time zone and is a popular point of departure for visitors to Guadalupe Mountains State Park 60 miles to the north. Some of Van Horn's downtown buildings are listed on the National Register of Historic Places.

Run, Spot, Run!
The Clark Hotel Museum. Housed in a former hotel which is one of the oldest buildings in town, the museum has several exhibits exploring the history of Van Horn as a ranching and railroad town. Dogs are not allowed inside but can be walked outside the museum on a leash. *Info: 110 W. Business Loop; (432) 424-6939; clarkhotelmuseum.com.*

Stay, Lie Down
Hotel El Capitan. Like its sister property Hotel Paisano in Marfa, the beautifully restored Hotel El Capitan is filled with history. Rooms are smallish but comfortable with modern bathrooms; some have private courtyards. The hotel is decidedly pet-

friendly, accepting all sizes of dogs for a $15 fee per night. Dogs are welcome to dine with their people on the restaurant patio, too. *Info: 100 East Broadway; (877) 283-1220; www.hotelinvanhorn.com.*

Sniff Out More Information
Van Horn Chamber of Commerce; (432) 283-2043; www.vanhorn chamber.com.

10. Resources

One of the most enjoyable aspects of dog travel is the trip planning. We'd like to share some of our favorite resources for planning your next dog vacation.

DOG-FRIENDLY ACCOMMODATIONS WEBSITES

BringFido.com. Along with searching for pet-friendly hotels (as well as restaurants, attractions, dog parks, events, and more) on this site, you can also call toll-free to speak with one of Bring Fido's travel agents. They'll help you book your next trip, and they don't charge a booking fee. *Info: (877) 411-FIDO; www.bringfido.com.*

DogFriendly.com. Since 1998, this site has identified dog-friendly US and Canada hotels, restaurants and attractions. *Info: www.dogfriendly.com.*

GoPetFriendly.com. Specializing in US and Canada coverage, this site features a handy Road Trip Planner to help you map out your next dog vacation, making recommendations from among the site's 60,000 listings that fall along your route. The husband-wife couple that created GoPetFriendly also run Take Paws Blog where you can follow their RV travels with their two dogs. *Info: www.gopetfriendly.com and gopetfriendlyblog.com.*

TripswithPets.com. This site is searchable by route and also includes special sections on air travel and airline policies. *Info: www.tripswithpets.com.*

NATIONAL MAGAZINES

Cesar's Way Magazine. Adoption, pet products, travel, celebrity canines, and more are featured in this bimonthly magazine. *Info: cesarsway.com.*

Dog Fancy Magazine. Although this magazine focuses on pure-bred dogs, it also includes a special section on rescue and frequently includes travel destinations. *Info: www.dogchannel.com.*

FIDO Friendly Magazine. This travel magazine whose motto is "Leave no dog behind"® showcases the best places to travel with your dog, from inexpensive retreats to dream vacations. *Info: www.fidofriendly.com.*

Life + Dog Magazine. Published in Houston but distributed to dog lovers across the country, this stylish magazine covers everything from rescue to pet products to dog-loving celebrities. *Info: www.lifeanddog.com.*

Modern Dog Magazine. Stylish dog accessories and gear take center stage in this bimonthly magazine which also features travel and dog-centric events. *Info: moderndogmagazine.com.*

TEXAS MAGAZINES & RESOURCES
Austin
Austin Pets Directory. Distributed free at many pet locations around town, back issues of this magazine featuring many local events are also available online. *Info: www.austinpetsdirectory.com.*

Haute Dog Magazine. You'll find dog parks, products, great photography, local events and more in this magazine and its annual "Ultimate Guide". *Info: hautedogmagazine.com.*

Dallas-Fort Worth
Dallas Dog Life. This online resource includes an extensive events calendar as well as information on local rescue groups, volunteer opportunities, and local pet businesses. *Info: dallasdoglife.com.*

DFW Dogs. This online resource features dog news, dog-centric events, and a large database of dog businesses in the Metroplex and listings of all dog parks in the Dallas-Fort Worth area. *Info: www.dfwdogs.com.*

For the Love of Dogs TV. "For the Love of Dogs" is a production of American Dog Rescue Foundation and the Arthur E. Benjamin Foundation. New episodes air Saturdays at 7:30 p.m. on Verizon UAN/Channel 27 in Dallas and now on KUGB/Channel 28.2 in Houston, and are available online. *Info: www.americandogrescue.org/for-the-love-of-dogs/.*

Houston

Houston Pet Talk. Available in both print and digital formats, this magazine features local events as well as a directory of pet-related businesses in Houston. *Info: www.houstonpettalk.com.*

Texas Dogs & Cats Magazine. This print magazine and website both serve as resources for Houston visitors and residents. You'll find information on special dog events. *Info: texasdogsandcats.com.*

San Antonio

Texas Dogs & Cats Magazine – San Antonio edition. Along with information on San Antonio pet events, you'll find local information on pet boarding, pet grooming, pet health, pet nutrition and more for your four-legged family members. *Info: texasdogsandcats.com/sa/.*

Index

236 TEXAS WITH DOGS!

Things Change!

Phone numbers, prices, addresses, quality of service – all change. If you come across any new information, let us know. No item is too small! Contact us at *www.dogtipper.com*.

"Hey, let's get moving, guys! I want to swim in the Gulf!"
– Tiki

About the Authors

Texans **Paris Permenter** and **John Bigley** are a husband-wife team of professional writers and the publishers of *DogTipper.com*. The pet parents of two mixed breed rescue dogs, Tiki and Irie, Paris and John enjoy traveling with their dogs as much as possible.

John and Paris have authored over 30 travel and pet books including *Caribbean with Kids, Best of National Parks with Kids, Best of the Caribbean, Insider's Guide to San Antonio, Texas Getaways for Two, Day Trips from San Antonion and Austin, Texas Barbecue*, and many others. Some of their other dog books include *Barkonomics: Tips for Frugal Fidos* and *My Dog Says I'm a Great Cook!*

In 2008, Paris and John launched *DogTipper.com*, an award-winning website featuring not only tips for dog lovers but also adoptable dogs, dog news, product reviews, give-aways, and more. Since that time, they've traveled the country speaking to dog lovers as well as pet professionals. Paris, a certified dog trainer, also speaks about ways to save money on pet care at Amazing Pet Expos and co-hosts the weekly "Dog Travel Experts" Internet radio show. Visit *www.dogtipper.com* and follow along with their tens of thousands of followers on Twitter at @dogtipper and on Facebook at www.facebook.com/dogtipper

Paris and John are also the "Bowser on a Budget" columnists for *FIDO Friendly* magazine, the country's only magazine dedicated solely to dog travel, and they are weekly columnists for *pet360*, the sister site of petMD. Dogtipper is consistently rated as Klout's number one dog-website account.

Paris and John live with their dogs and cats in the Texas Hill Country.

PRAISE FOR PARIS AND JOHN'S BOOKS

"The husband-and-wife team of Paris Permenter and John Bigley have been the most prolific travel writers in the state." - *Austin Chronicle*

"Paris and John know their territory well." - *Southern Living*

"If you're looking for a one- or two-day getaway but you're not sure where to go, then Paris Permenter and John Bigley may have just the ticket for you." - *Hill Country News*

"*Texas Barbecue* was written by a couple of the best Texas writers around, Paris Permenter and John Bigley." - Houston Post

"After logging 8,000 miles, Austinites Paris Permenter and John Bigley know the high roads and the back roads of Central and South Texas." - Austin American-Statesman

"An ideal reference tool for the aficionado of good food and high-quality accommodations." - Library Journal

"In Texas, barbecue is a religion. So when authors Paris Permenter and John Bigley made a pilgrimage to the Barbecue Belt...they were inspired to write *Texas Barbecue*." - *Texas Monthly*

"Boasts the beef on the state's best barbecue pits." - *Texas Highways*